The C# Helper Top 100

The 100 most popular posts at CSharpHelper.com

Rod Stephens

The C# Helper Top 100, The 100 most popular posts at CSharpHelper.com

Published by Rod Stephens, RodStephens@CSharpHelper.com

Copyright © 2017 by Rod Stephens

All rights reserved

ISBN–13: 978-1546886716

ISBN–10: 1546886710

About the Author

In a previous life, Rod Stephens studied mathematics, but during his stay at MIT he discovered the joys of computer algorithms and he hasn't looked back. Since then he's worked on an eclectic assortment of applications in such diverse fields as automated repair dispatching, billing, telephone switch programming, fuel tax collections, scientific visualization, wastewater treatment, concert ticket sales, cartography, optometry, and coaching tools for professional football players. His favorite topics remain algorithms and graphics.

Rod has been a Microsoft Most Valuable Professional (MVP) for more than 14 years. He consults (email him if you want help with an interesting application), maintains his web sites, and occasionally speaks at users' group meetings and conferences.

He has written more than 30 books, some of which have been translated into languages from all over the world, and more than 250 magazine articles. He's even created a few video training courses.

Rod's popular C# Helper website www.CSharpHelper.com contains thousands of example programs that demonstrate tips, tricks, and useful techniques for C# programmers. His VB Helper website www.vb-helper.com provides similar material for Visual Basic developers.

You can contact Rod (particularly if you want help on an interesting project) at RodStephens@CSharpHelper.com.

Contents

Introduction

I started the C# Helper web site (www.CSharpHelper.com) in 2009, partly to provide a place where people could get information and help for my C# books and partly just to provide a useful resource similar to my VB Helper web site (www.vb-helper.com). During the years since then, I've added more than 1,000 posts explaining useful tips, tricks, and techniques for C# developers.

Some of the examples are relatively simple, requiring just a few words of explanation. Others are extremely complex so they are spread across several posts.

Over the years, the site has received millions of visitors. This book describes the 100 examples that were most visited over the last few years. I only looked at views in the last couple of years to avoid giving the earliest posts too big an advantage. A post that has been around for five years should have received more visits that one that is only a year old. The most recent posts are probably under-represented, but I didn't want to turn this into a research project, so I just picked a range of dates and went with it.

The selected examples aren't necessarily the most important, best written, or most complicated. They're just the ones that people have visited the most. In some sense, I suppose that means they are the ones that people have found the most useful. I hope you find at least some of them useful, too!

Who This Book is For

This book is intended to help C# programmers. It explains useful C# programming tips and techniques.

This book doesn't assume that you're an expert C# developer, but it does assume that you have at least some familiarity with C# basics. If you know how to declare and use variables, write methods, and create classes, then you should be able to follow the examples.

How This Book is Structured

Each example's title includes an example number, description, and the example's ranking. For instance, consider the example, "41. Draw a Mandelbrot Fractal (24)." The first number, 41, means this is example number 41 in the book. The final number, 24, means this was the 24th most visited example on the C# Helper webs site.

To build this book, I first selected the 100 most visited examples. I grouped them into loose categories and then arranged them within the categories more or less in order of their popularity. That means the most popular posts tend to come at the beginning of the book, although the groups contain related examples that may have been visited less often.

Whatever their rankings, all of the examples are pretty interesting. As I was rewriting the examples for the book, I expanded those that seemed too simple, so even the least visited examples included in this book have something to teach you.

How to Use This Book

You can use the book as a sort of reference if you like. For example, if you need to write a WPF program that draws three-dimensional shapes, then you can look at the examples dealing with that topic.

However, these days there are better ways to find references for specific topics than looking in a book such as this one. If you need information on three-dimensional WPF programming in C#, you're probably better off searching the internet. In fact, I recommend that you search the C# Helper web site. It contains several dozen three-dimensional WPF examples, only a few of which are included here.

What this book is really intended to do is to introduce you to a wide variety of interesting examples and techniques that you can use in your programs. To get the most benefit from the book, I recommend that you just read it. You can jump to a particular section if you have a special interest in a particular topic, but I suggest that you just start reading and see what you learn.

Also be sure to download the book's source code and experiment with the example programs. Some of them are straightforward, but many are quite involved and it will be worth your time to do a little extra exploring. Some of the examples are also too long for the book to include all of their details. In those cases, you will need to download the example and study it to really understand what the program is doing.

Finally, engage with the book. Post comments on the book's web page and keep an eye out for other readers' comments. Sometimes another reader's comments may add a whole new dimension to an example that makes it even more interesting and useful.

What You Need to Use This Book

To read the book, you don't need anything special. (Except maybe a good lamp and reading glasses if you have them.) However, to get the most out of the book, you need to be able to run Visual Studio and build C# programs.

The book's example programs were written with Visual Studio Community 2017, which you can download for free at `tinyurl.com/juluzwl`.

None of the examples use any special features of that version of Visual Studio, however, so you can use their techniques in most recent versions of Visual Studio. I've run versions of most of the examples as far back as Visual Studio 2008 without major problems.

Note, however, that the text in the book only describes each example's key features. It does not explain every last little thing that might be necessary to make a program run. That means you cannot always start a new project, type in the code that's shown in the book, and expect the program to run. Often there are extra details that are too mundane to be worth describing in the text. To make a program run, you need to download it from the book's web site.

Unfortunately, Visual Studio isn't forward compatible so you can't load Visual Studio 2017 projects into earlier versions of Visual Studio. If you want to run an example in an earlier version, you'll have to retype, copy, and paste. (Or you could just install Visual Studio 2017.)

Conventions

To help the text make the most sense, I've adopted a few conventions. I've used the following styles in the text.

- ➢ Important words are *highlighted* when they are introduced.
- ➢ Keyboard strokes are shown as in Ctrl+A.
- ➢ Filenames, URLs, and code within the text are shown with a `monospaced font like this`.
- ➢ Blocks of code are shown as in the following.

```
for (int i=0; i<500; i++)
    Console.WriteLine("I will not throw paper airplanes in class.");
```

Particularly important notes are highlighted with a box and a notepad icon.

> **NOTE:** This is something important or interesting and you should take special notice.

Finally, some of the URLs used by the book are long. Really, *really* long. In fact, some are so long that they can't fit on one line in the book. To make reading and entering URLs in your browser easier, I've used TinyURL (`tinyurl.com`) to shorten most of them. For instance, the example, "44. Encrypt and Decrypt Files (11)," refers to `tinyurl.com/k9xgkn7` instead of the original 87 character URL `https://msdn.microsoft.com/library/system.security.cryptography.rfc2898derivebytes.aspx`.

Important URLs

The following sections describe the most important URLs associated with this book.

Web Page

This book's main web page is `www.CSharpHelper.com/top100.htm`. There you can find links to an overview, table of contents, discussions, and errata.

That page also includes links to some places where you can purchase the book. In addition to letting you buy the book, those pages provide reviews.

 NOTE: Please post a review when you have a chance!

This is a self-published book and self-published books live and die based on the reviews they receive.

Discussion

If there's some aspect of an example that you would like to discuss with others, please go to the book's web page, follow the discussion link, and post a comment. You can also post responses to previous comments in their own threads so others can follow the discussion.

Errata

I do my best to ensure that my books contain content of the highest possible quality, but mistakes do sneak through the editing process. Imagine trying to debug a 200,000+ word program without a compiler to help you find mistakes. For example, consider these three sentences.

> After lying on the floor for days, my brother finally washed his socks.
> I love cooking my dogs and my family.
> Time flies like a banana.

All of these are syntactically correct, so grammar checkers won't flag them, but they probably aren't saying what I mean. My brother wasn't lying on the floor for days (probably). I love cooking, my dogs, and my family, but I don't combine them in a cannibalistic way. Time may fly, and flies may like a banana, but I don't see how flying time is similar to a banana.

If you find one of these errors or some other mistake in the book, I would be grateful for your feedback. Posting errata may save other readers time and frustration, and will help me provide better information in the future.

To post errata, go to the book's web page and follow the errata link. First look to see if "your" error has already been reported and, if it has not, add it as a comment on that page. Please include your email address (which won't be posted publically) so I can contact you if I have questions. I'll review your comment and post a follow-up if necessary.

Email

If you have questions, comments, or suggestions while you're working through the book, please feel free to email me at RodStephens@CSharpHelper.com. I can't promise to solve all of your problems, but I'll do my best to point you in the right direction.

Summary

After reading this book, studying the examples, and working on some variations of your own, you should have an understanding of a wider variety of techniques that will make your C# programs more effective in the future. You'll have acquired new tools to add to your programming toolkit, and you'll be able to tackle problems in all sorts of new areas.

Now grab your favorite caffeinated beverage, launch Visual Studio, and start learning about *The C# Helper Top 100*.

Part I. Serialization

Serialization is the process of converting data into some sort of serial or stream-oriented representation. Deserialization is the process of converting a serialized representation back into the original data.

Currently XML (eXtensible Markup Language) and JSON (JavaScript Object Notation) are two of the most popular serialization formats, but there are many others. Some of those other formats, such as CSV (Comma-Separated Value) have been around for decades.

Microsoft's support for serialization tends to push C# programs towards using XML, but sometimes that may not be an option. For example, if you need to load data stored in JSON or CSV files, you have to learn how to work with those formats.

The examples in this part of the book show how to read and write CSV files and JSON serializations.

It's not clear why C# Helper's XML posts aren't more popular. They are certainly just as important as the CSV and JSON posts. Perhaps the .NET Framework's support for XML is good enough that people don't need as much help. Alternatively, it could be that the available books cover XML sufficiently.

It also seems likely that the number of hits on those posts is simply more diluted. If 10,000 visitors land on a dozen different XML posts, then the average number of visits per page small. If the visitors land on only one or two JSON posts, then those posts each get more hits.

Whatever the case, I invite you to visit C# Helper and look at its XML examples.

1. READ A CSV FILE INTO AN ARRAY (1)

A CSV file contains data in rows and columns. Rows are separated by carriage returns and the values in each row are separated by commas.

If a row is missing values, it must include adjacent commas to show where the missing data would be. That lets a program tell which values belong in the columns that come after the missing one.

Some CSV files, including the one used in this example, contain the names of the columns in the first row.

The following text shows part of the CSV data used by this example.

```
ZIP Code,City,State,State Abbrev,Area Code,Latitude,Longitude
00501,Holtsville,New York,NY,631,40.8147,-73.0451
00544,Holtsville,New York,NY,631,40.8128,-73.0480
00601,Adjuntas,Puerto Rico,PR,787,18.1650,-66.7240
00601,Jard de Adjuntas,Puerto Rico,PR,787,18.1650,-66.7240
00601,Urb San Joaquin,Puerto Rico,PR,787,18.1650,-66.7240
```

Each row in this file contains data for a city. The columns give the city's ZIP Code, city, state, state abbreviation, area code, latitude, and longitude.

This example reads and writes CSV data. First it reads a CSV file into an array of strings and displays the values in a `DataGridView`. It then writes the data back into a new file.

To make reading and writing CSV files easier, the example places the relevant methods in a tool class named `CsvTools`. This is a `static` class so you don't need to instantiate it to use its tools.

The following `LoadCsv` method loads a CSV file into an array of string arrays.

```
// Load a CSV file into an array of arrays of strings.
public static string[][] LoadCsv(string filename)
{
    // Get the file's lines.
    string[] lines = File.ReadAllLines(filename);

    // Allocate the result array.
    int numRows = lines.Length;
    string[][] values = new string[numRows][];

    // Load the values into the array.
```

```
        for (int r = 0; r < numRows; r++) values[r] = lines[r].Split(',');

        // Return the values.
        return values;
    }
```

The method first uses `File.ReadAllLines` to read the CSV file. That method, which is defined in the `System.IO` namespace, copies the file's lines into an array of strings.

The method then uses the array's length to determine the number of rows of data. It assumes that the file doesn't contain any blank lines.

NOTE: If the file *does* contain blank lines, use `File.ReadAllText` to read the file's contents as a single string that contains carriage return and newline characters. Then use that string's `Split` method to break the file into lines. An optional `StringSplitOptions` parameter to the `Split` method lets you remove any empty entries that were created by blank lines in the file.

The code creates the `values` array, an array of arrays of strings. It uses the number of rows to allocate the correct number of entries so the `values` array can hold one array of strings per row of CSV data.

The method then enters a loop where it uses each line's `Split` method to split the line into fields. After it has processed all of the lines, the method returns the `values` array.

The `CsvTools` class also defines the following `ArrayToCsv` method that converts an array of arrays of strings into a single string with the CSV format.

```
    // Return a string containing the data in CSV format.
    public static string ArrayToCsv(string[][] values)
    {
        // Make a StringBuilder to hold the data.
        StringBuilder sb = new StringBuilder();

        // Use string.Join to make each row into a CSV string.
        for (int r = 0; r <= values.GetUpperBound(0); r++)
            sb.AppendLine(string.Join(",", values[r]));

        // Remove the trailing newline and return the result.
        return sb.ToString().TrimEnd();
    }
```

You could build the result in a `string` variable and add pieces to it as you loop through the array. If the array is large, however, that would require a lot of string concatenations. In that case it is more efficient to use a `StringBuilder` object to create the string.

The method starts by creating a `StringBuilder`. It then loops through the entries in the array, each of which is an array of strings.

For each of those arrays, the code uses the `string.Join` method to turn the array into a single string with its values separated by commas. It uses the `StringBuilder` object's `AppendLine` method to add the result as a new line at the end of the `StringBuilder` contents.

After it has processed the array's rows, the method calls `StringBuilder.ToString` to convert the result into a single string.

Unfortunately, the result ends in a new line and in the CSV format that represents a blank row of data at the end of the file. The method uses the `string` class's `TrimEnd` method to remove any trailing whitespace from the string, and that includes carriage return and newline characters.

Finally, the method returns the result.

The `CsvTools` class includes one more tool for working with CSV data. The following code shows an extension method that converts a variable of type `string[][]` into a string with CSV format.

```
// An extension method to convert a string[][] into a CSV string.
public static string ToCsv(this string[][] values)
{
    return ArrayToCsv(values);
}
```

This code simply passes the `string[][]` object to the `ArrayToCsv` method described earlier and returns the result.

When you click the example program's Load button, the following code demonstrates the `CsvTools` methods.

```
// Load the data by parsing the CSV file.
private void loadButton_Click(object sender, EventArgs e)
{
    // Load the data.
    string[][] values = CsvTools.LoadCsv(fileTextBox.Text);

    // Display the values and elapsed time.
    DisplayValues(values, cityDataGridView);

    // Save the data into a new file.
    File.WriteAllText("test.csv", values.ToCsv());
    // File.WriteAllText("test.csv", TextTools.ToCsv(values));
}
```

This code first uses the `CsvTools.LoadCsv` method to load the CSV file into an array of arrays of strings. It then calls the `DisplayValues` method described shortly to show the data in a `DataGridControl`.

The code finishes by calling `values.ToCsv` to convert the data into a CSV format string. It then uses `File.WriteAllText` to save the string into a new file. You can then use an editor such as WordPad to open the file and verify that it contains the original data in CSV format.

The example program's final piece of code is the following `DisplayValues` method, which displays CSV data in a `DataGridView` control.

```
// Display an array of arrays of strings in a DataGridView.
// The first row of strings contains column headers.
private void DisplayValues(string[][] values, DataGridView dgv)
{
    int numRows = values.Length - 1;    // Don't count the header row.
    int numCols = values[0].Length;

    // Make column headers (stored in the first row).
    dgv.Columns.Clear();
    foreach (string header in values[0]) dgv.Columns.Add(header, header);

    // Add the required number of rows.
    dgv.Rows.Add(numRows);

    // Add the data.
    for (int r = 1; r <= numRows; r++)
        for (int c = 0; c < numCols; c++)
            dgv.Rows[r - 1].Cells[c].Value = values[r][c];

    // Autosize the columns.
    dgv.AutoResizeColumns();
}
```

The method starts by using the array's length to get the number of rows of data. It uses the number of items in the first row to get the number of columns of data.

Next, the code clears the `DataGridView` control's `Columns` collection and loops through the first row, adding its entries to the control's `Columns` collection to define the column headers.

The method adds enough `DataGridView` rows to hold all of the data and then loops through the data adding values to the appropriate `DataGridView` cells.

The method finishes by making the `DataGridView` control resize its columns to fit their data values.

Coma-separated value files may seem archaic. After all, they've been around since at least the early 1970s. They're still useful, however. Their simplicity, readability, and flexibility make them a reasonable choice for storing and retrieving simple data stored in rows and columns in a text file.

2. Use JSON to Serialize and Deserialize Objects (49)

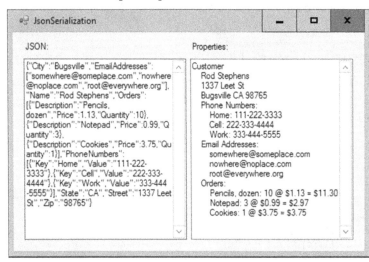

Comma-separated value files hold data in rows and columns. XML and JSON files store hierarchical data.

A JSON file can store objects that have properties. Properties can be simple values such as numbers or strings. They can also be arrays holding multiple values, and they can be other objects.

The following list summarizes some of JSON's more basic data types.

> Number
> String
> Boolean
> Array (a sequence of values separated by commas and enclosed in brackets [ ])
> Object (a collection of key:value pairs with pairs separated by commas and the whole collection surrounded by braces { })
> null (an empty value)

For example, the following text shows a JSON representation of a Customer object.

```
{
    "City":"Bugsville",
    "EmailAddresses":
    [
        "somewhere@someplace.com",
        "nowhere@noplace.com",
        "root@everywhere.org"
    ],
    "Name":"Rod Stephens",
    "Orders":
    [
        {"Description":"Pencils, dozen","Price":1.13,"Quantity":10},
        {"Description":"Notepad","Price":0.99,"Quantity":3},
        {"Description":"Cookies","Price":3.75,"Quantity":1}
    ],
    "PhoneNumbers":
    [
        {"Key":"Home","Value":"111-222-3333"},
```

```
        {"Key":"Cell","Value":"222-333-4444"},
        {"Key":"Work","Value":"333-444-5555"}
    ],
    "State":"CA",
    "Street":"1337 Leet St",
    "Zip":"98765"
}
```

Some of the properties such as City, Name, and State are simple string values. The EmailAddresses value is an array of strings.

The Orders property is an array of Order objects, each of which has a Description, Price, and Quantity.

Really the Orders property should probably be a collection of Order objects, each of which has a collection of OrderItem objects that have Description, Price, and Quantity properties, but the structure shown here is complicated enough for this example without all of that additional detail.

The PhoneNumbers value is a dictionary where the keys are phone number types (such as Home, Cell, Work) and the values are the phone number strings.

This example builds a Customer object. It then serializes it into a JSON format and then deserializes it to re-create the original object.

The following code shows the Order class.

```
using System.Runtime.Serialization;

[Serializable]
public class Order
{
    [DataMember] public string Description;
    [DataMember] public int Quantity;
    [DataMember] public decimal Price;

    // Return a textual representation of the order.
    public override string ToString()
    {
        decimal total = Quantity * Price;
        return Description + ": " +
            Quantity.ToString() + " @ " +
            Price.ToString("C") + " = " +
            total.ToString("C");
    }
}
```

To allow the program to serialize Order objects, the class must be marked with the Serializable attribute.

The fields within the class are marked with the DataMember attribute so the serializer knows to serialize them.

The Description, Quantity, and Price properties are straightforward. The last part of the class is an overridden ToString method that returns a textual representation of the object's values.

The following code shows the Customer class's property definitions.

```
using System.Runtime.Serialization;
using System.Runtime.Serialization.Json;
using System.IO;

...

[Serializable]
public class Customer
{
    [DataMember] public string Name = "";
    [DataMember] public string Street = "";
    [DataMember] public string City = "";
    [DataMember] public string State = "";
    [DataMember] public string Zip = "";
    [DataMember] public Dictionary<string, string> PhoneNumbers =
        new Dictionary<string, string>();
    [DataMember] public List<string> EmailAddresses = new List<string>();
    [DataMember] public Order[] Orders = null;

    ...
}
```

The module includes three using directives to make serializing and deserializing objects easier.

The Customer class defines several properties that are mostly straightforward. The last three properties, PhoneNumbers, EmailAddresses, and Orders, are respectively a dictionary, list, and array. I used three different methods for storing those values to demonstrate the JSON serializer's capabilities. The serializer will automatically convert them into the appropriate JSON data types.

The following list shows the basic steps to serialize an object.

1. Create a DataContractJsonSerializer object to perform the serialization.
2. Create some sort of stream to hold the serialization. For example, you could use a MemoryStream to write the serialization into memory or a FileStream to write the serialization into a file.
3. Use the serializer's WriteObject method to serialize the object into the stream.

To make serializing objects a bit easier, the Customer class includes the following ToJson method to convert the object into a string serialization.

```
// Return the JSON serialization of the object.
public string ToJson()
{
    // Make the serializer.
    DataContractJsonSerializer serializer
        = new DataContractJsonSerializer(typeof(Customer));
```

```
    // Make a stream to serialize into.
    using (MemoryStream stream = new MemoryStream())
    {
        // Serialize into the stream.
        serializer.WriteObject(stream, this);

        // Return the stream as text.
        byte[] bytes = stream.ToArray();
        return Encoding.UTF8.GetString(bytes, 0, bytes.Length);
    }
}
```

The method first creates a serializer. The parameter to the constructor gives the type of object that the serializer will manipulate, in this case Customer objects.

Next, the code creates a MemoryStream to hold the serialization. It then calls the serializer's WriteObject method to serialize the current Customer object into the stream.

The method then gets the bytes stored in the MemoryStream. It uses the static Encoding.UTF8.GetString method to convert the bytes into a string and returns the result.

The following list summarizes the steps you take to deserialize an object.

1. Create a serializer.
2. Create a stream holding the serialization.
3. Use the serializer's ReadObject method to deserialize the serialization.

The result has the non-specific object data type, so you will probably want to convert it into the correct type before saving it in a variable.

To make deserializing objects easier, the Customer class defines the following static FromJson method.

```
// Create a new Customer from a JSON serialization.
public static Customer FromJson(string json)
{
    // Make the serializer.
    DataContractJsonSerializer serializer =
        new DataContractJsonSerializer(typeof(Customer));

    // Make a stream from which to read.
    using (MemoryStream stream = new MemoryStream(Encoding.UTF8.GetBytes(json)))
    {
        // Deserialize and return the Customer object.
        return serializer.ReadObject(stream) as Customer;
    }
}
```

This method creates a serializer as before. It makes a MemoryStream and initializes it with the serialization string converted into bytes. The code calls the serializer's ReadObject method, converts the result into a Customer object, and returns the new object.

The following code shows how the example program serializes and deserializes a sample
Customer object.

```
// Serialize.
string serialization = cust.ToJson();
jsonTextBox.Text = serialization;
jsonTextBox.Select(0, 0);

// Deserialize.
Customer new_cust = Customer.FromJson(serialization);
propertiesTextBox.Text = new_cust.ToString();
propertiesTextBox.Select(0, 0);
```

The code first serializes the object and displays the serialization in a textbox. It then
deserializes the serialization and displays the restored object's values. (Download the
example and look at the code to see how the Customer class's ToString method works.)

The DataContractJsonSerializer isn't the only way you can serialize objects in .NET.
As I mentioned earlier, you can also use an XML serializer. In fact, you can even use other
JSON serializers. For example, the JavaScriptSerializer class defined in the
System.Web.Script.Serialization library lets you serialize and deserialize to and from
strings more easily.

You can also use third-party tools such as Newtonsoft's JSON.NET, which you can
download at www.newtonsoft.com/json.

I highly recommend that you give JavaScriptSerializer and JSON.NET a try as an
exercise.

Part II. Graphing

The examples in this part of the book show how to draw different kinds of graphs. Most of these show how to draw graphs in WPF and XAML. The final example in this part of the book draws a histogram in a Windows Forms application.

The reason that the the WPF examples are more popular than the Windows Forms examples may be because making graphs in WPF is a lot harder than it is in Windows Forms programs. That means more people need help with WPF, so they use those examples more.

These aren't the most complete graphing examples available on the C# Helper web site. For example, other programs show to draw rotated text and let the user move the mouse over a graph to see the graph's values. Search the site for those examples.

3. Draw a Graph in WPF (2)

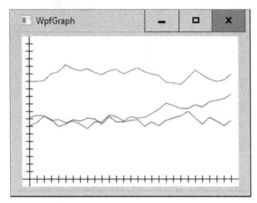

Drawing graphs is always a bit tricky because you typically need to work in at least two different coordinate systems. First, there's the *world coordinate system* that is natural for the data. For example, you might want X values to range over the years 2000 to 2020 and Y values to range over sales figures between $10,000 and $100,000.

The second coordinate system is the *device coordinate system* measured in pixels on the screen. Switching between the two systems is particularly difficult because Y coordinates typically increase upward world coordinates and downward in device coordinates.

The trickiest situation occurs when you need to position something in world coordinates but then draw it in device coordinates. For example, suppose you want to draw X and Y axes with tic marks that are five pixels wide. You need to use world coordinates to figure out where to draw the tic marks, but then you need to calculate the lengths of the tic marks in pixels.

Similarly suppose you want to draw some text on the graph to label something. You position the text in world coordinates, but you probably want to draw the text in device coordinates to make it easier to center and align the text.

The final weird problem I'll mention now is giving lines consistent widths. Suppose you draw the graph in some normalized space and then scale it to fit the device area. For example, you draw in the world coordinates $2000 \leq X \leq 2020$, $\$10,000 \leq Y \leq \$100,000$ and then you use a `LayoutTransform` to make the graph fit on a `Canvas` control.

When the transform stretches the graph, it also stretches the graph's lines. Unless the vertical and horizontal scale factors are the same, the lines will be stretched by different amounts vertically and horizontally. That means vertical and horizontal lines will have different thicknesses.

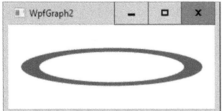

For example, the picture on the left shows a circle with width and height 50, and line thickness five. It has been scaled by factors of five horizontally and one vertically. You can see that its sides are much thicker than its top and bottom.

Anyway, to really place everything exactly where you want it, you need to be able to work freely in both world and device coordinates. This example shows how to draw a basic graph in device coordinates. The next example shows how to use transformations to work in world coordinates.

This example creates lines and polylines on a `Canvas` control. Because it uses device coordinates, the control's upper left corner has coordinates (0, 0). The X and Y coordinates are measured in pixels and increase to the right and downward respectively.

The following code shows the example program's XAML code.

```
<Window x:Class="WpfGraph.MainWindow"
    xmlns="http://schemas.microsoft.com/winfx/2006/xaml/presentation"
    xmlns:x="http://schemas.microsoft.com/winfx/2006/xaml"
    xmlns:d="http://schemas.microsoft.com/expression/blend/2008"
    xmlns:mc="http://schemas.openxmlformats.org/markup-compatibility/2006"
    xmlns:local="clr-namespace:WpfGraph"
    mc:Ignorable="d"
    Title="WpfGraph"
    Height="250" Width="335"
    Loaded="Window_Loaded">
    <Grid Background="LightGreen">
        <Canvas Name="graphCanvas" Background="White"
            Width="300" Height="200"
            VerticalAlignment="Center" HorizontalAlignment="Center"/>
    </Grid>
</Window>
```

The window's main child is a `Grid` that contains a `Canvas` named `graphCanvas`.

In WPF you don't normally draw directly on a drawing surface. You can if you really must, but normally you use `Line`, `Ellipse`, `Rectangle`, and other shape controls to draw.

You can include those objects in the XAML code if you like, but if you're going to draw a non-trivial graph, you're going to need to use code to do it.

Notice the `Loaded="Window_Loaded"` part of the window's XAML declaration. That tells the program that the `Window_Loaded` method is the event handler for the window's `Loaded` event.

When the example starts, the following `Window_Loaded` event handler builds the graph.

```
// Draw a simple graph.
private void Window_Loaded(object sender, RoutedEventArgs e)
{
    const double margin = 10;
    double xmin = margin;
    double xmax = graphCanvas.Width - margin;
    double ymin = margin;
    double ymax = graphCanvas.Height - margin;
    const double step = 10;

    // Make the X axis.
    GeometryGroup xaxisGeom = new GeometryGroup();
    xaxisGeom.Children.Add(new LineGeometry(
        new Point(0, ymax), new Point(graphCanvas.Width, ymax)));
    for (double x = xmin + step; x <= graphCanvas.Width - step; x += step)
    {
```

```
            xaxisGeom.Children.Add(new LineGeometry(
                new Point(x, ymax - margin / 2),
                new Point(x, ymax + margin / 2)));
        }

        Path xaxisPath = new Path();
        xaxisPath.StrokeThickness = 1;
        xaxisPath.Stroke = Brushes.Black;
        xaxisPath.Data = xaxisGeom;

        graphCanvas.Children.Add(xaxisPath);

        // Make the Y axis.
        GeometryGroup yaxisGeom = new GeometryGroup();
        yaxisGeom.Children.Add(new LineGeometry(
            new Point(xmin, 0), new Point(xmin, graphCanvas.Height)));
        for (double y = step; y <= graphCanvas.Height - step; y += step)
        {
            yaxisGeom.Children.Add(new LineGeometry(
                new Point(xmin - margin / 2, y),
                new Point(xmin + margin / 2, y)));
        }

        Path yaxisPath = new Path();
        yaxisPath.StrokeThickness = 1;
        yaxisPath.Stroke = Brushes.Black;
        yaxisPath.Data = yaxisGeom;

        graphCanvas.Children.Add(yaxisPath);

        // Make some data sets.
        Brush[] brushes = { Brushes.Red, Brushes.Green, Brushes.Blue };
        Random rand = new Random();
        for (int dataset = 0; dataset < 3; dataset++)
        {
            int lastY = rand.Next((int)ymin, (int)ymax);

            PointCollection points = new PointCollection();
            for (double x = xmin; x <= xmax; x += step)
            {
                lastY = rand.Next(lastY - 10, lastY + 10);
                if (lastY < ymin) lastY = (int)ymin;
                if (lastY > ymax) lastY = (int)ymax;
                points.Add(new Point(x, lastY));
            }

            Polyline polyline = new Polyline();
            polyline.StrokeThickness = 1;
            polyline.Stroke = brushes[dataset];
            polyline.Points = points;

            graphCanvas.Children.Add(polyline);
        }
    }
}
```

The code first defines some boundaries for the graph.

Next the program creates a `GeometryGroup` object to represent the X axis. You can use a `GeometryGroup` to hold other geometry objects such as lines. The code creates a `Line` to represent the axis's baseline and adds it to the group. It then uses a loop to create a sequence of small `Line` objects to represent tic marks and adds them to the group.

After it finishes defining the X axis's geometry, the program creates a `Path` object and sets its `StrokeThickness` and `Stroke` properties. It then sets the path's `Data` property to the `GeometryGroup` so the `Path` will draw the objects defined by the `GeometryGroup`.

The program then adds the `Path` to the canvas's `Children` collection to give it a home on the window.

The code repeats those steps to create the Y axis.

Next, the code makes some random values for three sets of data. For each data set, the code creates a `PointCollection` object. It generates some random points and adds them to the collection. When it's finished defining the data set's points, the program creates a `Polyline`, sets its drawing properties, and sets its `Points` property to the point collection. Finally, the code adds the `Polyline` to the canvas's `Children` collection.

That's all the program needs to do. After the `Window_Loaded` event handler creates the `Line` and `Polyline` objects, the program doesn't need to do anything to draw the graph. The `Line` and `Polyline` objects draw themselves automatically as needed.

4. USE TRANSFORMATIONS TO DRAW A GRAPH IN WPF (88)

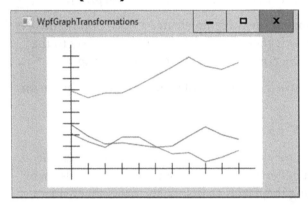

In two-dimensional graphics, *transformations* let you translate, scale, rotate, and skew the objects you draw. The preceding post, "Draw a graph in WPF," draws using device coordinates. This example shows how you can use transformations to let you draw in a world coordinate system that's more convenient for the data.

WPF provides a Transform class and several sub-classes (ScaleTransform, TranslateTransform, RotateTransform, and SkewTransform) to let you apply transformations to controls. You can set a control's LayoutTransform or RenderTransform property to a transform object to transform the control. For example, these properties let you rotate or skew a label relatively easily.

The LayoutTransform is applied when the window is arranged. The RenderTransform is applied when the control is drawn. Often you should use a LayoutTransform instead of a RenderTransform so container controls such as StackPanel and ScrollViewer can use the control's transformed dimensions.

If you want to apply multiple transforms to a control, you can combine them in a TransformGroup and then set the LayoutTransform or RenderTransform property to the group. For example, you can use that technique to both scale and rotate a label.

Unfortunately, that technique doesn't let you easily convert back and forth between world and device coordinates. As I mentioned in the preceding previous post, you often need to perform those conversions to draw a graph.

Fortunately, there's another way that you can represent transformations. Instead of using the transform classes, you can use the Matrix class. A Matrix object represents a 3×3 matrix that can store information about a transformation.

One of the nice features of matrices is that you can combine them to represent multiple transformations. For example, you can use a single Matrix to represent a translation, followed by a rotation, followed by a scaling, followed by another translation.

Another nice feature of matrices is that you can invert them to get a transformation representing the opposite of the original transformation.

Finally, your code can you can use a matrix to transform a point from one coordinate system to another.

By putting all of those features together, you can make a matrix to transform points from world to device coordinates. Then you can invert that matrix to transform points from device to world coordinates. That's just the approach that this example takes.

When the program starts, its `Window_Loaded` event handler performs several tasks such as creating the X and Y axes and generating some random data. It then uses the following `PrepareTransformations` method to create the two transformation matrices.

```
// Prepare values for perform transformations.
private Matrix WtoDMatrix, DtoWMatrix;
private void PrepareTransformations(
    double wxmin, double wxmax, double wymin, double wymax,
    double dxmin, double dxmax, double dymin, double dymax)
{
    // Make WtoD.
    WtoDMatrix = Matrix.Identity;
    WtoDMatrix.Translate(-wxmin, -wymin);

    double xscale = (dxmax - dxmin) / (wxmax - wxmin);
    double yscale = (dymax - dymin) / (wymax - wymin);
    WtoDMatrix.Scale(xscale, yscale);

    WtoDMatrix.Translate(dxmin, dymin);

    // Make DtoW.
    DtoWMatrix = WtoDMatrix;
    DtoWMatrix.Invert();
}
```

This method takes as parameters the coordinate bounds for the world and device coordinate systems. It uses those values to initialize the two transformation matrices `WtoDMatrix` and `DtoWMatrix`.

The method first creates the `WtoDMatrix` matrix and initializes it to the identity transformation. (If you apply the identity transformation to a point, the result is the same as the original untransformed point.)

Next, the code adds a translation to the matrix to translate the point (`wxmin, wymin`) so it sits at the origin.

The code then calculates the amounts by which the program must scale the world coordinates so they have the same size as the device coordinates. It adds a scaling transformation to the matrix to stretch the data to fit the device coordinates.

Next, the code adds another translation to move the origin (where the point (`wxmin, wymin`) was mapped earlier) so it ends up at the device coordinate location (`dxmin, dymin`).

NOTE: This code stretches the world coordinates to fit the device coordinates even if the two coordinate systems don't have the same shape. For example, if the world coordinate space is square and the device coordinate space is tall and thin, then the result is stretched so it looks tall and thin.

If you want to preserve the drawing's aspect ratio (the coordinate system's width-to-height ratio), then `xscale` and `yscale` must be the same. For example, you could use the smaller of the two ratios for both scales. With some extra work, you can also adjust the translations to center the result.

At this point, the matrix `WtoDMatrix` represents a transformation that maps world coordinates to device coordinates. The code sets the new matrix `DtoWMatrix` equal to matrix `WtoDMatrix` and then inverts it. Now `DtoWMatrix` represents the inverse transformation from device coordinates to world coordinates.

The following code shows how the program uses the `PrepareTransformations` method.

```
const double wxmin = -10;
const double wxmax = 110;
const double wymin = -1;
const double wymax = 11;
const double xstep = 10;
const double ystep = 1;
const double xtic = 5;
const double ytic = 0.5;

const double dmargin = 10;
double dxmin = dmargin;
double dxmax = graphCanvas.Width - dmargin;
double dymin = dmargin;
double dymax = graphCanvas.Height - dmargin;

// Prepare the transformation matrices.
PrepareTransformations(
    wxmin, wxmax, wymin, wymax,
    dxmin, dxmax, dymax, dymin);
```

This code defines the world coordinate bounds and the tic mark parameters as constants. It then uses the size of the `Canvas` control to set the device coordinates. It makes the device coordinates fill the `Canvas` minus a 10-pixel margin around the edges.

The code then calls `PrepareTransformations` to define the transformation matrices.

Notice that the device minimum and maximum Y coordinates are switched in the call to `PrepareTransformations`. That makes the resulting transformation flip the drawing area upside down. In other words, `WtoDMatrix` makes things drawn normally in world coordinates appear upside down in device coordinates. That's handy if Y values in the world coordinate system increase moving upwards as they usually do when you're graphing and performing other mathematical operations.

To make using the transformation matrices easier, the program defines the following two helper methods.

```
// Transform a point from world to device coordinates.
private Point WtoD(Point point)
{
    return WtoDMatrix.Transform(point);
}

// Transform a point from device to world coordinates.
private Point DtoW(Point point)
{
    return DtoWMatrix.Transform(point);
}
```

These methods use the matrices to transform points from one coordinate system to the other. This example doesn't actually use the DtoW method; it's just included for completeness. It does, however, use WtoD to convert all of the points it draws into device coordinates. For example, the following code creates the X axis.

```
// Make the X axis.
GeometryGroup xaxisGeom = new GeometryGroup();
Point p0 = new Point(wxmin, 0);
Point p1 = new Point(wxmax, 0);
xaxisGeom.Children.Add(new LineGeometry(WtoD(p0), WtoD(p1)));

for (double x = xstep; x <= wxmax - xstep; x += xstep)
{
    Point tic0 = new Point(x, -ytic);
    Point tic1 = new Point(x, ytic);
    xaxisGeom.Children.Add(new LineGeometry(WtoD(tic0), WtoD(tic1)));
}

Path xaxisPath = new Path();
xaxisPath.StrokeThickness = 1;
xaxisPath.Stroke = Brushes.Black;
xaxisPath.Data = xaxisGeom;
```

The code generates the points that it wants to use in world coordinates. It then uses WtoD to convert them into device coordinates before it uses them to create LineGeometry objects.

As a result, all of the drawing objects are in device coordinates so we don't need to transform the program's WPF controls. In turn that means we don't need to worry about weird effects such as scaling lines differently vertically and horizontally.

In fact, the preceding code sets the xaxisPath object's StrokeThickness property to 1. Because neither that object nor the Canvas control use transformations, the resulting lines are not scaled so they appear one pixel wide.

5. DRAW A GRAPH WITH LABELS IN WPF (85)

This example adds labels to the preceding example.

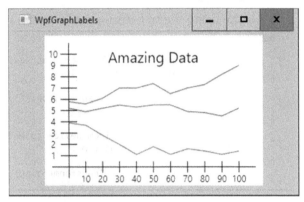

The basic idea is simple: create a `Label` control and add it to the `Canvas` that contains the other graph controls. To avoid weird transformation effects like the ones described in the preceding example, you can position the label in device coordinates. You can even use the transformation methods described in the preceding example to convert locations from world to device coordinates.

To make creating labels easier, the program defines the following `DrawText` method.

```
// Position a label at the indicated point in device coordinates.
private void DrawText(Canvas can, string text, Point location, double font_size,
    HorizontalAlignment halign, VerticalAlignment valign)
{
    // Make the label.
    Label label = new Label();
    label.Content = text;
    label.FontSize = font_size;
    can.Children.Add(label);

    // Position the label.
    label.Measure(new Size(double.MaxValue, double.MaxValue));

    double x = location.X;
    if (halign == HorizontalAlignment.Center)
        x -= label.DesiredSize.Width / 2;
    else if (halign == HorizontalAlignment.Right)
        x -= label.DesiredSize.Width;
    Canvas.SetLeft(label, x);

    double y = location.Y;
    if (valign == VerticalAlignment.Center)
        y -= label.DesiredSize.Height / 2;
    else if (valign == VerticalAlignment.Bottom)
        y -= label.DesiredSize.Height;
    Canvas.SetTop(label, y);
}
```

This method first makes a `Label` control, sets its `Content` and `FontSize` properties, and adds it to the `Canvas`.

In order to position the control correctly, the program needs to know how big the label is. The code uses the control's `Measure` method to get the control's size. It passes the method a huge `Size` object so the `Label` can be as large as it wants to be.

The method then uses the control's size and its alignment parameters to set the control's left and top coordinates within the Canvas. For example, if the Label should be centered horizontally at X position x, then the control's Left value should be x - width / 2.

That's all the method needs to do. After the method creates and positions it, the Label control automatically draws itself as needed.

The following code shows how the program draws and labels the tic marks on the X axis.

```
for (double x = xstep; x <= wxmax - xstep; x += xstep)
{
    Point tic0 = WtoD(new Point(x, -ytic));
    Point tic1 = WtoD(new Point(x, ytic));
    xaxisGeom.Children.Add(new LineGeometry(tic0, tic1));

    // Label the tic mark's X coordinate.
    DrawText(graphCanvas, x.ToString(), new Point(tic0.X, tic0.Y - 5), 12,
        HorizontalAlignment.Center, VerticalAlignment.Top);
}
```

As it loops over the tic marks, the code converts each tic mark's endpoints into device coordinates and creates a LineGeometry object to draw the mark.

The code then calls DrawText to display the tic mark's X coordinate value. The tic mark's endpoints tic0 and tic1 are in device coordinates so the DrawText method can use their X and Y values. The code subtracts five pixels from the Y value to move the label up slightly so it fits better on the graph.

NOTE: Normally when you draw text, there is a margin between its bounds and the actual text. As in this example, you may sometimes want to fudge the text's location a bit to make the result look better.

The program uses the following code to draw the graph's title.

```
// Make a title
Point titleLocation = new Point((dxmin + dxmax) / 2, 10);
DrawText(graphCanvas, "Amazing Data", titleLocation, 20,
    HorizontalAlignment.Center, VerticalAlignment.Top);
```

The code calculates the point where the top middle of the text should be. It calculates the position in device coordinates so the point doesn't need to be mapped from world coordinates before it's passed into the DrawText method. The DrawText method does the rest.

6. ZOOM ON A GRAPH IN WPF (60)

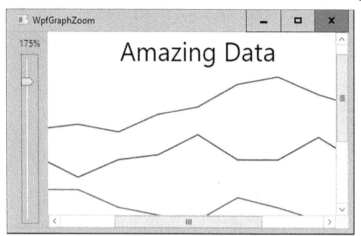

It's remarkably easy to make a program zoom in on something in WPF. This example draws a graph similar to the one created by the preceding example. It also lets you use the slider on the left to zoom in and out on the graph.

This program is very similar to the preceding one with just a few changes.

Obviously, the user interface now includes the slider and label on the left. They occupy two cells in the same column in the window's main `Grid` control.

It's less obvious that the `Canvas` holding the graph now sits inside a `ScrollViewer` control. The following XAML code defines those two controls.

```
<ScrollViewer Name="scvGraph"
    Grid.Row="0" Grid.Column="1" Grid.RowSpan="2"
    HorizontalScrollBarVisibility="Auto"
    VerticalScrollBarVisibility="Auto">
    <Canvas Name="graphCanvas" Background="White"
        Width="400" Height="250"
        VerticalAlignment="Center"
        HorizontalAlignment="Center"/>
</ScrollViewer>
```

The `ScrollViewer` is a remarkably useful control that lets you easily scroll and zoom on other controls. If the viewer's contents are too big to fit, then the viewer automatically displays scroll bars and adjusts the position of its contents as necessary. That means the program merely needs to adjust the size of the `Canvas` control and the `ScrollViewer` will do the rest.

When you adjust the value of the slider, the following code executes.

```
// Zoom.
private void zoomSlider_ValueChanged(object sender,
    RoutedPropertyChangedEventArgs<double> e)
{
    // Make sure the controls are ready.
    if (!IsInitialized) return;

    // Display the zoom factor as a percentage.
    zoomLabel.Content = zoomSlider.Value + "%";

    // Get the scale factor as a fraction 0.25 - 2.00.
    double scale = (double)(zoomSlider.Value / 100.0);
```

```
    // Scale the graph.
    graphCanvas.LayoutTransform = new ScaleTransform(scale, scale);
}
```

This code first checks the window's IsInitialized property and it exits if the window isn't initialized yet. The zoomSlider_ValueChanged event handler executes when the Slider is first created. At that time the graphCanvas control doesn't yet exist. If the code tried to set the canvas control's LayoutTransform property before the canvas existed, the program would crash.

If the window is initialized, the code displays the new scale factor in zoomLabel. It then converts the new value into a fraction, uses it to create a ScaleTransform, and applies the transformation to the Canvas control.

The rest is automatic. The Canvas uses the ScaleTransform to resize itself and its contents. The ScrollViewer then adjusts the Canvas and displays scroll bars if necessary.

You should take two lessons from this example. First, the ScrollViewer is remarkably useful and easy to use. Second, it's relatively easy to add a ScrollViewer to an existing program to add scrolling and zooming features.

7. Draw a Simple Histogram (37)

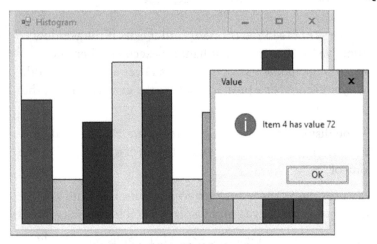

This Windows Forms example draws a simple histogram. If you resize the form, the histogram resizes to fill it. If you click on or above one of the histogram's bars, the program displays the bar's value in a dialog box, as shown in the picture on the right.

When the program starts, it uses the following code to generate some random data.

```
private const int MinValue = 0;
private const int MaxValue = 100;
private float[] DataValues = new float[10];

// Make some random data.
private void Form1_Load(object sender, EventArgs e)
{
    Random rnd = new Random();

    // Create data.
    for (int i = 0; i < DataValues.Length; i++)
        DataValues[i] = rnd.Next(MinValue + 5, MaxValue - 5);
}
```

This code defines minimum and maximum values, and an array to hold the data. The form's Load event handler uses a Random object to generate values and saves them in the array.

When the form's main PictureBox needs to be repainted, its Paint event handler calls the following DrawHistogram method to do all of the interesting work.

```
// Draw a histogram.
private void DrawHistogram(Graphics gr, Color bgcolor,
    float[] values, int width, int height)
{
    Color[] colors = new Color[] {
        Color.Red, Color.LightGreen, Color.Blue,
        Color.Pink, Color.Green, Color.LightBlue,
        Color.Orange, Color.Yellow, Color.Purple
    };

    gr.Clear(bgcolor);

    // Make a transformation to the PictureBox.
    RectangleF dataBounds = new RectangleF(0, 0, values.Length, MaxValue);
    PointF[] points =
```

```
    {
        new PointF(0, height),
        new PointF(width, height),
        new PointF(0, 0)
    };
    Matrix transformation = new Matrix(dataBounds, points);
    gr.Transform = transformation;

    // Draw the histogram.
    using (Pen pen = new Pen(Color.Black, 0))
    {
        for (int i = 0; i < values.Length; i++)
        {
            RectangleF rect = new RectangleF(i, 0, 1, values[i]);
            using (Brush brush = new SolidBrush(colors[i % colors.Length]))
            {
                gr.FillRectangle(brush, rect);
                gr.DrawRectangle(pen, rect);
            }
        }
    }

    gr.ResetTransform();
    gr.DrawRectangle(Pens.Black, 0, 0, width - 1, height - 1);
}
```

This method first defines an array of colors that it will use to fill the histogram's rectangles. It then clears the Graphics object gr with the background color it received as a parameter.

Next, the code sets up a transformation to map from world coordinates to device coordinates. It creates a RectangleF representing the world coordinates. The X coordinates range from 0 to the number of data values. That allows the program to treat the histogram's bars as if they are one unit wide.

The world coordinates have Y coordinates between 0 and MaxValue, the largest value that the program could have generated earlier. That way the tallest possible bar will fit in world coordinates.

The program then makes an array containing three points. Those points indicate in device coordinates where the world coordinate rectangle's upper left, upper right, and lower left corners should be mapped. This is the most interesting, important, and confusing part of the example, so I want to spend a few extra seconds explaining it.

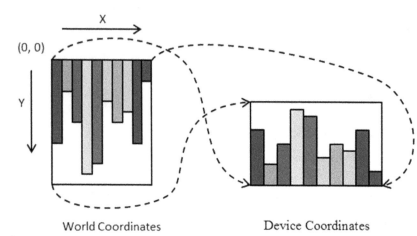

World Coordinates   Device Coordinates

The picture on the left shows how the program maps world coordinates to device coordinates. To make drawing easier, the program draws the histogram's rectangles with their bases sitting at Y = 0 and their tops with larger values of Y.

If you think about that in terms of your middle school math classes, the result is a normal histogram. The rectangles sit on the same baseline and grow upward.

Unfortunately, in C# the coordinate system has Y values increasing downward. That means the actual result in world coordinates looks like the left in the picture above.

The array of points used by this method maps the rectangle's corners as shown by the dashed arrows in the picture so the result is flipped right side up and stretched to fit the device coordinates.

After it defines the world coordinate rectangle and the device coordinate points, the code uses them to create a new `Matrix` object that represents the transformation between the two coordinate systems. The program assigns the `Matrix` to the `Transform` property of the `Graphics` object that it is using to draw.

The result is similar to placing a transformation on a WPF object; any drawing produced by the `Graphics` object will be automatically transformed.

> **NOTE:** Windows Forms and WPF have different definitions for `Matrix`. Windows Forms uses the `System.Drawing.Drawing2D.Matrix` class. WPF uses the `System.Windows.Media.Matrix` structure.
>
> Both of these represent transformations but they are not interchangeable. You need to use the right one with Windows Forms or WPF programs.

Now the code draws the histogram's rectangles. It loops through the data and defines a `RectangleF` that's one unit wide and as tall as its data value. The program uses the `Graphics` object's `FillRectangle` method to fill the rectangle with a color selected form the `colors` array.

Next, the code needs to outline the rectangle and that raises two interesting issues.

The first issue is that transformations scale not only the points that make up a shape but also the thickness of the lines used to draw the shapes. For example, if you draw something with a standard pen such as Pens.Black, that pen has thickness one. In this example, the transformation would make the one-pixel wide pen fill the entire rectangle, which also has width one in the world coordinate system.

The example program solves this problem by using a pen with thickness zero. When you use a pen that has thickness zero, the drawing system draws any lines one pixel wide even if it applies a transformation to the drawing.

The second issue is that the Graphics object's DrawRectangle method doesn't have an overloaded version that takes a RectangleF as a parameter. It can draw a Rectangle, or an area defined by an upper left corner, a width, and a height, but it can't draw a RectangleF.

To make drawing a RectangleF easier, the program uses the following extension method.

```
public static class GraphicsTools
{
    public static void DrawRectangle(this Graphics gr, Pen pen, RectangleF rect)
    {
        gr.DrawRectangle(pen, rect.X, rect.Y, rect.Width, rect.Height);
    }
}
```

This adds a new version of DrawRectangle to the Graphics class that takes a Pen and a RectangleF as parameters. The method simply invokes one of the other versions of DrawRectangle to draw the rectangle.

After the DrawHistogram method finishes drawing the rectangles, it resets the Graphics object's transformation and outlines the drawing surface with a black rectangle.

NOTE: This example resets the transformation so it can outline the drawing area in device coordinates. It's generally a good idea to reset the transformation when you're done with it in any case. That way if other parts of the program need to draw something, perhaps a caption on top of the histogram, the transformation isn't in some weird state left over from a previous drawing operation.

If you compare this example to the previous few, you can see the major difference between using WPF and Windows Forms to produce graphics. In WPF you define objects that draw themselves as needed. In Windows Forms you define code that draws shapes as needed. Both systems provide features such as transformations, so the choice is mostly a matter of which approach seems more intuitive to you.

Part III. Text Processing

The examples in this part of the book demonstrate some handy text processing techniques. They show how to change a string's capitalization, how to convert numbers to file sizes such as 1.35 MB, and how to convert between byte values and strings containing the hexadecimal equivalent.

8. CONVERT BETWEEN CASES (3)

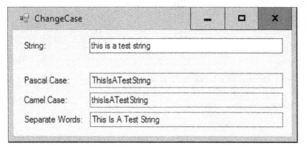

This example uses extension methods to convert strings between Pascal case, camel case, and proper case.

In *Pascal case*, each word is capitalized as in ThisStringIsPascalCased. In *camel case*, each word except the first is capitalized as in thisStringIsCamelCased. In *proper case*, each word is capitalized and separated by spaces as in "This String Is Proper Cased."

This example uses the `ToPascalCase` string extension method shown in the following code.

```
// Convert the string to Pascal case.
public static string ToPascalCase(this string theString)
{
    // If the string is null, just return it.
    if (theString == null) return theString;

    // If there are 0 or 1 characters, return the string capitalized.
    if (theString.Length < 2) return theString.ToUpper();

    // Split the string into words.
    string[] words = theString.Split(
        new char[] { },
        StringSplitOptions.RemoveEmptyEntries);

    // Capitalize and rejoin the words.
    string result = "";
    foreach (string word in words)
    {
        result +=
            word.Substring(0, 1).ToUpper() +
            word.Substring(1).ToLower();
    }
    return result;
}
```

This method splits a string containing spaces into words. It then loops through the words combining them. As it does so, it capitalizes each word's first character and converts their remaining characters to lowercase. When it's finished, the method returns the combined result.

The example also uses the `ToCamelCase` extension method shown in the following code.

```
// Convert the string to camel case.
public static string ToCamelCase(this string theString)
{
    // If the string is null, just return it.
    if (theString == null) return theString;
```

```
    // If there are 0 or 1 characters, return the string in lowercase.
    if (theString.Length < 2) return theString.ToLower();

    // Convert to Pascal case.
    theString = theString.ToPascalCase();

    // Convert the first character to lowercase and return the string.
    return theString.Substring(0, 1).ToLower() + theString.Substring(1);
}
```

This method uses the first method to convert the string into Pascal case. It then converts the string's first character into lowercase, adds on the rest of the string, and returns the result.

The following code shows the `ToProperCase` extension method.

```
// With input a Pascal cased or camel cased string,
// capitalize the first character and add a space before
// each following capitalized letter.
public static string ToProperCase(this string theString)
{
    // If the string is null, just return it.
    if (theString == null) return theString;

    // If there are 0 or 1 characters, return the string capitalized.
    if (theString.Length < 2) return theString.ToUpper();

    // Start with the first character capitalized.
    string result = theString.Substring(0, 1).ToUpper();

    // Add the remaining characters, inserting a space before capital letters.
    foreach (char ch in theString)
    {
        if (char.IsUpper(ch)) result += " ";
        result += ch;
    }
    return result;
}
```

This method loops through the characters in the string and inserts a space in front of each capital letter. Notice how it uses `char.IsUpper` to determine whether a character is upper case.

Note that these extension methods do not handle multi-character abbreviations such as "USSenator."

The rest of the example is straightforward. Download it to see additional details.

9. CONVERT BETWEEN CASES, PART 2 (66)

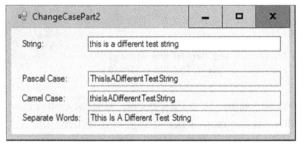

Like the previous example, this one shows how to use string extension methods to convert strings into various case types. (Thanks to Gary Winey for this version.)

Instead of splitting strings at spaces and examining the strings one character at a time, this version uses `StringInfo` objects and regular expressions.

The extension methods use several new namespaces so the class that defines them includes the following using directives.

```
using System.Globalization;
using System.Threading;
using System.Text.RegularExpressions;
```

The following code shows the new `ToPascalCase` method.

```
// Convert the string to Pascal case.
public static string ToPascalCase(this string theString)
{
    // If the string is null, just return it.
    if (theString == null) return theString;

    // If there are 0 or 1 characters, return the string capitalized.
    if (theString.Length < 2) return theString.ToUpper();

    TextInfo info = Thread.CurrentThread.CurrentCulture.TextInfo;
    theString = info.ToTitleCase(theString);
    return theString.Replace(" ", "");
}
```

This method uses `Thread.CurrentThread.CurrentCulture.TextInfo` to get a `TextInfo` object that has properties and methods dealing with the way the computer's culture handles text. It uses that object's `ToTitleCase` method to capitalize the first letter of each of the string's words.

The `ToTitleCase` method does not remove the spaces from the string, so the code replaces spaces with an empty string. It then returns the result.

The following code shows the new `ToCamelCase` extension method.

```
// Convert the string to camel case.
public static string ToCamelCase(this string theString)
{
    // If the string is null, just return it.
    if (theString == null) return theString;

    // If there are 0 or 1 characters, return the string in lowercase.
    if (theString.Length < 2) return theString.ToLower();
```

```
    // Convert to Pascal case.
    theString = theString.ToPascalCase();

    // Convert the first character to lowercase and return the string.
    return theString.Substring(0, 1).ToLower() + theString.Substring(1);
}
```

This code uses the preceding ToPascalCase method to convert the string into Pascal case. It then converts the string's first character into lowercase just as the preceding example did.

The following code shows the new ToProperCase method.

```
    // With input a Pascal cased or camel cased string,
    // capitalize the first character and add a space before
    // each following capitalized letter.
    public static string ToProperCase(this string theString)
    {
        // If the string is null, just return it.
        if (theString == null) return theString;

        // If there are 0 or 1 characters, return the string capitalized.
        if (theString.Length < 2) return theString.ToUpper();

        const string pattern = @"(?<=\w)(?=[A-Z])";
        string result = Regex.Replace(theString, pattern, " ", RegexOptions.None);
        return result.Substring(0, 1).ToUpper() + result.Substring(1);
    }
```

This method defines a constant to hold the following regular expression pattern.

```
    (?<=\w)(?=[A-Z])
```

The first part of this pattern, (?<=\w), marks the ending of a string of word characters. The second part, (?=[A-Z]), marks the beginning of a sequence of uppercase letters. Together these mark boundaries between sequences of letters and the beginning of a run of uppercase letters. Because the input string is in either Pascal or camel case, it basically finds the positions just before capital letters.

The method uses the regular expression method Regex.Replace to replace the matches found with space characters. The result is a string with a space before each capital letter.

The method finishes by capitalizing the strings' first letter.

For more information about regular expressions, see the article ".NET Framework Regular Expressions" at tinyurl.com/ydd6t6ry.

10. Format File Sizes (35)

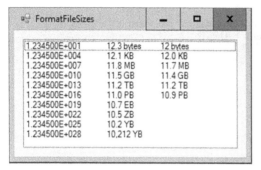

This example shows how to format file sizes in KB, MB, GB, and so forth. It defines two extension methods that convert numeric values into strings representing a number of bytes. The first method uses an API (Application Programming Interface) function. The second method uses only C# code.

To make displaying the results easier, the program also defines an extension method that lets you easily set tab stops for `ListBox` controls.

The following code shows the `SetTabs` extension method.

```
public static class ListBoxExtensions
{
    // Set tab stops inside a ListBox.
    public static void SetTabs(this ListBox lst, IList<int> tabs)
    {
        // Make sure the control will use them.
        lst.UseTabStops = true;
        lst.UseCustomTabOffsets = true;

        // Get the control's tab offset collection.
        ListBox.IntegerCollection offsets = lst.CustomTabOffsets;

        // Define the tabs.
        foreach (int tab in tabs)
        {
            offsets.Add(tab);
        }
    }
}
```

This method sets the control's `UseTabStops` and `UseCustomTabOffsets` properties so the `ListBox` will use the tab stops.

Next, the method saves a reference to the `ListBox` control's `CustomTabOffsets` property in the variable `offsets`. The method finishes by looping through the list of tab values and adding them to the control's tab offsets.

NOTE: The tab stops are measured in quarters of the average width of the characters in the control's font. In practice, you may need to fiddle with the values to make the result look nice. If you really want values to line up, use a grid-like control such as a `DataGrid` or `ListView`.

The following code shows the first file size extension method.

```
using System.Runtime.InteropServices;
```

```
...
[DllImport("Shlwapi.dll", CharSet = CharSet.Auto)]
public static extern Int32 StrFormatByteSize(
    long fileSize,
    [MarshalAs(UnmanagedType.LPTStr)] StringBuilder buffer,
    int bufferSize);

// Return a file size created by the StrFormatByteSize API function.
public static string ToFileSizeApi(this long value)
{
    StringBuilder sb = new StringBuilder(20);
    StrFormatByteSize(value, sb, 20);
    return sb.ToString();
}
```

This method uses the `StrFormatByteSize` API function so the class begins with a `DllImport` statement to declare that function. That statement is defined in the `System.Runtime.InteropServices` namespace so the module begins with a `using` directive to include that namespace.

> **NOTE:** The word "Interop" in the library's name is short for "interoperability." Interoperability is the ability of different kinds of programs and libraries to work together. In this case, it refers to the C# program interoperating with the Windows API functions.
>
> Later examples in the book, such as those that demonstrate Microsoft Office Integration, use other interop tools.

The extension method creates a `StringBuilder` to hold the result. Initially the `StringBuilder` has capacity to hold 20 characters. You can change that if the result will be longer.

The method calls `StrFormatByteSize` passing it the size to convert, the `StringBuilder`, and the maximum allowed length of the result. The method then returns the contents of the `StringBuilder`.

In Windows 10, the `StrFormatByteSize` function uses base 10. That means its idea of a kilobyte is 1,000 bytes instead of 1,024 bytes. If you want to format file sizes using 1,024 byte kilobytes, then you can use the example's second extension method, which is shown in the following code.

```
// Return a string describing the value as a file size.
// For example, 1.23 MB.
public static string ToFileSize(this double value)
{
    string[] suffixes =
        { "bytes", "KB", "MB", "GB", "TB", "PB", "EB", "ZB", "YB" };
    for (int i = 0; i < suffixes.Length; i++)
    {
        if (value <= (Math.Pow(1024, i + 1)))
        {
```

```
            return ThreeNonZeroDigits(value / Math.Pow(1024, i)) +
                " " + suffixes[i];
        }
    }

    return ThreeNonZeroDigits(value / Math.Pow(1024, suffixes.Length - 1)) +
        " " + suffixes[suffixes.Length - 1];
}
```

This method first creates an array holding the suffixes that it will use. It then enters a loop that compares the input value with powers of 1,024. When it reaches a point where the value is less than 1,024 to a power, the method divides the value by the next smaller power and then returns it followed by the appropriate suffix.

For example, consider the value 1,000,000. The program makes the following comparisons.

Value	i	$1,024^{i+1}$
1,000,000	0	1
1,000,000	1	1,024
1,000,000	2	1,048,576

The final test value 1,048,576 is greater than 1,000,000, so the if test succeeds. The program divides 1,000,000 by the next smaller power (which is $1,024^1 = 1,024$) to get 976.56.

The code uses the ThreeNonZeroDigits method described shortly to get that value's three most significant digits. In this example, that's 977.

The method then appends the corresponding prefix. In this example, the largest value of i that was tested is 2, so the program uses the prefix in position 2 - 1 = 1 in the prefixes array. That entry is "KB," so the final result is "977 KB."

If the value is too big for any of the prefixes, the program divides it by the largest prefix's power of 1,024 and then uses the largest prefix. For example, if the value is 10^{27}, then the result is 1,000 YB.

The final piece to this example is the following ThreeNonZeroDigits method.

```
// Return the value formatted to include at most three
// non-zero digits and at most two digits after the
// decimal point.
private static string ThreeNonZeroDigits(double value)
{
    if (value >= 100)
    {
        // No digits after the decimal.
        return value.ToString("0,0");
    }
    else if (value >= 10)
```

```
    {
        // One digit after the decimal.
        return value.ToString("0.0");
    }
    else
    {
        // Two digits after the decimal.
        return value.ToString("0.00");
    }
}
```

If the value is at least 100, then it needs three digits anyway so the method simply returns the value formatted as a string with no values after the decimal point.

> **NOTE:** If the original file size was small enough to display using the available prefixes, then this value will have at most three digits. For larger values such as 1,234 YB, the method returns all of the value's digits.
>
> If you would rather have the method reduce this to three significant digits and return 1,230 YB, feel free to modify the code.

If the value is at least 10 but less than 100, the method returns the value formatted as a string with two digits before the decimal point and one after.

Finally, if the value is less than 10, the method returns the value formatted as a string with one digit before the decimal point and two after.

The main program displays several sample values. It displays the file size value, the result of the method that uses the API function, and the result of the C# extension method.

The StrFormatByteSize API function works with long integers so it can't handle values that won't fit in a long integer. If you look at the program's results, you'll see that the API method only handles sizes up to petabytes, but the C# solution works up to yottabytes.

11. Convert between Byte Arrays and Hex Strings (57)

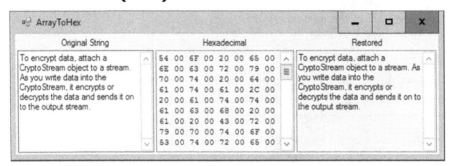

Sometimes it's useful to be able to visualize the values in an array of bytes. For example, in cryptography many values are handled as arrays of bytes and it's occasionally useful to have a textual representation of those bytes. This example's methods convert between byte arrays and hexadecimal strings.

In addition to those methods, the example defines two other methods that convert strings to and from byte arrays. They allow the program to work with the bytes as strings instead of arbitrary bytes that don't have much meaning.

The following string extension methods convert between strings and arrays of bytes.

```
// Convert a string into an array of bytes holding the string's Unicode.
public static byte[] UnicodeBytes(this string text)
{
    UnicodeEncoding encoder = new UnicodeEncoding();
    return encoder.GetBytes(text);
}

// Convert an array holding Unicode bytes into a string.
public static string ToUnicodeString(this byte[] bytes)
{
    UnicodeEncoding encoder = new UnicodeEncoding();
    return encoder.GetString(bytes);
}
```

The first method simply creates a `UnicodeEncoding` object and uses its `GetBytes` method to return an array of bytes holding the string's Unicode data.

The second method also creates a `UnicodeEncoding` object. It uses the object's `GetString` method to convert the array of bytes back into a string.

The following extension method converts a byte array into a string that holds the hexadecimal representation of the array's bytes.

```
// Return a string that represents the byte array as a series
// of hexadecimal values separated by a separator character.
public static string ToHex(this byte[] bytes, char separator)
{
```

```
            return BitConverter.ToString(bytes, 0).Replace('-', separator);
    }
```

The method first calls the `BitConverter` class's static `ToString` method to create a string representation of the byte array. The `ToString` method returns the hexadecimal values separated by dashes as in the following text.

```
54-00-6F-00-20-00-65-00-6E-00-63-00-72-00-79-00-70-00-74-00-20-00-64
```

The method takes as a parameter a separator character that it should use in place of the dash character. The code replaces the dash character with the new separator and returns the result. For example, the preceding result with spaces as separators looks like the following.

```
54 00 6F 00 20 00 65 00 6E 00 63 00 72 00 79 00 70 00 74 00 20 00 64
```

The final extension method, which is shown in the following code, converts a string that contains hexadecimal values back into a byte array.

```
// Convert a string containing 2-digit hexadecimal values into a byte array.
public static byte[] ToBytes(this string text)
{
    // Get the separator character.
    char separator = text[2];

    // Split at the separators.
    string[] pairs = text.Split(separator);
    byte[] bytes = new byte[pairs.Length];
    for (int i = 0; i < pairs.Length; i++)
        bytes[i] = Convert.ToByte(pairs[i], 16);
    return bytes;
}
```

This method first looks at the string's third character (with index 2) to discover the separator character. It then uses the string's `Split` method to divide the string into an array of smaller strings each containing one of the hexadecimal values.

Next the code allocates the `bytes` array to hold the result. It loops through the hexadecimal values, uses `Convert.ToByte` to convert each value into a byte, and saves the result in the `bytes` array.

NOTE: If you change the second parameter to `Convert.ToByte` to 2, 8, or 10, it can convert a binary, octal, or decimal value into a byte.

12. REMOVE NONPRINTABLE ASCII CHARACTERS (84)

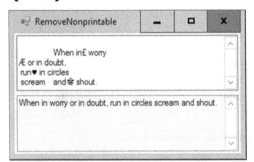

This is actually a tricky problem these days. In the good old days of simple ASCII text, you could easily remove whitespace characters such as carriage returns and tabs from a string. You could also remove odd characters such as windings and other non-alphabetic shapes. The result would be a string containing only letters, numbers, and other typewriter characters such as # and %.

Today most programs use Unicode instead of ASCII. It's much harder to determine which characters should be removed from a Unicode string. You can try to remove whitespace characters as before, but should you remove characters from other language sets such as Kanji, Cyrillic, or Vietnamese? If a character set defines a character that is actually some odd kind of whitespace, can you detect that and remove it?

Unfortunately, I don't know the answers to those questions. Until someone solves those mysteries, this example does something much simpler. It removes all characters from a string that lie outside of the range between the space character and the tilde (~) character. That leaves only the normal typewriter characters.

The example program uses the following string extension method.

```
using System.Text.RegularExpressions;
...
public static class StringExtensions
{
    // Remove characters that are not between ~ and space.
    public static string TrimNonAscii(this string value)
    {
        string pattern = "[^ -~]+";
        return Regex.Replace(value, pattern, "");
    }
}
```

This method uses regular expressions, so its module includes the following `using` directive.

```
using System.Text.RegularExpressions;
```

The method itself creates the pattern [^ -~]+, which matches any character that is *not* between the space and tilde characters. It then uses the `Regex` class's static `Replace` method to replace occurrences of the pattern with an empty string, and that removes the unwanted characters from the string.

Part IV. DataGridView

The `DataGridView` control displays data in rows and columns. Usually a program binds a data source to it, and the control displays the data automatically. Because that's the way people usually use this control, that's what's covered in most programming books.

The posts in this section explain some other ways that you can use the `DataGridView` control. For example, they show how to handle `DataGridView` errors, use a `DataGridView` control without an underlying data set, and define `DataGridView` column styles.

13. BIND A DATATABLE TO A DATAGRIDVIEW CONTROL (4)

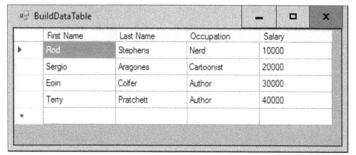

This example shows how to build a DataTable at runtime and bind it to a DataGridView control.

A DataTable is an in-memory representation of a relational database table. It can define columns of particular data types and even enforce uniqueness and foreign key constraints much as a relational database can. This example shows how to build a DataTable in code that uses specific data types for its columns and that has a two-column uniqueness constraint.

When the program starts, it uses the following code to create and display the DataTable.

```csharp
private void Form1_Load(object sender, EventArgs e)
{
    // Make the DataTable object.
    DataTable dt = new DataTable("People");

    // Add columns to the DataTable.
    dt.Columns.Add("First Name", System.Type.GetType("System.String"));
    dt.Columns.Add("Last Name", System.Type.GetType("System.String"));
    dt.Columns.Add("Occupation", System.Type.GetType("System.String"));
    dt.Columns.Add("Salary", System.Type.GetType("System.Int32"));

    // Make all columns required.
    for (int i = 0; i < dt.Columns.Count; i++)
    {
        dt.Columns[i].AllowDBNull = false;
    }

    // Make First Name + Last Name require uniqueness.
    DataColumn[] unique_cols =
    {
        dt.Columns["First Name"],
        dt.Columns["Last Name"]
    };
    dt.Constraints.Add(new UniqueConstraint(unique_cols));

    // Add items to the table.
    dt.Rows.Add(new object[] { "Rod", "Stephens", "Nerd", 10000 });
    dt.Rows.Add(new object[] { "Sergio", "Aragones", "Cartoonist", 20000 });
    dt.Rows.Add(new object[] { "Eoin", "Colfer", "Author", 30000 });
    dt.Rows.Add(new object[] { "Terry", "Pratchett", "Author", 40000 });

    // Prohibited: First Name is missing.
    //dt.Rows.Add(new object[] { null, "Aragones", "Cartoonist", 20000 });
```

```
        // Prohibited: Duplicate First Name + Last Name.
        //dt.Rows.Add(new object[] { "Eoin", "Colfer", "President", 200000 });

        // Make the DataGridView use the DataTable as its data source.
        peopleDataGridView.DataSource = dt;
    }
```

This code makes a DataTable object and adds columns to it, specifying their data types. It then loops through all of the columns setting their AllowDBNull properties to false so every column is required.

Next, the program makes an array containing references to the First Name and Last Name columns. It uses that array to make a UniqueConstraint object and adds it to the DataTable object's Constraints collection.

Finally, the program uses the DataTable object's Rows.Add method to add arrays of objects to the DataTable. The code includes two commented out statements that try to violate the required field and uniqueness constraints. Uncomment them to see what happens.

The code finishes by setting the DataGridView control's DataSource property to the DataTable. After that, the DataGridView and DataTable display the data automatically.

You can use this technique to display data generated at runtime in a DataGridView control without using a database.

14. HANDLE DATAGRIDVIEW ERRORS (52)

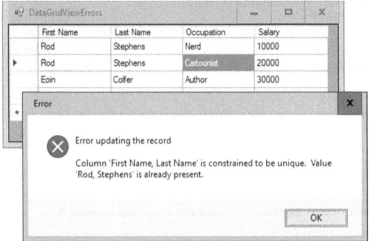

This example shows how you can handle data errors in a `DataGridView` control.

If you create a `DataTable` as in the preceding example, the `DataGridView` control allows the user to modify the program's data. If the user tries to violate the `DataTable` object's constraints, the `DataGridView` control raises its `DataError` event.

In this example, all of the data columns are required and the {First Name, Last Name} pair must be unique. If the user tries to modify the data to remove one of the values or to make a duplicate {First Name, Last Name} pair, the control raises its `DataError` event.

If you don't handle the event, the `DataGridView` control displays an ugly error message that includes a stack trace. If you would rather not show this intimidating message to the user, make your code handle the `DataError` event. Your event handler can try to figure out what went wrong or at least tell the user that the data is invalid in more friendly terms.

> **NOTE:** The error doesn't actually occur until the `DataGridView` control tries to update the `DataTable`. That happens when the user tries to move out of the updated row. That means the user may be able to see an invalid change for a while until trying to move to a new row.

This example uses the following `DataError` event handler.

```
// Display information about the error.
private void peopleDataGridView_DataError(object sender,
    DataGridViewDataErrorEventArgs e)
{
    // Display an error message.
    string text = "Error updating the record" +
        "\n\n" + e.Exception.Message;
    MessageBox.Show(text, "Error",
        MessageBoxButtons.OK, MessageBoxIcon.Error);
}
```

This code displays a simple error message without scaring the user with a stack trace.

15. ADD ROWS TO AN UNBOUND DATAGRIDVIEW CONTROL (9)

The preceding example binds a DataTable to a DataGridView control. This example uses a DataGridView control that is not bound to any data source.

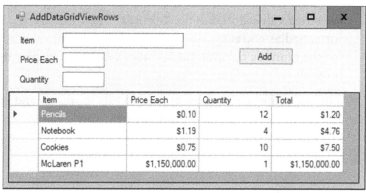

Before you can add data to the DataGridView control, you need to prepare it. Add the control to the form and select it. Click its Smart Tag (the little right-pointing arrow at the control's upper right edge), click the Edit Columns link, and use the Edit Columns editor to create and define the columns.

Set each column's HeaderText property to determine what the control will display above the column. Set other column properties such as Width if you like.

To make the control properly format the values in a column, click the column's DefaultCellStyle property and then click the ellipsis to the right. Use the CellStyle Builder that appears to set such properties as the column's colors, format, alignment, and wrapping.

After you perform all of that setup, the control is ready to use at runtime. This example executes the following code when you click the Add button.

```csharp
// Add a new item to the DataGridView.
private void addButton_Click(object sender, EventArgs e)
{
    // Create the new row.
    decimal priceEach = decimal.Parse(priceEachTextBox.Text);
    decimal quantity = decimal.Parse(quantityTextBox.Text);
    decimal total = priceEach * quantity;
    valuesDataGridView.Rows.Add(itemTextBox.Text, priceEach, quantity, total);

    // Get ready for the next entry.
    itemTextBox.Clear();
    priceEachTextBox.Clear();
    quantityTextBox.Clear();
    itemTextBox.Focus();
}
```

The code first gets the Price Each and Quantity values that you entered and uses them to calculate total cost.

Next the code uses the `DataGridView` control's `Rows.Add` method to create the new row, passing in the row's values. (The item value is just text, so the code passes the value that you entered directly from its `TextBox`.)

It is important that the call to `Rows.Add` passes a decimal value for Price Each rather than the string value stored in the `TextBox`. The Price Each column's cell style displays the value formatted as currency, but that only works if the value is numeric. If you use a string value for the numeric column, the `DataGridView` will display the value, but it won't format it properly.

The code finishes by clearing the `TextBox` controls and setting focus back to the Item `TextBox` so you can easily enter the next row's values.

16. SET DATAGRIDVIEW COLUMN STYLES (95)

You can set a `DataGridView` column's default cell styles by setting its `DefaultCellStyle` property. That property determines the column's appearance including its foreground color, background color, font, alignment, and selected item color.

Item	Price Each	Quantity	Total
Pencils, dozen	$1.24	4	$4.96
Cookies, box	$2.17	1	$2.17
Notebook	$1.95	2	$3.90
Paper, ream	$3.75	2	$7.50
Pencil sharpener	$12.95	1	$12.95
Paper clips, 100	$0.75	1	$0.75

To set a column's style at design time, select the control, click the Columns property in the Properties window, and click the ellipsis to the right.

In the Column Editor that appears, select a column, click its `DefaultCellStyle` property, and click the ellipsis to its right. Finally, in the CellStyle Builder that pops up, set the properties that you want the column to use. In this example, I used this method to set the first column's style at design time.

To set a column's style at runtime, create a `DataGridViewCellStyle` object, set its properties, and assign it to a column's `DefaultCellStyle` property. This example uses the following code to set the style for the `DataGridView` control's fourth column.

```
// Define a column style at run time.
DataGridViewCellStyle style = new DataGridViewCellStyle();
style.BackColor = Color.LightGreen;
style.Alignment = DataGridViewContentAlignment.MiddleRight;
style.Format = "C2";
valuesDataGridView.Columns[3].DefaultCellStyle = style;
```

This gives the column a light green background, aligns values on the right horizontally and in the middle vertically, and displays values with the C2 format, which displays numeric values as currency with two digits after the decimal point.

NOTE: By default, the `DataGridView` control uses styles that more or less make sense. For example, if a column contains integer data, it aligns that column on the right. If a column contains decimal data, it displays the values in that column as currency. If you use `DataGridView` column styles of your own, then you should probably use similar settings.

Part V. Microsoft Office Integration

Microsoft Office integration lets a C# program manipulate a Microsoft Office program. For example, you could use these kinds of programs to create PowerPoint presentations, copy data in and out of Excel workbooks, or add pictures to Word documents.

Often the hardest part in these kinds of programs is figuring out what objects in the Office object model do the things you want. For example, to create and format pictures in a Word document, you need to understand how to use Word's InlineShape and Shape objects.

If you want to do a lot of this kind of programming, my book *Microsoft Office Programming: A Guide for Experienced Developers* (Rod Stephens, APress, 2003) may help. The code is in Visual Basic for Applications (VBA) and it's a few years old, but it should help you figure out how to manipulate the Microsoft Word, Excel, PowerPoint, Access, and Outlook object models.

Office integration is a huge topic and the C# Helper web site contains dozens of posts that deal with it. This section describes the site's four most popular Office integration posts.

17. READ DATA FROM EXCEL (5)

To read Excel data, you open the Excel application and use it as a server to manipulate Excel workbooks.

Before you can use the Excel application and the objects it defines, you need to add a reference to the Excel object library. To do that, open the Project menu and select Add Reference. In the Reference Manager, expand the Assemblies section on the left.

Next click the Extensions category and scroll down until you see `Microsoft.Office.Interop.Excel`. You may have several versions installed. Check the box next to the most recent version and click OK.

The following picture shows the Reference Manager on my computer with the library selected.

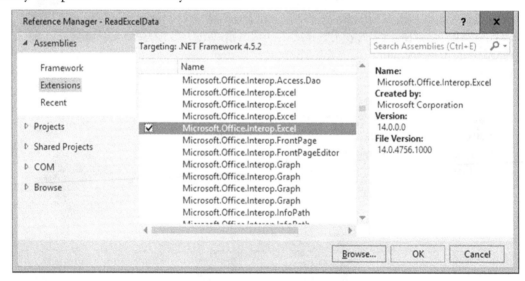

To make using the library easier, the example program includes the following `using` directive.

```
using Excel = Microsoft.Office.Interop.Excel;
```

This defines the alias `Excel` so it refers to the interop library's namespace.

When you enter the full path to an Excel workbook and click Read, the example program executes the following code.

```
// Read the data in the workbook's first two columns.
private void readButton_Click(object sender, EventArgs e)
```

```
{
    Cursor = Cursors.WaitCursor;

    // Get the Excel application object.
    Excel.Application excel = new Excel.Application();

    // Uncomment to make Excel visible.
    //excel.Visible = true;

    // Open the workbook read-only.
    Excel.Workbook workbook = excel.Workbooks.Open(
        Filename: fileTextBox.Text,
        ReadOnly: true);

    // Get the first worksheet.
    Excel.Worksheet sheet = (Excel.Worksheet)workbook.Sheets[1];

    // Get the titles and values.
    SetTitleAndListValues(sheet, 1, 1, title1Label, items1ListBox);
    SetTitleAndListValues(sheet, 1, 2, title2Label, items2ListBox);

    // Close the workbook without saving changes.
    workbook.Close(SaveChanges: false);

    // Close the Excel server.
    excel.Quit();

    Cursor = Cursors.Default;
}
```

This code makes the form display a wait cursor and then creates a new object of type
`Excel.Application`. This is an Excel application server that the program can use to
manipulate Excel.

Uncomment the next statement if you want to make Excel visible while the program is
using it. Normally you probably don't want Excel to pop up while your program is running
so you can leave this statement commented out.

However, if your program halts without calling Excel's Quit method, then the Excel server
remains running. For example, if your program crashes or if you use Visual Studio to halt
the program, then Excel is left running.

If you make Excel visible, then you can at least see it and close it after your program stops
unexpectedly. For that reason, you may want to make Excel visible while you are testing
your program. That also lets you see what Excel is doing, although its actions may happen
so quickly that you can't really understand them clearly.

Even if you stop the visible instance of Excel, the system will have another Excel process
running in the background. You can use the Task Manager to hunt down and stop those
kinds of zombie instances.

Having created the Excel server and possibly made it visible, the example program then
uses the server's `Workbooks` collection's `Open` method to open the Excel workbook.

Note that the Office interop libraries tend to provide only one version of any particular method. Instead of providing overloaded versions to do different things, they tend to include all sorts of parameters that you may never use to handle every conceivable situation. There are two ways you can deal with those unwanted parameters.

First, you can use named parameters as in the preceding code. Simply give the names and values of the parameters that you want to use and omit the other parameters.

Second, you can include all of the parameters and use the special value `Type.Missing` for any parameters that you don't want to set. Generally, you cannot use `null`, an empty string, or some other value to indicate a missing parameter—you must use `Type.Missing`.

The following code shows the call to the `Open` method using this approach.

```
Excel.Workbook workbook = excel.Workbooks.Open(fileTextBox.Text,
    Type.Missing, true, Type.Missing, Type.Missing,
    Type.Missing, Type.Missing, Type.Missing, Type.Missing,
    Type.Missing, Type.Missing, Type.Missing, Type.Missing,
    Type.Missing, Type.Missing);
```

After it opens the workbook, the program gets a reference to the opened workbook's first worksheet. It then calls the `SetTitleAndListValues` method described shortly to read data from the worksheet.

Next, the code closes the workbook and calls the server's `Quit` method. Remember, if you don't call `Quit`, the server keeps running in the background.

The code finishes by resetting the program's cursor to the default.

The following code shows the `SetTitleAndListValues` method.

```
// Set a title Label and the values in a ListBox.
// Get the title from cell (row, col). Get the values from
// cell (row + 1, col) to the end of the column.
private void SetTitleAndListValues(Excel.Worksheet sheet,
    int row, int col, Label lbl, ListBox lst)
{
    Excel.Range range;

    // Get the title.
    range = sheet.Cells[row, col];
    lbl.Text = (string)range.Value;
    lbl.ForeColor = System.Drawing.ColorTranslator.FromOle(
        (int)range.Font.Color);
    lbl.BackColor = System.Drawing.ColorTranslator.FromOle(
        (int)range.Interior.Color);

    // Get the values.
    // Find the last cell in the column.
    range = (Excel.Range)sheet.Columns[col];
    Excel.Range lastCell = range.get_End(Excel.XlDirection.xlDown);

    // Get a Range holding the values.
    Excel.Range firstCell = sheet.Cells[row + 1, col];
    Excel.Range valueRange = sheet.get_Range(firstCell, lastCell);
```

```
        // Copy the values into a list.
        List<string> values = new List<string>();
        foreach (object value in valueRange.Value)
        {
            values.Add((string)value);
        }

        // Display the values in the ListBox.
        lst.DataSource = values;
    }
```

This method takes the following parameters.

➢ The Excel worksheet that holds the data
➢ The row and column where the desired data starts
➢ The Label control where the method should display the first data value (as a header)
➢ The ListBox that should display the rest of the data

When working with Excel, a program uses Range objects to represent cells in a worksheet. A Range object can represent a single cell, a contiguous group of cells, or even a non-contiguous collection of groups of cells. The Range object controls the cells' contents, colors, font, and formatting.

The SetTitleAndListValues method starts by creating a Range variable that it will use to manipulate different parts of the worksheet. It then sets that variable equal to the first cell that the method will examine.

If a Range object represents a single cell, then its value is the value contained in that cell. In this example, the Range does represent a single cell, so the program gets its value, casts it into a string, and displays it in the label named lbl.

A Range object represents colors using a dynamic data type, so Visual Studio doesn't really understand it at design time. At runtime the value is a double. To convert that value into a Color that the C# program can understand, the code casts the value into an int and passes the result to the System.Drawing.ColorTranslator.FromOle method.

The code performs that conversion twice to copy the cell's foreground and background colors to the program's label.

Next, the code makes the Range object represent the entire column. It calls the object's get_End method to get the last cell in the column.

The code gets the cell where the data values start (the cell below the title cell). It then makes variable valueRange refer to the cells between the first and last data cells.

Next, the program loops through the range's values and adds them to a list of strings. The method finishes by making the ListBox use that list as its data source.

This code may seem complicated, but that's mostly because you're not familiar with the Excel object model. If you read it again now that you know a bit about how to work with Range objects, it will probably seem simpler.

> **NOTE:** The libraries that let a C# program work with the Office applications are called the Microsoft Office Primary Interop Assemblies (PIAs). They should be installed on your system when you install Visual Studio or Office.
>
> The PIAs should also be automatically embedded in any installation project that you build so you won't need to install them separately on a computer where you install your projects.

18. WRITE DATA INTO EXCEL (6)

This example shows how to write data into an Excel workbook. When you run the example program and click its Write button, the program opens an Excel workbook, adds a worksheet named after the current date, writes some data onto that worksheet, and saves the changes.

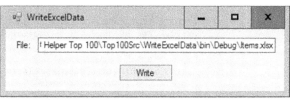

Start by adding a reference to the `Microsoft.Office.Interop.Excel` library as described in the preceding example. Also add a `using` directive as described in that example.

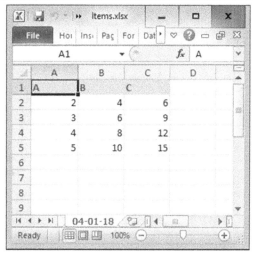

When you click the example's button, the following code does all of the work.

```
// Write into the Excel workbook.
private void writeButton_Click(object sender, EventArgs e)
{
    // Get the Excel application object.
    Excel.Application excel = new Excel.Application();

    // Uncomment to make Excel visible.
    //excel.Visible = true;

    // Open the workbook.
    Excel.Workbook workbook = excel.Workbooks.Open(Filename: fileTextBox.Text);

    // See if a worksheet with today's date already exists.
    string sheetName = DateTime.Now.ToString("MM-dd-yy");
    Excel.Worksheet sheet = FindSheet(workbook, sheetName);
    if (sheet == null)
    {
        // Add the worksheet at the end.
        sheet = (Excel.Worksheet)workbook.Sheets.Add(
            After: workbook.Sheets[workbook.Sheets.Count]);
        sheet.Name = DateTime.Now.ToString("MM-dd-yy");
    }

    // Add some data to individual cells.
```

```
    sheet.Cells[1, 1] = "A";
    sheet.Cells[1, 2] = "B";
    sheet.Cells[1, 3] = "C";

    // Make that range of cells bold and red.
    Excel.Range headerRange = sheet.get_Range("A1", "C1");
    headerRange.Font.Bold = true;
    headerRange.Font.Color =
        System.Drawing.ColorTranslator.ToOle(System.Drawing.Color.Red);
    headerRange.Interior.Color =
        System.Drawing.ColorTranslator.ToOle(System.Drawing.Color.Pink);

    // Add some data to a range of cells.
    int[,] values =
    {
        { 2,  4,  6},
        { 3,  6,  9},
        { 4,  8, 12},
        { 5, 10, 15},
    };
    Excel.Range valueRange = sheet.get_Range("A2", "C5");
    valueRange.Value = values;

    // Save the changes and close the workbook.
    workbook.Close(SaveChanges: true);

    // Close the Excel server.
    excel.Quit();

    MessageBox.Show("Done");
}
```

This example begins much as the preceding one does. It creates an Excel server, optionally makes the server visible, and opens the workbook, although this time it doesn't set the ReadOnly parameter to true when it opens the workbook.

Next, the program uses the current date to build a worksheet name. It calls the FindSheet method described shortly to see if the workbook already contains a worksheet with that name.

If the worksheet doesn't yet exist, the program adds one by calling the worksheet collection's Add method. It sets the After parameter to the last worksheet currently in the collection so the new sheet is added at the end. The program then sets the new worksheet's name to the current date.

Having found or created the worksheet, the program places some values in the worksheet's cells.

The code then creates a Range representing the modified cells and uses the Range to make the cells bold and to give them colors. Notice how the program uses System.Drawing .ColorTranslator.ToOle to translate from Windows Forms style Color values to the numeric values that Excel understands.

Next, the program creates a two-dimensional array holding some values. It creates a Range representing a corresponding number of cells and sets the Range object's value to the array.

The program calls the workbook's Close method, setting its SaveChanges parameter to true, so the changes are saved into the Excel file. The program finishes by shutting down the Excel server and displaying a success message.

> **NOTE:** As in the preceding example, if the program doesn't call the server's Quit method, the server remains running in the background.

The following code shows the FindSheet method.

```
// Return the worksheet with the given name if it exists.
private Excel.Worksheet FindSheet(Excel.Workbook workbook, string sheetName)
{
    foreach (Excel.Worksheet sheet in workbook.Sheets)
        if (sheet.Name == sheetName) return sheet;
    return null;
}
```

This method loops through a workbook's worksheets looking for one with a particular name. If it finds that worksheet, the method returns it. If no worksheet has that name, the method returns null.

19. CREATE A WORD DOCUMENT (10)

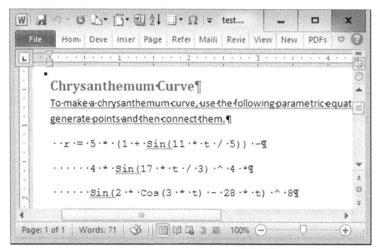

This example shows how a C# program can create a Microsoft Word document. It adds some text to the document and changes its format.

As in the previous two examples, this example requires a reference to a Microsoft Office interop library. As before, open the Project menu and select Add Reference. This time add a reference to the `Microsoft.Office.Interop.Word` library. Then you can add the following using directive to make using the library easier.

```
using Word = Microsoft.Office.Interop.Word;
```

When you click the example program's Make button, it uses the following code to create the new Word document.

```csharp
// Make a Word document.
private void makeButton_Click(object sender, EventArgs e)
{
    // Get the Word application object.
    Word.Application word = new Word.Application();

    // Uncomment to make Word visible.
    //word.Visible = true;

    // Create the Word document.
    Word.Document doc = word.Documents.Add();

    // Create a header paragraph.
    Word.Paragraph para = doc.Paragraphs.Add();
    para.Range.Text = "Chrysanthemum Curve";
    object style = "Heading 1";
    para.Range.set_Style(ref style);
    para.Range.InsertParagraphAfter();

    // Add more text.
    para.Range.Text = "To make a chrysanthemum curve, use the following " +
        "parametric equations as t goes from 0 to 21 * π to generate " +
        "points and then connect them.";
    para.Range.InsertParagraphAfter();

    // Save the current font and start using Courier New.
    string oldFont = para.Range.Font.Name;
    float oldSize = para.Range.Font.Size;
    para.Range.Font.Name = "Courier New";
```

```
        para.Range.Font.Size -= 2;

        // Add the equations.
        para.Range.Text =
            "  r = 5 * (1 + Sin(11 * t / 5)) -\n" +
            "      4 * Sin(17 * t / 3) ^ 4 *\n" +
            "      Sin(2 * Cos(3 * t) - 28 * t) ^ 8\n" +
            "  x = r * Cos(t)\n" +
            "  y = r * Sin(t)";

        // Start a new paragraph and then switch back to the original font.
        para.Range.InsertParagraphAfter();
        para.Range.Font.Name = oldFont;
        para.Range.Font.Size = oldSize;

        // Add a little more text.
        para.Range.Text = "That's all for this example.";
        para.Range.InsertParagraphAfter();

        // Save the document.
        object filename = Application.StartupPath + "\\test.docx";
        doc.SaveAs(ref filename);

        // Close.
        doc.Close();
        word.Quit();

        MessageBox.Show("Done");
    }
```

As in the previous examples, the program starts by creating a server application. Uncomment the second statement if you want the Word server to be visible.

The code then adds a new document to the server's Documents collection.

Now the program adds new content to the document. It first adds a new Paragraph object to the document's Paragraphs collection. To modify the paragraph, the program must use the Paragraph object's Range property. The program sets that property's Text value to a string.

The code then uses the Range object's set_Style method to set the paragraph's style. The syntax here is common when you work with Word. The set_Style method expects its parameter to be an *object* passed *by reference*. Even though the value is a actually string, the program must save it in an object variable and then pass it into the method by reference. In particular, you cannot pass a string literal into the method because that's not an object and you can't pass a literal by reference. You also cannot pass a string variable into the method because that's not an object either.

NOTE: The style whose name is passed into the set_Style method must exist in the Word document or the interop library will throw an exception.

After it sets the paragraph's style, the program calls the Range object's InsertParagraphAfter method. That appends a new paragraph mark to the current paragraph and then updates the Range so it represents the position after the paragraph mark. This is intended to make it easier for you to add several paragraphs one after another.

The code adds more text and inserts another paragraph.

Now the program will add some text that should be formatted as code. Before doing that, it saves the Range object's current font name and size. It then makes the Range use the Courier New font two point sizes smaller than normal. That produces a reasonably nice result.

The program adds the code, appends a new paragraph, and restores the original font name and size.

The program adds one final paragraph of text, just to show that the font properties were properly restored.

Having finished building the document, the program uses the SaveAs method to save it. Notice again that the Word method needs a parameter that is an object passed by reference.

Also note that Word, and the Office applications in general, work best if you give them full paths to files. If you only provide a file name, such as "test.docx," the servers tend to place the file wherever they think best. For example, that may be in your Documents folder.

Finally, the program closes the document, calls the Word server's Quit method, and displays a success message.

NOTE: As in the previous Excel examples, if the program doesn't call the server's Quit method, or if the program halts before calling Quit, then the server remains running in the background and you need to use the Task Manager to stop it.

20. ADD A PICTURE TO A WORD DOCUMENT (25)

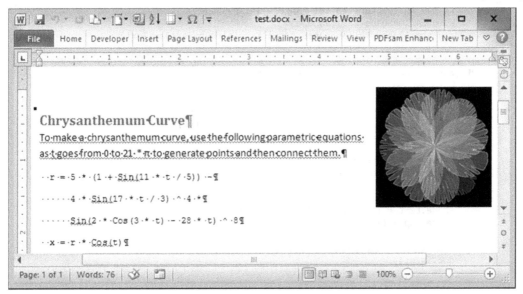

This example opens a Microsoft Word document, uses a bookmark to find the document's beginning, adds a picture to the document, and formats the picture to scale it and make text flow around it.

Before you start, add a reference to the `Microsoft.Office.Interop.Word` library as in the preceding example. Also add a reference to the `office` library. Be sure to use libraries with matching versions or Visual Studio will complain.

To make using the libraries easier, add the following two `using` directives.

```
using Word = Microsoft.Office.Interop.Word;
using Core = Microsoft.Office.Core;
```

This example uses the following code to open and modify the Word document.

```
// Add the picture to the Word document.
private void insertButton_Click(object sender, EventArgs e)
{
    // Get the Word application object.
    Word.Application word = new Word.Application();

    // Uncomment to make Word visible.
    //word.Visible = true;

    // Open the existing Word document.
    object filename = Application.StartupPath + "\\test.docx";
    Word.Document doc = word.Documents.Open(ref filename);

    // Find the beginning of the document bookmark.
    object start = "\\startofdoc";
```

```
        // Get a Range at the start of the document.
        Word.Range startRange = doc.Bookmarks.get_Item(ref start).Range;

        // Add the picture to the Range's InlineShapes.
        Word.InlineShape inlineShape =
            startRange.InlineShapes.AddPicture(pictureTextBox.Text);

        // Format the picture.
        Word.Shape shape = inlineShape.ConvertToShape();

        // Scale uniformly by 50%.
        shape.LockAspectRatio = Core.MsoTriState.msoTrue;
        shape.ScaleHeight(0.5f, Core.MsoTriState.msoTrue,
            Core.MsoScaleFrom.msoScaleFromTopLeft);

        // Wrap text around the picture's square.
        shape.WrapFormat.Type = Word.WdWrapType.wdWrapSquare;

        // Align the picture on the upper right.
        shape.Left = (float)Word.WdShapePosition.wdShapeOutside;
        shape.Top = (float)Word.WdShapePosition.wdShapeTop;

        // Save the document.
        doc.Save();

        // Close.
        doc.Close();
        word.Quit();

        MessageBox.Show("Done");
    }
```

The code starts by creating a `Word` application server and optionally making it visible.

Next, the code uses the `Documents` collection's `Open` method to open an existing Word document. Notice that, as is so often the case, the method expects a parameter that is an `object` passed by reference.

The program then uses the `Bookmarks` collection's `get_Item` method to get the `Range` object representing the predefined bookmark named "startofdoc."

> **NOTE:** To learn about other predefined bookmarks see
> `tinyurl.com/yasafy6p`.

Next the code adds the picture to the `Range` object's `InlineShapes` collection. This is one of the unusual cases when a Word method takes a `string` as a parameter instead of an `object` passed by reference.

Before it can format the picture, the program must convert it from an `InlineShape` into a `Shape` object. It does that by calling the `InlineShape` object's `ConvertToShape` method.

The program then sets the shape's size parameters. The `LockAspectRatio` parameter ensures that the picture is is scaled by the same amount vertically and horizontally. The `ScaleHeight` method then scales the picture by a factor of 0.5.

Next, the program sets the shape so text wraps around it in a square. It also aligns the picture to the top and outside edge of the document.

> **NOTE:** The outside edge switches for odd and even pages. It's on the right for odd pages and on the left for even pages. That puts the image on the outside edge of the pages if the pages are arranged as in a book.

To finish, the program saves the document's changes, closes the document, quits the Word server, and displays a success message.

Part VI. WPF

WPF is a big topic. So big, in fact, that I wrote a whole book about it: *WPF Programmer's Reference* (Rod Stephens, Wrox, 2010).

The user interfaces for Windows Forms applications are usually easier to build than those for WPF applications, so the C# Helper web site focuses mostly on Windows Forms programs. The code behind the user interfaces is usually the same for Windows Forms and WPF applications, at least if it doesn't deal directly with the user interface, so many of the C# Helper examples are useful in both kinds of applications.

WPF is still important, however, so a few of the site's examples use WPF.

This part of the book describes a few of the most popular WPF-related posts on C# Helper. You'll also find a few other WPF examples dealing with such topics as image processing, graphics, and three-dimensional drawing scattered throughout the rest of the book.

21. MOVE AND RESIZE RECTANGLES AT RUNTIME IN WPF (7)

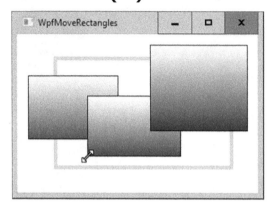

This example shows how you can let the user move and resize `Rectangle` controls at runtime in a WPF program.

The program's XAML code defines a `Canvas` object that contains three `Rectangle` controls. It also contains a `Border` control, just to show that the program doesn't need to move every kind of control inside the `Canvas`.

The program catches the `Canvas` object's `MouseDown`, `MouseMove`, and `MouseUp` events and uses them to move and resize the `Rectangle` controls.

One oddity of the `Canvas` controls is that it doesn't generate mouse events if it has a `null` background. To work around that restriction in this example, I set its background to `Transparent`. It's still invisible but it's not `null`.

The program uses the following code to track the moving and resizing operations.

```
// The part of the rectangle the mouse is over.
private enum HitType
{
    None, Body, UL, UR, LR, LL, L, R, T, B
};

// True if a drag is in progress.
private bool DragInProgress = false;

// The drag's last point.
private Point LastPoint;

// The part of the rectangle under the mouse.
HitType MouseHitType = HitType.None;

// The Rectangle that was hit.
private Rectangle HitRectangle = null;

// The Rectangles that the user can move and resize.
private List<Rectangle> Rectangles;
```

The `HitType` enumeration indicates parts of the rectangle. The variable `DragInProgress` is true when the user is moving or resizing the rectangle. The `LastPoint` variable stores the last recorded position of the mouse during a drag.

The variable MouseHitType indicates the part of the rectangle under the mouse at various times while the program runs. Variable HitRectangle tracks the Rectangle control under the mouse.

Finally, the Rectangles list holds all of the Rectangles that the user is allowed to move. When the program starts, it uses the following code to initialize the Rectangles list.

```
// Make a list of the Rectangles that the user can move.
private void Window_Loaded(object sender, RoutedEventArgs e)
{
    Rectangles = new List<Rectangle>();
    foreach (UIElement child in dragCanvas.Children)
    {
        if (child is Rectangle)
            Rectangles.Add(child as Rectangle);
    }

    // Reverse the list so the Rectangles on top come first.
    Rectangles.Reverse();
}
```

This code allocates the Rectangles list. It then loops through the Canvas control's children and adds the Rectangle controls to the list.

This code finishes by reversing the list so the Rectangle controls that are at the top of the stacking order come first. That allows the program to consider the controls on top first when it later loops through the list to see if the mouse is over a Rectangle.

The program uses three important helper methods: GetHitType, FindHit, and SetMouseCursor.

The GetHitType method, which is shown in the following code, returns a HitType value to indicate what part of a Rectangle is at a particular point.

```
// Return a HitType indicating the part of the Rectangle at the Point.
private HitType GetHitType(Rectangle rect, Point point)
{
    double left = Canvas.GetLeft(rect);
    double top = Canvas.GetTop(rect);
    double right = left + rect.Width;
    double bottom = top + rect.Height;
    if (point.X < left) return HitType.None;
    if (point.X > right) return HitType.None;
    if (point.Y < top) return HitType.None;
    if (point.Y > bottom) return HitType.None;

    const double GAP = 10;
    if (point.X - left < GAP)
    {
        // Left edge.
        if (point.Y - top < GAP) return HitType.UL;
        if (bottom - point.Y < GAP) return HitType.LL;
        return HitType.L;
    }
    if (right - point.X < GAP)
```

```
    {
        // Right edge.
        if (point.Y - top < GAP) return HitType.UR;
        if (bottom - point.Y < GAP) return HitType.LR;
        return HitType.R;
    }
    if (point.Y - top < GAP) return HitType.T;
    if (bottom - point.Y < GAP) return HitType.B;
    return HitType.Body;
}
```

First, the method needs to find the rectangle's left and top coordinates. Those values are not properties of the `Rectangle` object. They are *attached properties* provided by the `Canvas` control for the `Rectangle`. That means you can't get them by looking at the `Rectangle` object's properties. Instead, the program uses the `Canvas` class's `GetLeft` and `GetTop` methods to get the values for the rectangle.

After it gets the left and top values, the program adds the rectangle's `Width` and `Height` (which *are* `Rectangle` properties) to get the coordinates of the rectangle's bottom and right edges.

Next, the method compares the target point with the rectangle's edges. If the point lies outside of the rectangle, the method returns `None`.

The method determines whether the point is over a rectangle corner, edge, or body, and it returns the appropriate `HitType`.

The following code shows the second helper method: `FindHit`. This method uses `GetHitType` to see if a point is over any of the `Rectangle` controls.

```
// If the point is over any Rectangle, return the Rectangle and hit type.
private void FindHit(Point point)
{
    HitRectangle = null;
    MouseHitType = HitType.None;

    foreach (Rectangle rect in Rectangles)
    {
        MouseHitType = GetHitType(rect, point);
        if (MouseHitType != HitType.None)
        {
            HitRectangle = rect;
            return;
        }
    }

    // We didn't find a hit.
    return;
}
```

This method loops through the `Rectangle` controls in top-to-bottom order. If `GetHitType` finds that the point is over a `Rectangle`, the method returns that `Rectangle` and the hit type.

The following code shows the third helper method, `SetMouseCursor`.

```
// Set a mouse cursor appropriate for the current hit type.
private void SetMouseCursor()
{
    // See what cursor we should display.
    Cursor desiredCursor = Cursors.Arrow;
    switch (MouseHitType)
    {
        case HitType.None:
            desiredCursor = Cursors.Arrow;
            break;
        case HitType.Body:
            desiredCursor = Cursors.ScrollAll;
            break;
        case HitType.UL:
        case HitType.LR:
            desiredCursor = Cursors.SizeNWSE;
            break;
        case HitType.LL:
        case HitType.UR:
            desiredCursor = Cursors.SizeNESW;
            break;
        case HitType.T:
        case HitType.B:
            desiredCursor = Cursors.SizeNS;
            break;
        case HitType.L:
        case HitType.R:
            desiredCursor = Cursors.SizeWE;
            break;
    }

    // Display the desired cursor.
    if (Cursor != desiredCursor) Cursor = desiredCursor;
}
```

This code simply sets the cursor that is appropriate for the mouse's hit type.

When the user presses the mouse down over the `Canvas`, the following event handler executes.

```
// Start dragging.
private void dragCanvas_MouseDown(object sender, MouseButtonEventArgs e)
{
    FindHit(Mouse.GetPosition(dragCanvas));
    SetMouseCursor();
    if (MouseHitType == HitType.None) return;

    LastPoint = Mouse.GetPosition(dragCanvas);
    DragInProgress = true;
}
```

This method calls `FindHit` to see whether the mouse is over a `Rectangle`. If the mouse isn't over a `Rectangle`, the method returns.

If the mouse is over a `Rectangle`, the method saves the mouse's current location in the `LastPoint` variable and then sets `DragInProgress` to `true`.

When the user moves the mouse, the following code executes.

```csharp
// If a drag is in progress, continue the drag.
// Otherwise display the correct cursor.
private void dragCanvas_MouseMove(object sender, MouseEventArgs e)
{
    if (!DragInProgress)
    {
        FindHit(Mouse.GetPosition(dragCanvas));
        SetMouseCursor();
    }
    else
    {
        // See how much the mouse has moved.
        Point point = Mouse.GetPosition(dragCanvas);
        double offsetX = point.X - LastPoint.X;
        double offsetY = point.Y - LastPoint.Y;

        // Get the rectangle's current position.
        double newX = Canvas.GetLeft(HitRectangle);
        double newY = Canvas.GetTop(HitRectangle);
        double newWidth = HitRectangle.Width;
        double newHeight = HitRectangle.Height;

        // Update the rectangle.
        switch (MouseHitType)
        {
            case HitType.Body:
                newX += offsetX;
                newY += offsetY;
                break;
            case HitType.UL:
                newX += offsetX;
                newY += offsetY;
                newWidth -= offsetX;
                newHeight -= offsetY;
                break;
            case HitType.UR:
                newY += offsetY;
                newWidth += offsetX;
                newHeight -= offsetY;
                break;
            case HitType.LR:
                newWidth += offsetX;
                newHeight += offsetY;
                break;
            case HitType.LL:
                newX += offsetX;
                newWidth -= offsetX;
                newHeight += offsetY;
                break;
            case HitType.L:
                newX += offsetX;
                newWidth -= offsetX;
                break;
            case HitType.R:
                newWidth += offsetX;
                break;
            case HitType.B:
```

```
                newHeight += offsetY;
                break;
            case HitType.T:
                newY += offsetY;
                newHeight -= offsetY;
                break;
        }

        // Don't use negative width or height.
        if ((newWidth > 0) && (newHeight > 0))
        {
            // Update the rectangle.
            Canvas.SetLeft(HitRectangle, newX);
            Canvas.SetTop(HitRectangle, newY);
            HitRectangle.Width = newWidth;
            HitRectangle.Height = newHeight;

            // Save the mouse's new location.
            LastPoint = point;
        }
    }
}
```

This code does one of two things depending on whether a drag is in progress.

If a drag is not in progress, the method calls FindHit to see whether the mouse is over a Rectangle and SetMouseCursor to display an appropriate cursor.

If a drag is in progress, the code gets the mouse's current position and subtracts its coordinates from LastPoint to see how far the mouse has moved since that point was recorded. It gets the hit rectangle's current position and then initializes variables to hold the rectangle's new size and position.

Depending on the part of the rectangle that was under the mouse, the method updates the rectangle's size and position.

Next, the method checks that the rectangle's new width and height are at least 10. You could allow smaller sizes, but then the rectangle wouldn't be very useful. If the new width and height are at least 10, the method updates the rectangle's size and position.

Finally, the code saves the mouse's current location for the next time it moves.

The following code shows the last piece of the program.

```
// Stop dragging.
private void dragCanvas_MouseUp(object sender, MouseButtonEventArgs e)
{
    DragInProgress = false;
}
```

When the user releases the mouse button, this code simply ends the drag.

22. MAKE A BLINKING LABEL IN WPF (21)

As is the case for many tasks, WPF makes this harder than it is in Windows Forms but it gives you some extra flexibility. This example demonstrates two approaches for making a blinking label in WPF. The first approach is somewhat similar to the approach you can use in Windows Forms.

In Windows Forms, you can add a `Timer` component to the form and then make its `Tick` event handler switch a `Label` control's foreground and background colors. WPF doesn't have a `Timer` component, and a label's `ForeColor` and `BackColor` properties are brushes instead of simple colors, but you can still do something sort of similar. The following code shows this approach.

```
using System.Windows.Threading;
...
// Create a timer.
private DispatcherTimer TheTimer;
private void Window_Loaded(object sender, RoutedEventArgs e)
{
    TheTimer = new DispatcherTimer();
    TheTimer.Tick += TheTimer_Tick;
    TheTimer.Interval = new TimeSpan(0, 0, 0, 0, 500);
    TheTimer.Start();
}

// The timer's Tick event.
private bool BlinkOn = false;
private void TheTimer_Tick(object sender, EventArgs e)
{
    if (BlinkOn)
    {
        timerLabel.Foreground = Brushes.Red;
        timerLabel.Background = Brushes.LightGreen;
    }
    else
    {
        timerLabel.Foreground = Brushes.LightGreen;
        timerLabel.Background = Brushes.Red;
    }
    BlinkOn = !BlinkOn;
}
```

This code uses the `DispatcherTimer` class, which is defined in the `System.Windows.Threading` namespace, so it starts with a `using` directive for that namespace.

The code then declares a `DispatcherTimer` variable named `TheTimer`.

When the program starts, the window's `Loaded` event handler initializes the timer and sets its `Tick` event handler. It sets the timer's interval to 500 milliseconds (half a second) and starts the timer.

When the timer's `Tick` event handler fires, it checks the `BlinkOn` variable to see which colors the label should display. It then sets the label's `Foreground` and `Background` properties appropriately and switches the value of `BlinkOn`.

This is a lot more complicated than it is in Windows Forms, but it's a lot simpler than doing this in the truly WPFish way used by the example's second approach. A truly WPFish approach can do this by using only XAML code with no C# code in sight, but it requires a `Storyboard` and an `EventTrigger`.

The following code shows how the program defines its `Storyboard`.

```
<Window.Resources>
    <Storyboard x:Key="blinkStory" Duration="0:0:1"
        RepeatBehavior="Forever">
        <ColorAnimationUsingKeyFrames
            Storyboard.TargetName="storyboardLabel"
            Storyboard.TargetProperty="Background.(SolidColorBrush.Color)">
            <DiscreteColorKeyFrame KeyTime="0:0:0" Value="Blue" />
            <DiscreteColorKeyFrame KeyTime="0:0:0.5" Value="Yellow" />
        </ColorAnimationUsingKeyFrames>
        <ColorAnimationUsingKeyFrames
            Storyboard.TargetName="storyboardLabel"
            Storyboard.TargetProperty="Foreground.(SolidColorBrush.Color)">
            <DiscreteColorKeyFrame KeyTime="0:0:0" Value="Yellow" />
            <DiscreteColorKeyFrame KeyTime="0:0:0.5" Value="Blue" />
        </ColorAnimationUsingKeyFrames>
    </Storyboard>
</Window.Resources>
```

This code places the `Storyboard` inside the window's `Resources` dictionary. It defines a `Storyboard` named `blinkStory` with a total duration of one second. Its `RepeatBehavior` is set to `Forever` so the `Storyboard` repeats itself whenever it finishes its one-second cycle.

The `Storyboard` contains two `ColorAnimationUsingKeyFrames` objects. The first targets the `storyboardLabel` control's `Background.(SolidColorBrush.Color)` value. This value means the object looks at the `Background` property. That property isn't a simple value like a color, so the program must look more closely at it.

The syntax `(SolidColorBrush.Color)` tells the program to look at a `SolidColorBrush` object's `Color` property. The parentheses indicate a partially qualified property name. In this case, it's basically saying the `Background` property needs to be set to a `SolidColorBrush` object. The rest of the value indicates that the storyboard is setting that object's `Color` property.

To summarize, the code `Background.(SolidColorBrush.Color)` means the storyboard should look at the `Background` property, find the `SolidColorBrush` object that it holds, and set its `Color` property.

Next, the code gives the `ColorAnimationUsingKeyFrames` object two color frames. The first sets the target's color to blue when the storyboard starts. The second sets the target's color to yellow 0.5 seconds into the storyboard. The result is that the label's text turns blue when the animation starts, turns yellow 0.5 seconds later, and then the storyboard repeats after 1 second.

The second `ColorAnimationUsingKeyFrames` object is similar to the first except it sets the label's `Foreground` color to yellow and then blue.

That's the end of the code that defines the `Storyboard` object to animate the label's colors. Now the program needs a way to start the `Storyboard` running. To do that, the example uses the following trigger.

```
<Window.Triggers>
    <EventTrigger RoutedEvent="FrameworkElement.Loaded">
        <BeginStoryboard Storyboard="{StaticResource blinkStory}"/>
    </EventTrigger>
</Window.Triggers>
```

This `Trigger`, which is defined in the window's `Triggers` collection, executes when the window raises its `FrameworkElement.Loaded` routed event. That event occurs when the window is loaded and ready to go.

When that event occurs, the trigger creates a `BeginStoryboard` object for the `Storyboard` that is a static resource (in the window's `Resources` dictionary) named `blinkStory`. Creating the `BeginStoryboard` object starts the `Storyboard` running.

If this whole thing seems absurdly arcane and cryptic, I agree. The problem is that the code is trying to use static XAML statements to do something that is naturally dynamic. That's why you get strange constructs such as creating a `BeginStoryboard` object to start the `Storyboard` when in code you would simply call a `Storyboard` method.

Once you have all of this working, however, you do get some extra flexibility. For example, instead of making the label's colors jump between blue and yellow, you could make them fade gradually from one color to another. You probably wouldn't want to do that in this example, but you could.

NOTE: About three percent of people who have epilepsy have a condition known as *photosensitive epilepsy*. If you have that condition, certain patterns of flashing lights can induce seizures. In particular, lights flashing at certain frequencies can trigger that kind of response.

Lights flashing between around five and 30 times per second are most likely to cause this reaction. Partly to avoid causing seizures, a few standards bodies have defined guidelines that specify frequencies for blinking lights in software applications.

The World Wide Web Consortium's Web Content Accessibility Guidelines (WCAG) Version 2.0 says that content should not flash more than three times per second.

The United States Rehabilitation Act of 1973 indicates that content should not flash between two and 55 times per second.

To be safe, I recommend making text blink at most two times per second.

Or better still, don't use blinking text at all. Blinking or moving objects on a computer screen are extremely attention-grabbing so they may distract the user from other items on the screen.

Or if you really want to use blinking to direct the user's attention, you could make the text blink two or three times and then stop.

23. UNDERSTAND EVENT BUBBLING AND TUNNELING IN WPF (75)

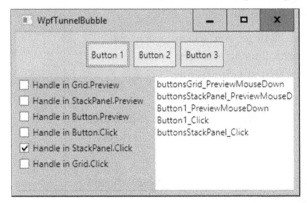

This example demonstrates event bubbling and tunneling in WPF programs. In a Windows Forms application, a control raises an event and that's that. WPF uses more complicated *routed events* that are guided through a sequence of controls.

First, the event "tunnels" down through the control hierarchy in a sequence of preview events. It starts at the highest level of the control hierarchy and moves down into container controls until it reaches the control that actually launched the event.

Then the event "bubbles" back up through the control hierarchy in a sequence of final, possibly converted events.

All of the controls in the tunneling and bubbling chain can handle the event and take action. They can also set their e.Handled parameters to true to prevent the event from continuing on its little adventure.

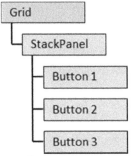

This example contains a main Grid control at the top of the control hierarchy. That control contains another Grid that holds a StackPanel holding three Button controls. If you ignore the top-level Grid, which doesn't participate in the events used by this example, the hierarchy looks like the picture on the left.

When you click the Button1 control, PreviewMouseDown events start at the Grid control and tunnel their way down the hierarchy until they reach the button. After that, Click events bubble up from the button through the hierarchy to the Grid.

The following picture shows the sequence of events.

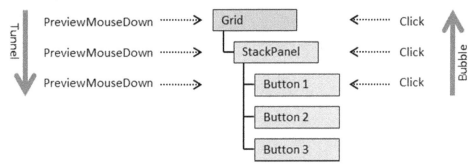

In the example program, you can use the check boxes to make an event handler set its e.Handled parameter to true to interrupt the flow of events. For example, if you check the Handle in Button.Preview box, then the Button control's PreviewMouseDown event handler flags its event as handled so none of the Click events occur.

Here's the XAML code that creates the first button.

```
<Button Name="Button1" Content="Button 1"
    PreviewMouseDown="Button1_PreviewMouseDown"
    Click="Button1_Click" />
```

This code creates the button and assigns event handlers to its PreviewMouseDown and Click events. The following code shows the corresponding event handlers.

```
private void Button1_PreviewMouseDown(object sender, MouseButtonEventArgs e)
{
    e.Handled = buttonPreviewCheckBox.IsChecked.Value;
    ShowMethodName();
}

private void Button1_Click(object sender, RoutedEventArgs e)
{
    e.Handled = buttonClickCheckBox.IsChecked.Value;
    ShowMethodName();
}
```

The event handlers set e.Handled appropriately, depending on whether the corresponding check boxes are checked. They then call the following ShowMethodName method to record the name of the executing event handler.

```
// Record the name of the method that called this one.
private void ShowMethodName()
{
    resultsTextBox.AppendText(
        new StackTrace(1).GetFrame(0).GetMethod().Name + '\n');
}
```

The parameter passed to the StackTrace constructor skips one frame up the call stack to the method that called ShowMethodName. The code gets that call's stack frame, gets the method, and adds its name to the results text box.

Part VII. Graphics

Over the years I've written a lot of graphics programs. I've probably written hundreds of articles and blog posts dealing with graphics. I've even written a two editions of a graphics book: *Visual Basic Graphics Programming* (Rod Stephens, Wiley, 2000).

I enjoy writing complicated algorithms in general and I find graphics algorithms particularly satisfying. I'm always fascinated when I dump a bunch of numbers into a program and a complicated picture pops out.

The examples in this part of the book deal with basic graphics. They show how to draw and manipulate simple shapes and text. Examples in other parts of the book deal with other graphics-related topics such as image processing, three-dimensional graphics, and geometry.

24. DRAW IN A PAINT EVENT HANDLER (26)

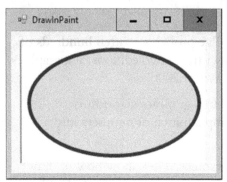

There are two main ways you can produce graphics in a Windows Forms application. First, you can draw in a control's Paint event handler. Second, you can create a bitmap and then display it in a PictureBox or other control.

This example demonstrates the first technique. The next example demonstrates the second.

The basic idea is to catch a control's Paint event. The Paint event handler has a parameter e with property Graphics. That object provides methods that let you draw on the control being painted.

This example's form contains a PictureBox control. When the PictureBox needs to redraw, the following Paint event handler executes.

```
// Draw an ellipse.
private void ellipsePictureBox_Paint(object sender, PaintEventArgs e)
{
    Rectangle rect = new Rectangle(10, 10,
        ellipsePictureBox.ClientSize.Width - 20,
        ellipsePictureBox.ClientSize.Height - 20);
    DrawEllipse(e.Graphics, rect);
}
```

This event handler makes a Rectangle to represent the PictureBox control's client area (the area inside the control's borders, if it is displaying them) minus a 10-pixel margin. It then passes the Rectangle and the e.Graphics object to the following DrawEllipse method.

```
// Draw the ellipse.
private void DrawEllipse(Graphics gr, Rectangle rect)
{
    gr.Clear(Color.White);
    gr.SmoothingMode = SmoothingMode.AntiAlias;

    gr.FillEllipse(Brushes.Pink, rect);
    using (Pen thick_pen = new Pen(Color.Blue, 5))
    {
        gr.DrawEllipse(thick_pen, rect);
    }
}
```

This method does the actual drawing. It uses the Graphics object's Clear method to give the PictureBox a white background.

Next, the code sets the Graphics object's SmoothingMode property to make it draw smooth shapes. The System.Drawing.Drawing namespace defines the SmoothingMode enumeration, so the program includes a using directive to make using that namespace easier.

The code then uses the Graphics object's FillEllipse method to fill the ellipse with pink pixels

To outline the ellipse, the code creates a blue, five-pixel wide pen. It then uses the DrawEllipse method to draw the ellipse's outline.

The Pen class has a Dispose method, so the code defines it in a using block to make the program automatically call Dispose when the Pen is no longer needed.

The PictureBox is anchored so it resizes when the form does. When the form resizes, the PictureBox resizes and raises its Resize event, so the following event handler executes.

```
// Redraw the ellipse.
private void ellipsePictureBox_Resize(object sender, EventArgs e)
{
    ellipsePictureBox.Refresh();
}
```

This method simply calls the PictureBox control's Refresh method. That method raises the control's Paint event and the event handler redraws the ellipse at a new size.

There are several things to note about this example. First, the program draws on a PictureBox instead of directly on the form. You can catch the form's Paint event and draw directly on it, but I've found that in many programs you later decide to rearrange the drawing. If you draw on a PictureBox instead of the form, it's easier to move the picture to a new location, change its size, or move it into some container control such as a Panel.

Second, the Paint event handler doesn't actually do any drawing. Instead it calls the DrawEllipse method to do all of the work. This is more a matter of style than necessity. Sometimes it's handy to perform the drawing in a separate method so you can reuse the code later. For example, if you needed to draw ellipses in several different PictureBox controls, you could simply catch their Paint events and pass their e.Graphics parameters into the same DrawEllipse method.

Finally, calling a control's Refresh method, as the Resize event handler does in this example, is a common way to make a control redraw. A program can do that when the control resizes or when the underlying data used to generate the picture changes.

Even the Paint event itself has a couple of features worth noting. A control raises its Paint event whenever it needs to redraw part of itself. For example, if the control is covered by another program and then brought back to the top, it *may* need to be repainted. Its image may also still be available to the graphics system, so it might not raise its Paint event.

Similarly, if the control is resized, it may or may not need repainting. If the control shrinks, then the parts in its upper left corner that were not cut off are presumably still valid, so the control doesn't raise its `Paint` event. In contrast, if the control grows bigger, then it raises its `Paint` event because it has newly exposed areas.

Even if the control is growing, you may not get the results you expect. If the control enlarges, the `Graphics` object that the `Paint` event handler receives as a parameter only affects the areas that were exposed. If you try to use that `Graphics` object to draw on the parts of the control in the upper left corner that were already visible, you won't see any result. The `Graphics` object will only draw on the new areas.

There's one last warning that I want to give. Controls have a `CreateGraphics` method that returns a `Graphics` object that can draw on them. Unfortunately, anything you draw using that object will only be visible until the control repaints, at which time it will draw over anything you drew with the object returned by `CreateGraphics`.

Probably the most confusing situation occurs if you use `CreateGraphics` inside the `Paint` event handler. In that case, you draw on the object returned by `CreateGraphics`, but as soon as the event handler finishes it overwrites whatever you drew. As a result you don't see any of your drawing.

All of those details together can lead to some very confusing bugs. You can avoid them if you obey the following relatively simple rules.

➢ When you handle the `Paint` event, clear the control and redraw everything.
➢ If the drawing has a fixed size, for example a 100×100 circle in the upper left corner, then the `Paint` event handler can handle all of the drawing.
➢ If the drawing depends on the control's size, for example if it contains an ellipse that fills the control, make a `Resize` event handler call the control's `Refresh` method. Then let the `Paint` event handler do all of the drawing.
➢ Never use `CreateGraphics`.

25. DRAW ON A BITMAP (29)

The preceding example explains the most common method for producing graphics: drawing in a control's `Paint` event handler. This example demonstrates a second technique: drawing on a bitmap.

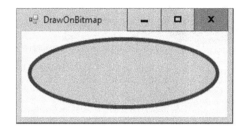

If you make a bitmap and then display it in a control's `Image` property, that control automatically redisplays the bitmap whenever necessary. That means you don't need to write a `Paint` event handler to update the display whenever the control is displayed or resized.

Much of this example's code is similar to the code used to draw in a `Paint` event handler. The only real difference is that the program must create a `Bitmap` object and an associated `Graphics` object instead of using the `Paint` event handler's `e.Graphics` parameter.

When this example starts, it uses the following code to create a bitmap displaying an ellipse.

```
// Make and display a Bitmap.
private void Form1_Load(object sender, EventArgs e)
{
    drawingPictureBox.SizeMode = PictureBoxSizeMode.AutoSize;
    drawingPictureBox.Location = new Point(0, 0);

    Bitmap bm = new Bitmap(280, 110);
    using (Graphics gr = Graphics.FromImage(bm))
    {
        gr.SmoothingMode = SmoothingMode.AntiAlias;
        Rectangle rect = new Rectangle(10, 10, 260, 90);
        gr.FillEllipse(Brushes.LightGreen, rect);
        using (Pen pen = new Pen(Color.Blue, 5))
        {
            gr.DrawEllipse(pen, rect);
        }
    }

    drawingPictureBox.Image = bm;
}
```

The code starts by setting the `PictureBox` control's `SizeMode` property to `AutoSize`. Later, when the code sets the control's `Image` property, the `PictureBox` automatically resizes itself to fit the image.

Next, the code moves the `PictureBox` to the form's upper left corner. The code then creates a 280×110 pixel `Bitmap` and makes a `Graphics` object associated with the `Bitmap`. This `Graphics` object allows the program to draw on the `Bitmap`.

The `Graphics` class provides a `Dispose` method, so the program creates the object in a `using` statement to make the program call `Dispose` automatically.

The code then sets the `Graphics` object's `SmoothingMode` property to produce smooth shapes.

Now the program fills and outlines an ellipse much as the preceding example does.

After it has finished making the drawing, the code sets the `PictureBox` control's `Image` property equal to the `Bitmap`. After that, the `PictureBox` displays the image automatically.

> **NOTE:** Like the `Graphics` class, the `Bitmap` class has a `Dispose` method. However, the program needs to use the `Bitmap` any time it needs to redraw the image. If you call `Dispose`, the program will later crash (with a remarkably uninformative error message) when it tries to redisplay the `Bitmap`.
>
> For that reason, you shouldn't call the `Bitmap` object's `Dispose` method directly and you can't create it in a `using` block.

Whether you should draw in the `Paint` event handler or make a bitmap depends on the nature of the graphics. If the drawing is relatively simple, then the `Paint` event handler can draw it whenever it needs to relatively quickly. In that case, you might prefer to use the `Paint` event handler to save the memory needed by a `Bitmap` object.

In contrast, suppose the drawing is very complicated so it takes a second or two to draw. Every time the user enlarges or exposes the `PictureBox`, the `Paint` event handler will spend a considerable amount of time redrawing, and the user will see the image redraw. In that case, you might be better off drawing the image once on a `Bitmap`. That will use a bit more memory, but memory is cheap and it will allow the program to redisplay its image practically instantly.

If the drawing is complex and also depends on the size of the `PictureBox` control, then you're kind of stuck. Using a `Bitmap` will save you time when the control is exposed, but you'll probably need to regenerate the `Bitmap` when the control is resized.

You might also try making the `Bitmap` as large as you will ever need it and then scaling it to fit the `PictureBox` control by setting the control's `ScaleMode` property to `Zoom`.

26. Double Buffer (93)

If you draw a complex image in a form's
`Paint` event handler, the user may see the
incomplete drawing while it is being drawn.

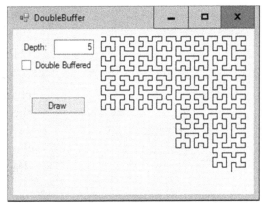

The preceding example shows one solution.
Instead of drawing in the form's `Paint` event
handler, draw on a bitmap and then display
the bitmap when the drawing is finished.

When you're drawing on a form, there's an
even easier solution. If you set a form's
`DoubleBuffered` property to `true`, then the
form basically does the same thing automatically. It generates the graphics produced by the
`Paint` event handler in a hidden bitmap. When the `Paint` event handler is finished, the
form displays the result.

> **NOTE:** This technique is called *double buffering* because the image is first
> drawn in a *back buffer* and then copied to the computer's video RAM (the
> *front buffer*).

This example draws a space-filling curve called a *Hilbert curve*. Exactly how the curve works
isn't important for this example, so I won't explain it here. Look online (for example, on
the C# Helper web site) for details.

When you click the program's **Draw** button, the following line of code sets the form's
`DoubleBuffered` property.

```
DoubleBuffered = doubleBufferCheckBox.Checked;
```

This turns on double buffering if the box is checked. The code then draws the curve.

The program's Depth value determines how complicated the curve is. If you set depth to 5
or 6, the curve takes long enough to draw that, if double buffering is off, you can see it
partially drawn.

You can often still save time if you use your own `Bitmap` as described in the preceding
example instead of relying on double buffering. If the image seldom changes, there's no
need to recreate it every time the form or `PictureBox` generates a `Paint` event. In the
extreme case, if the image is generated when the program starts and then never changes,
you can just build the image once when the program starts and then never change it.

27. DRAW AND MOVE LINE SEGMENTS (8)

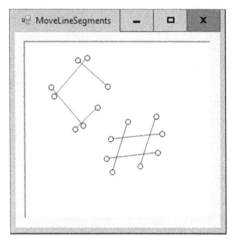

This example lets you draw and move line segments at runtime. It lets you perform three different operations depending on what is below the mouse.

➤ When the mouse is over a segment, the cursor changes to a hand. You can then click and drag to move the segment.

➤ When the mouse is over a segment's endpoint, the cursor changes to an arrow. You can then click and drag to move the endpoint.

➤ When the mouse is over nothing, the cursor changes to a crosshair. You can then click and drag to create a new line segment.

The program handles all of these cases using MouseDown, MouseMove, and MouseUp events, but handling all of the possible combinations in one set of event handlers would be confusing. To make things easier to manage, the example program uses separate MouseMove and MouseUp event handlers to perform its different tasks.

This example is fairly complicated (it has the longest description in this book), so I've divided it into several sections corresponding to the program's basic states. The following list shows those states.

➤ Drawing
➤ Not Moving Anything
➤ Drawing a New Segment
➤ Moving an Endpoint
➤ Moving a Line Segment

Even broken into sections this is a pretty long example, so grab your favorite caffeinated beverage and take it slowly one section at a time.

Drawing

The program uses the following code to create two lists where it will store the coordinates of line segment endpoints.

```
// The points that make up the line segments.
private List Pt1 = new List<Point>();
private List Pt2 = new List<Point>();
```

The following code defines three variables to represent a new line segment's endpoints.

```
// Points for the new line.
private bool IsDrawing = false;
private Point NewPt1, NewPt2;
```

The variable IsDrawing is true while the program is in the process of drawing a new segment. While it is drawing a new segment, the variables NewPt1 and NewPt2 hold the new segment's endpoints.

The following Paint event handler draws whatever segments are currently defined.

```
// Draw the lines.
private void picCanvas_Paint(object sender, PaintEventArgs e)
{
    e.Graphics.SmoothingMode = SmoothingMode.AntiAlias;

    // Draw the segments.
    for (int i = 0; i < Pt1.Count; i++)
        e.Graphics.DrawLine(Pens.Blue, Pt1[i], Pt2[i]);

    // Draw the endpoints.
    foreach (Point pt in Pt1)
    {
        Rectangle rect = new Rectangle(
            pt.X - ObjectRadius, pt.Y - ObjectRadius,
            2 * ObjectRadius + 1, 2 * ObjectRadius + 1);
        e.Graphics.FillEllipse(Brushes.White, rect);
        e.Graphics.DrawEllipse(Pens.Black, rect);
    }
    foreach (Point pt in Pt2)
    {
        Rectangle rect = new Rectangle(
            pt.X - ObjectRadius, pt.Y - ObjectRadius,
            2 * ObjectRadius + 1, 2 * ObjectRadius + 1);
        e.Graphics.FillEllipse(Brushes.White, rect);
        e.Graphics.DrawEllipse(Pens.Black, rect);
    }

    // If there's a new segment under constructions, draw it.
    if (IsDrawing)
    {
        e.Graphics.DrawLine(Pens.Red, NewPt1, NewPt2);
    }
}
```

The Paint event handler sets the Graphics object's SmoothingMode property to draw smooth lines. It then loops through the point lists and draws the old line segments. Next, the code loops through the point lists and draws the segments' endpoints. If the program is in the middle of drawing a new segment, the method finishes by drawing it.

Not Moving Anything

When the program isn't drawing anything, the mouse cursor indicates the type of item under the mouse. For example, if the mouse is above a line segment's body, the cursor is a hand.

While the program isn't drawing or moving anything, the `PictureBox` uses the following `MouseMove` event handler to set the cursor appropriately.

```csharp
// The mouse is up. See whether we're over an endpoint or segment.
private void canvasPictureBox_MouseIsUp_MouseMove(
    object sender, MouseEventArgs e)
{
    Cursor newCursor = Cursors.Cross;

    // See what we're over.
    Point hitPoint;
    int segmentNumber;

    if (MouseIsOverEndpoint(e.Location, out segmentNumber, out hitPoint))
        newCursor = Cursors.Arrow;
    else if (MouseIsOverSegment(e.Location, out segmentNumber))
        newCursor = Cursors.Hand;

    // Set the new cursor.
    if (canvasPictureBox.Cursor != newCursor)
        canvasPictureBox.Cursor = newCursor;
}
```

This code calls the `MouseIsOverEndPoint` and `MouseIsOverSegment` methods described later to see if the mouse is over anything interesting. It then displays the appropriate cursor.

If the program isn't currently moving anything and you press the mouse button, the following event handler executes.

```csharp
// See what we're over and start doing whatever is appropriate.
private void canvasPictureBox_MouseDown(object sender, MouseEventArgs e)
{
    // See what we're over.
    Point hitPoint;
    int segmentNumber;

    if (MouseIsOverEndpoint(e.Location, out segmentNumber, out hitPoint))
    {
        // Start moving this endpoint.
        canvasPictureBox.MouseMove -= canvasPictureBox_MouseIsUp_MouseMove;
        canvasPictureBox.MouseMove += canvasPictureBox_MovingEndPoint_MouseMove;
        canvasPictureBox.MouseUp += canvasPictureBox_MovingEndPoint_MouseUp;

        // Remember the segment number.
        MovingSegment = segmentNumber;

        // See if we're moving the start endpoint.
        MovingStartEndPoint = (Pt1[segmentNumber].Equals(hitPoint));
```

```
            // Remember the offset from the mouse to the point.
            OffsetX = hitPoint.X - e.X;
            OffsetY = hitPoint.Y - e.Y;
        }
        else if (MouseIsOverSegment(e.Location, out segmentNumber))
        {
            // Start moving this segment.
            canvasPictureBox.MouseMove -= canvasPictureBox_MouseIsUp_MouseMove;
            canvasPictureBox.MouseMove += canvasPictureBox_MovingSegment_MouseMove;
            canvasPictureBox.MouseUp += canvasPictureBox_MovingSegment_MouseUp;

            // Remember the segment number.
            MovingSegment = segmentNumber;

            // Remember the offset from the mouse to the segment's first point.
            OffsetX = Pt1[segmentNumber].X - e.X;
            OffsetY = Pt1[segmentNumber].Y - e.Y;
        }
        else
        {
            // Start drawing a new segment.
            canvasPictureBox.MouseMove -= canvasPictureBox_MouseIsUp_MouseMove;
            canvasPictureBox.MouseMove += canvasPictureBox_Drawing_MouseMove;
            canvasPictureBox.MouseUp += canvasPictureBox_Drawing_MouseUp;

            IsDrawing = true;
            NewPt1 = new Point(e.X, e.Y);
            NewPt2 = new Point(e.X, e.Y);
        }
    }
```

This event handler uses the MouseIsOverEndPoint and MouseIsOverSegment methods, which are described in the next section, to see if the mouse is over anything interesting. If the mouse is over an endpoint or segment, the code starts moving it.

Notice how the code uninstalls the old MouseMove event handler and installs new MouseMove and MouseUp event handlers for the operation that it's starting. Instead of forcing every event handler to deal with many different situations, this technique of uninstalling old event handlers and then installing new ones on the fly allows each event handler to work under a limited set of circumstances. That makes them much simpler.

Determining What's under the Mouse

The program uses the ObjectRadius and OverDistSquared constants defined in the following code to determine whether an object is at a particular point.

```
// The "size" of an object for mouse over purposes.
private const int ObjectRadius = 3;

// We're over an object if the distance squared
// between the mouse and the object is less than this.
private const int OverDistSquared = ObjectRadius * ObjectRadius;
```

This code sets the constant ObjectRadius to 3. The program uses this value to decide whether the mouse is over an object. For example, if the mouse is within three pixels of a line segment endpoint, then the program considers it over that endpoint.

When it calculates a distance, the program actually examines the distance squared. If the distance squared between the mouse and an object is less than ObjectRadius squared, then the mouse is over the object. Using the OverDistSquared value lets the program compare distances without calculating square roots, which is relatively slow.

The following code shows the MouseIsOverEndPoint method.

```
// See if the mouse is over an endpoint.
private bool MouseIsOverEndpoint(Point mousePoint, out int segmentNumber,
    out Point hitPoint)
{
    for (int i = 0; i < Pt1.Count; i++)
    {
        // Check the starting point.
        if (FindDistanceToPointSquared(mousePoint, Pt1[i]) < OverDistSquared)
        {
            // We're over this point.
            segmentNumber = i;
            hitPoint = Pt1[i];
            return true;
        }

        // Check the endpoint.
        if (FindDistanceToPointSquared(mousePoint, Pt2[i]) < OverDistSquared)
        {
            // We're over this point.
            segmentNumber = i;
            hitPoint = Pt2[i];
            return true;
        }
    }

    segmentNumber = -1;
    hitPoint = new Point(-1, -1);
    return false;
}
```

The MouseIsOverEndpoint method loops through the endpoints and uses the FindDistanceToPointSquared method, which is described in the next section, to find the distance squared between the mouse and each endpoint. If it finds a point close enough to the mouse, the method returns its information.

The following code shows the MouseIsOverSegment method.

```
// See if the mouse is over a line segment.
private bool MouseIsOverSegment(Point mousePoint, out int segmentNumber)
{
    for (int i = 0; i < Pt1.Count; i++)
    {
        // See if we're over the segment.
        PointF closest;
```

```
        if (FindDistanceToSegmentSquared(
            mousePoint, Pt1[i], Pt2[i], out closest)
                < OverDistSquared)
        {
            // We're over this segment.
            segmentNumber = i;
            return true;
        }
    }

    segmentNumber = -1;
    return false;
}
```

This method loops through the segments and calls FindDistanceToSegmentSquared to determine whether a segment is close to the mouse position. That method is described in the next section.

Finding Distances

The following code shows the FindDistanceToPointSquared method.

```
// Calculate the distance squared between two points.
private int FindDistanceToPointSquared(Point pt1, Point pt2)
{
    int dx = pt1.X - pt2.X;
    int dy = pt1.Y - pt2.Y;
    return dx * dx + dy * dy;
}
```

This method uses the Pythagorean Theorem to calculate the distance squared between two points. It finds the differences in the points' X and Y coordinates, squares them, adds them together, and returns the result.

To return the actual distance instead of the distance squared, the method would simply take the square root of the sum of the squares.

The FindDistanceToSegmentSquared method finds the shortest distance (squared) between a point and a line segment. It's much more complicated than the FindDistanceToPointSquared method so I don't want to take the space to explain it here. You can read about it and download an example program at the C# Helper web site's post, "Find the shortest distance between a point and a line segment in C#," at tinyurl.com/gpw5441. (The last character in the URL is a lowercase L not a numeral 1.)

Drawing a New Segment

The following code shows the MouseMove and MouseUp event handlers that are active while you're drawing a new segment.

```
// We're drawing a new segment.
private void canvasPictureBox_Drawing_MouseMove(object sender, MouseEventArgs e)
```

```
    {
        // Save the new point.
        NewPt2 = new Point(e.X, e.Y);

        // Redraw.
        canvasPictureBox.Invalidate();
    }

    // Stop drawing.
    private void canvasPictureBox_Drawing_MouseUp(object sender, MouseEventArgs e)
    {
        IsDrawing = false;

        // Reset the event handlers.
        canvasPictureBox.MouseMove -= canvasPictureBox_Drawing_MouseMove;
        canvasPictureBox.MouseMove += canvasPictureBox_MouseIsUp_MouseMove;
        canvasPictureBox.MouseUp -= canvasPictureBox_Drawing_MouseUp;

        // Create the new segment.
        Pt1.Add(NewPt1);
        Pt2.Add(NewPt2);

        // Redraw.
        canvasPictureBox.Invalidate();
    }
```

When the mouse moves, the `MouseMove` event handler updates the value of `NewPt2` to hold the mouse's current position. It then invalidates the program's `PictureBox` to make its `Paint` event handler draw the current line segments plus the new one.

When you release the mouse, the `MouseUp` event handler restores the "not moving anything" event handlers, adds the new segment's points to the `Pt1` and `Pt2` lists, and invalidates the `PictureBox` to make it redraw.

Moving an Endpoint

The following code shows the `MouseMove` and `MouseUp` event handlers that are active while you're moving an endpoint.

```
    // We're moving an endpoint.
    private void canvasPictureBox_MovingEndPoint_MouseMove(
        object sender, MouseEventArgs e)
    {
        // Move the point to its new location.
        if (MovingStartEndPoint)
            Pt1[MovingSegment] =
                new Point(e.X + OffsetX, e.Y + OffsetY);
        else
            Pt2[MovingSegment] =
                new Point(e.X + OffsetX, e.Y + OffsetY);

        // Redraw.
        canvasPictureBox.Invalidate();
    }
```

```
// Stop moving the endpoint.
private void canvasPictureBox_MovingEndPoint_MouseUp(
    object sender, MouseEventArgs e)
{
    // Reset the event handlers.
    canvasPictureBox.MouseMove += canvasPictureBox_MouseIsUp_MouseMove;
    canvasPictureBox.MouseMove -= canvasPictureBox_MovingEndPoint_MouseMove;
    canvasPictureBox.MouseUp -= canvasPictureBox_MovingEndPoint_MouseUp;

    // Redraw.
    canvasPictureBox.Invalidate();
}
```

When the mouse moves, the MouseMove event handler updates the position of the point you are moving and then invalidates the PictureBox to make it redraw. The MouseUp event handler simply restores the "not moving anything" event handlers and redraws.

Moving a Line Segment

The following code shows the MouseMove and MouseUp event handlers that are active while you're moving a segment.

```
// We're moving a segment.
private void canvasPictureBox_MovingSegment_MouseMove(
    object sender, MouseEventArgs e)
{
    // See how far the first point will move.
    int newX1 = e.X + OffsetX;
    int newY1 = e.Y + OffsetY;

    int dx = newX1 - Pt1[MovingSegment].X;
    int dy = newY1 - Pt1[MovingSegment].Y;

    if (dx == 0 && dy == 0) return;

    // Move the segment to its new location.
    Pt1[MovingSegment] = new Point(newX1, newY1);
    Pt2[MovingSegment] = new Point(
        Pt2[MovingSegment].X + dx,
        Pt2[MovingSegment].Y + dy);

    // Redraw.
    canvasPictureBox.Invalidate();
}

// Stop moving the segment.
private void canvasPictureBox_MovingSegment_MouseUp(
    object sender, MouseEventArgs e)
{
    // Reset the event handlers.
    canvasPictureBox.MouseMove += canvasPictureBox_MouseIsUp_MouseMove;
    canvasPictureBox.MouseMove -= canvasPictureBox_MovingSegment_MouseMove;
    canvasPictureBox.MouseUp -= canvasPictureBox_MovingSegment_MouseUp;

    // Redraw.
    canvasPictureBox.Invalidate();
```

```
    }
```

When the mouse moves, the MouseMove event handler updates the positions of the segment's endpoints and redraws to show the new position. The MouseUp event handler simply restores the "not moving anything" event handlers and redraws.

Summary

This example is rather long, but the pieces aren't too complicated as long as you take them one at a time. The way the program uninstalls event handlers and installs new ones lets you write the code in pieces and that helps keep the pieces simpler. It's a useful technique for any program that uses complex interactions among event handlers and the program's state.

The following list describes a few other features that you might like to add to a drawing program such as this one.

> Other drawing tools such as polylines, polygons, scribbles, rectangles, ellipses, and so forth.
> A different selection model so, for example, the user must select an object before moving its endpoints.
> Grab handles that let the user resize a selected object. You don't need this if you're only drawing line segments and you can move their endpoints, but you might want it if you're drawing other shapes.
> Snap-to-grid features.
> The ability to save and restore drawings.
> A method for selecting multiple objects at the same time.
> Alignment tools such as Align Tops and Align Middles.
> The ability to remove objects and change their stacking order.
> Shapes with different foreground and background colors.

This example stores line segment endpoints in two lists. An approach that might be better if you want to provide those more flexible features would be to use classes to represent the objects in the drawing. The following example uses that approach to draw bouncing balls.

28. Animate Bouncing Balls (20)

This example shows how to make a bouncing ball animation. This version of the program is actually a bit more elaborate than the version posted on the web site. That version displays a single ball bouncing around on the form. The basic approach is to store the ball's position and velocity in form-level variables similar to the way the preceding example stores line segment endpoints.

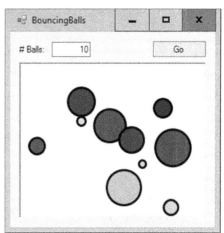

This version of the program uses a `Ball` class to manage many balls bouncing around inside a `PictureBox`.

The following code shows the `Ball` class.

```
public class Ball
{
    public Rectangle Bounds;
    public int Vx, Vy;
    public Brush TheBrush;
    public Pen ThePen;

    public Ball(int x, int y, int width, int height,
        int vx, int vy, Brush brush, Pen pen)
    {
        Bounds = new Rectangle(x, y, width, height);
        Vx = vx;
        Vy = vy;
        TheBrush = brush;
        ThePen = pen;
    }

    // Update the ball's position. Return true if it bounces off an edge.
    public void Move(int xmax, int ymax)
    {
        // Update the X coordinate.
        Bounds.X += Vx;
        if (Bounds.X < 0)
        {
            Bounds.X = -Bounds.X;
            Vx = -Vx;
        }
        else if (Bounds.Right > xmax)
        {
            Bounds.X = xmax - (Bounds.Right - xmax) - Bounds.Width;
            Vx = -Vx;
        }

        // Update the Y coordinate.
        Bounds.Y += Vy;
        if (Bounds.Y < 0)
        {
```

```
                Bounds.Y = -Bounds.Y;
                Vy = -Vy;
            }
            else if (Bounds.Bottom > ymax)
            {
                Bounds.Y = ymax - (Bounds.Bottom - ymax) - Bounds.Height;
                Vy = -Vy;
            }
        }

        // Draw the ball.
        public void Draw(Graphics gr)
        {
            gr.FillEllipse(TheBrush, Bounds);
            gr.DrawEllipse(ThePen, Bounds);
        }
    }
```

The class uses a `Rectangle` field named `Bounds` to store a ball's location and size. The `Vx` and `Vy` values hold the X and Y components of the ball's velocity. The class also stores a brush and a pen that it will use to draw the ball.

After it defines fields to hold those values, the class defines a constructor to make initializing `Ball` objects easier.

This type of class that represents an animated object is sometimes called a *sprite*. Normally a sprite class includes methods for updating the object's position and drawing the object.

The `Move` method adds the ball's `Vx` and `Vy` velocity components to its X and Y positions. It also checks that the new X and Y coordinates are between 0 and the values `xmax` and `ymax` passed in as parameters. If the ball has moved so it extends beyond the edge of the allowed area, the code reverses the corresponding velocity component and moves the ball back within bounds. The result is that the ball bounces off of the edge of the allowed area.

The `Ball` class's `Draw` method simply uses the ball's brush, pen, and bounds to draw the ball on a `Graphics` object.

The main program uses the `Balls` list defined in the following code to manage its list of balls.

```
// The balls.
private List<Ball> Balls = null;
```

When you click the Go button, the program fills the list with random `Ball` objects. That code is relatively straightforward so I won't take up space to show it here. Download the example to see all of the details.

When you click the button, the program also starts a `Timer` component named `moveBallTimer`. I set the timer's `Interval` property to 50 at design time so it ticks every 50 milliseconds or 20 times per second.

When the timer fires, the following `Tick` event handler executes.

```
// Move the balls.
private void moveBallTimer_Tick(object sender, EventArgs e)
{
    // Update the ball positions.
    int xmax = pictureBox1.ClientSize.Width;
    int ymax = pictureBox1.ClientSize.Height;
    foreach (Ball ball in Balls) ball.Move(xmax, ymax);

    // Draw the balls.
    pictureBox1.Refresh();
}
```

This code gets the PictureBox control's client area width and height. It then loops through the balls, calling each ball's Move method and passing in the available width and height.

After it has moved all of the balls, the code refreshes the program's PictureBox. The following Paint event handler then draws the balls in their new positions.

```
// Draw the balls on this PictureBox.
private void pictureBox1_Paint(object sender, PaintEventArgs e)
{
    if (Balls == null) return;

    e.Graphics.Clear(pictureBox1.BackColor);
    e.Graphics.SmoothingMode = SmoothingMode.AntiAlias;
    foreach (Ball ball in Balls) ball.Draw(e.Graphics);
}
```

This code clears the Graphics object's background and sets its SmoothingMode property to make smooth shapes. It then loops through the balls and calls their Draw methods.

That's about all there is to this example, other than a few details that deal with generating random balls. Using a sprite class that provides Move and Draw methods makes it much easier to update and draw animated objects.

29. ALIGN DRAWN TEXT (31)

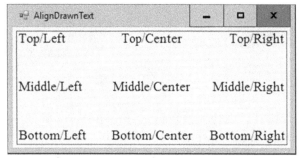

You can use labels and other controls to display text. This example shows how you can draw text aligned in various ways within a target rectangle.

The example's `Paint` event handler draws nine strings inside a rectangle, aligning them vertically and horizontally in the nine possible combinations of top/left, top/center, bottom/right, and so forth.

The `Graphics` class's `DrawString` method draws text. One of the parameters that you can pass into that method is a `StringFormat` object that determines how the text should be aligned.

The `StringFormat` class's `LineAlignment` property determines how the text is aligned vertically. It can take the values `Near` (top), `Center` (middle), or `Far` (bottom).

The `Alignment` property determines how the text is aligned horizontally. It can take the same values `Near` (left), `Center` (middle), or `Far` (right).

NOTE: This is a good example of overusing a piece of code, in this case, an enumeration. Instead of creating two separate enumerations Top/Center/Bottom and Left/Middle/Right, the `StringFormat` class uses the single `StringAlignment` enumeration to represent both. The single enumeration is trying to serve two purposes and that makes it harder to figure out what the values mean.

The similar property names `Alignment` and `LineAlignment` also make it hard to remember which value represents vertical alignment and which represents horizontal alignment.

This would be much more straightforward if the `StringFormat` class had properties named `VerticalAlignment` and `HorizontalAlignment` and they used separate enumerations for their values.

The following code shows how the `Paint` event handler draws text aligned in the rectangle's upper left corner.

```
// Draw text aligned in various ways.
private void Form1_Paint(object sender, PaintEventArgs e)
{
    Rectangle rect = new Rectangle(5, 5,
        ClientSize.Width - 10, ClientSize.Height - 10);
```

```
e.Graphics.DrawRectangle(Pens.Red, rect);

using (Font font = new Font("Times New Roman", 18, GraphicsUnit.Pixel))
{
    using (StringFormat sf = new StringFormat())
    {
        ...

        // Top/Left.
        sf.Alignment = StringAlignment.Near;          // Left.
        e.Graphics.DrawString("Top/Left", font, Brushes.Black, rect, sf);

        ...
    }
}
}
```

The code creates a `Rectangle` slightly smaller than the form and outlines it in red. It then creates `Font` and `StringFormat` objects.

To draw the text at the top of the rectangle, the code sets the `StringFormat` object's `LineAlignment` property to `Near`. To draw the text in the upper left corner, it also sets the object's `Alignment` property to `Near`.

The code then uses the `Graphics` object's `DrawString` method to draw the text "Top/Left" using the `StringFormat` object as a parameter. The result is the text drawn in the form's upper left corner.

The rest of the code is similar. It uses different `Alignment` and `LineAlignment` values to align text in various ways. Download the example to see all of the details.

30. GET FONT METRICS (77)

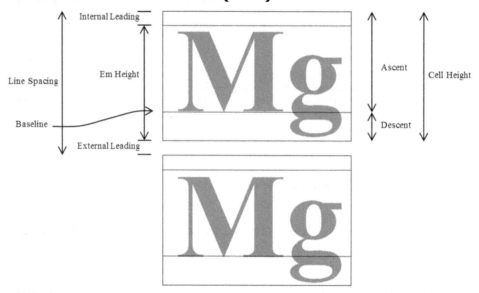

The `Font` and `FontFamily` classes provide a lot of information about a font's metrics, but that information is fairly hard to understand. The following list describes the key metrics shown in the picture above.

> ➤ Internal Leading – Space above the characters that is still considered part of the character's height. (Here "leading" is pronounced to rhyme with "sledding." The term comes from the old days when printers laid out letters with little lead stamps. Internal leading was lead added inside the letter's cell.)
> ➤ Em Height – The height of the characters not counting the internal leading.
> ➤ Ascent – The height of the characters from the baseline to the top of the cell including the internal leading.
> ➤ Descent – The distance the characters may extend below the baseline.
> ➤ Cell Height – The total height of the characters from bottom to top including the internal leading.
> ➤ Line Spacing – The distance between the top of one line and the top of the next line.
> ➤ External Leading – The distance between the bottom of one line and the top of the next line.

This example defines a `FontInfo` class to hold information about a font. The `Font` and `FontFamily` classes provide a lot of information about font dimensions, but much of it is in design units instead of something useful such as pixels or points. The `FontInfo` class converts values from design units into pixels to make using the dimensions easier.

The following code shows most of the `FontInfo` class.

```
class FontInfo
{
    // Heights and positions in pixels.
    public float EmHeightPixels;
    public float AscentPixels;
    public float DescentPixels;
    public float CellHeightPixels;
    public float InternalLeadingPixels;
    public float LineSpacingPixels;
    public float ExternalLeadingPixels;

    // Distances from the top of the cell in pixels.
    public float RelTop;
    public float RelBaseline;
    public float RelBottom;

    // Initialize the properties.
    public FontInfo(Graphics gr, Font font)
    {
        float emHeight = font.FontFamily.GetEmHeight(font.Style);
        EmHeightPixels = ConvertUnits(gr, font.Size,
            font.Unit, GraphicsUnit.Pixel);
        float designToPixels = EmHeightPixels / emHeight;

        AscentPixels = designToPixels *
            font.FontFamily.GetCellAscent(font.Style);
        DescentPixels = designToPixels *
            font.FontFamily.GetCellDescent(font.Style);
        CellHeightPixels = AscentPixels + DescentPixels;
        InternalLeadingPixels = CellHeightPixels - EmHeightPixels;
        LineSpacingPixels = designToPixels *
            font.FontFamily.GetLineSpacing(font.Style);
        ExternalLeadingPixels = LineSpacingPixels - CellHeightPixels;

        RelTop = InternalLeadingPixels;
        RelBaseline = AscentPixels;
        RelBottom = CellHeightPixels;
    }
}
```

The class first defines some public variables that will hold the font metrics in pixels. The `RelTop`, `RelBaseline`, and `RelBottom` values give the distance from the top of the character cell to the top of the character (below the internal leading), the baseline, and the bottom of the character (below the descent).

The class's constructor initializes the public fields for a particular font. This code simply uses the `Font` and `FontFamily` properties and methods to get information about the font's dimensions. There are two tricks to this part of the code.

First, the `Font` object's `Size` property returns the font's size in whatever units were used to create the font. If you specified the font's size in pixels when you created it, then this value is in pixels, which is what we need. If you specified the font's size in points, however, then this value is in points and the code needs to convert it into pixels before continuing. The code does this by calling the `ConvertUnits` method described shortly to convert from the font's unit into pixels.

The second trick is contained in the value `designToPixels`. This is a scale factor that converts font design units into pixels. The `FontFamily` class's `GetEmHeight` method returns the font's height in design units. The `Font` class's `Size` property returns the font's absolute height, and the code converts that value into pixels. That means the values `emHeight` and `EmHeightPixels` give the font's height in design units and pixels respectively. The code uses those values to calculate the conversion factor `designToPixels`.

After calculating `designToPixels`, the code simply uses other `Font` and `FontFamily` properties and methods to get the metric values. It then scales the values to convert them into pixels. It finishes by calculating the `RelTop`, `RelBaseline`, and `RelBottom` values for convenience.

The following code shows the `ConvertUnits` method.

```
// Convert from one type of unit to another.
// I don't know how to handle Display or World. Email me if you figure them out.
private float ConvertUnits(Graphics gr, float value,
    GraphicsUnit fromUnit, GraphicsUnit toUnit)
{
    if (fromUnit == toUnit) return value;

    // Convert to pixels.
    switch (fromUnit)
    {
        case GraphicsUnit.Document:
            value *= gr.DpiX / 300;
            break;
        case GraphicsUnit.Inch:
            value *= gr.DpiX;
            break;
        case GraphicsUnit.Millimeter:
            value *= gr.DpiX / 25.4F;
            break;
        case GraphicsUnit.Pixel:
            // Do nothing.
            break;
        case GraphicsUnit.Point:
            value *= gr.DpiX / 72;
            break;
        default:
            throw new Exception("Unknown input unit " +
                fromUnit.ToString() + " in FontInfo.ConvertUnits");
    }

    // Convert from pixels to the new units.
    switch (toUnit)
    {
        case GraphicsUnit.Document:
            value /= gr.DpiX / 300;
            break;
```

```
        case GraphicsUnit.Inch:
            value /= gr.DpiX;
            break;
        case GraphicsUnit.Millimeter:
            value /= gr.DpiX / 25.4F;
            break;
        case GraphicsUnit.Pixel:
            // Do nothing.
            break;
        case GraphicsUnit.Point:
            value /= gr.DpiX / 72;
            break;
        default:
            throw new Exception("Unknown output unit " +
                toUnit.ToString() + " in FontInfo.ConvertUnits");
    }

    return value;
}
```

This code checks the original unit and scales the value by an appropriate amount to convert the value into pixels.

By definition, the unit Document is 1/300th of an inch and the unit Point is 1/72nd of an inch. The code uses a Graphics object's DpiX property to determine the number of pixels per inch if necessary.

Next, the code converts the value, which is now in pixels, into the desired unit and returns the result.

The main program creates some fonts and makes FontInfo objects for them. It then uses the FontInfo values to draw the font metrics. That requires a bunch of drawing code that is complicated but not very interesting, so it isn't shown here. Download the example to see all of the details.

The picture below shows the example program in action.

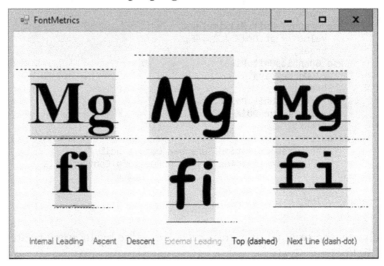

When you run the program, the colored labels at the bottom match colored lines in the drawing. You may be able to see the dashed lines, but the colors aren't visible in this book.

Notice that the exact result varies depending on the font. For example, in the middle font (80-point Comic Sans MS) the lowercase "f" extends below the baseline and in the font on the right (80-point Courier New) the lowercase "g" does not use the full descent.

To mangle a quote from the movie *Pirates of the Caribbean: Curse of the Black Pearl*, "The font metrics are more what you'd call 'guidelines' than actual rules."

31. DRAW ROTATED TEXT (79)

Drawing rotated text in a Windows Forms application isn't hard. Simply apply a RotateTransform to a Graphics object and draw the text using DrawString.

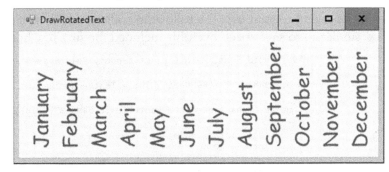

Positioning the rotated text is a bit harder. The transformation rotates the text's position as well as its orientation, so making it appear where you want it can be confusing.

A much simpler approach is to draw the text at the origin and then use a translation transformation to move the text where you want it. The following DrawRotatedTextAt method does this.

```
// Draw a rotated string at a particular position.
private void DrawRotatedTextAt(Graphics gr, float angle, string text,
    int x, int y, Font font, Brush brush)
{
    // Save the graphics state.
    GraphicsState state = gr.Save();
    gr.ResetTransform();

    // Rotate.
    gr.RotateTransform(angle);

    // Translate to the desired position. Be sure to append
    // the translation so it occurs after the rotation.
    gr.TranslateTransform(x, y, MatrixOrder.Append);

    // Draw the text at the origin.
    gr.DrawString(text, font, brush, 0, 0);

    // Restore the graphics state.
    gr.Restore(state);
}
```

This method first saves the Graphics object's state so it doesn't lose any other transformations that may be in effect. It then resets the transform to remove any previous effects.

Next, the code applies a rotation transformation followed by a translation to position the text as desired. It uses DrawString to draw the text at the origin and the transformation moves it to the desired location.

Finally, the code restores the saved graphical state to put the `Graphics` object back the way it was.

The main program uses the following code to display rotated text. All of the entries are similar so to save space I've only included the first few here.

```
private void Form1_Paint(object sender, PaintEventArgs e)
{
    e.Graphics.TextRenderingHint = TextRenderingHint.AntiAliasGridFit;

    using (Font font = new Font("Comic Sans MS", 20))
    {
        const int dx = 40;
        int x = 10;
        int y = ClientSize.Height - 10;
        DrawRotatedTextAt(e.Graphics, -90, "January", x, y, font, Brushes.Red);
        x += dx;
        DrawRotatedTextAt(e.Graphics, -90, "February", x, y, font, Brushes.Red);
        x += dx;
        DrawRotatedTextAt(e.Graphics, -90, "March", x, y, font, Brushes.Red);
        x += dx;
        ...
    }
}
```

This code sets the `Graphics` object's `TextRenderingHint` to make it produce smoothly drawn text. It then creates a 20-point Comic Sans MS font.

> **NOTE:** Rotated text usually looks best if you use a relatively large font.

The code makes some variables to track its position on the form and then calls `DrawRotatedTextAt` to draw text rotated by -90°. It updates the text's X coordinate and draws the next string.

The code continues, updating the text's X coordinate and calling `DrawRotatedTextAt`, until it has drawn all of the strings.

> **NOTE:** This same approach of drawing things rotated at the origin and then translating them to their final destinations works with other drawing objects, too. For example, it lets you draw and position rotated shapes or images.

32. RENDER POLYGONS AND POLYLINES IN WPF (89)

WPF lets you do all sorts of interesting things that are much harder to do in Windows Forms applications. Unfortunately, there are also some things that WPF makes much harder. For example, in a Windows Forms application, you can catch the `Paint` event raised by a form or `PictureBox` and produce graphics at runtime.

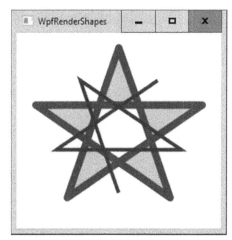

In contrast, a WPF application normally creates objects, such as a `Line` or `Polygon` object, to represent graphics and then displays them on the window. You *can* draw graphics on the fly in WPF if you really want to, but it's much harder and the process is poorly documented. In WPF this kind of drawing without an object is called *rendering*.

To render on the window, you override the window's `OnRender` method. That method's single parameter is a `DrawingContext` object that you can use to draw on the window.

> **NOTE:** The `Window` performs some extra drawing tasks on its own such as drawing its background. Unfortunately, anything that you draw in `OnRender` will be covered by the window's background so you won't see anything.
>
> To avoid that problem, set the window's background color to `Transparent`.

The following code shows the declaration for the example program's `OnRender` method.

```
protected override void OnRender(DrawingContext drawingContext)
{
}
```

The `DrawingContext` class provides a few drawing methods such as `DrawEllipse`, `DrawLine`, and `DrawRectangle`. Logically that class should also provide `DrawPolygon`, `DrawPolyline`, and other drawing methods but it doesn't. To make drawing in the example more consistent, I decided to add those methods to `DrawingContext` as extension methods.

The following code shows a private `DrawPolygonOrPolyline` method that draws either polygons or polylines.

```
// Draw a polygon or polyline.
private static void DrawPolygonOrPolyline(this DrawingContext drawingContext,
    Brush brush, Pen pen, Point[] points, FillRule fillRule, bool drawPolygon)
{
    // Make a StreamGeometry to hold the drawing objects.
    StreamGeometry geo = new StreamGeometry();
    geo.FillRule = fillRule;

    // Open the context to use for drawing.
    using (StreamGeometryContext context = geo.Open())
    {
        // Start at the first point.
        context.BeginFigure(points[0], true, drawPolygon);

        // Add the points after the first one.
        context.PolyLineTo(points.Skip(1).ToArray(), true, false);
    }

    // Draw.
    drawingContext.DrawGeometry(brush, pen, geo);
}
```

This method creates a `StreamGeometry` object to represent the shape. The `StreamGeometry` class is a geometry class (there are others such as `LineGeometry` and `RectangleGeometry`) that represents a sequence of drawing commands that can include shapes such as lines, arcs, ellipses, and rectangles. (The `PathGeometry` class is similar but heavier because it supports data binding, animation, and modification. Because this example doesn't need those, it uses the lighter-weight `StreamGeometry` class.)

After it creates the `StreamGeometry` object, the code sets its `FillRule` property. This can have the value `EvenOdd` or `Nonzero`. This example uses the `EvenOdd` setting so there is an unfilled hole in the middle of the outer star. (See the picture at the beginning of this example.) If this property were set to `Nonzero`, then the interior of the star would be filled completely.

Next, the program "opens" the `StreamGeometry` to get a context that it can use to draw. It calls the context's `BeginFigure` method to start a drawing sequence. You need to call this method before you start drawing. Its first parameter indicates where drawing should start, in this case at the `points` array's first point.

The second parameter to `BeginFigure` indicates whether the shape should be filled. This example sets this value to `true`. If you don't want to fill the shape, you can simply pass this method a `null` brush to make the method "fill" the shape with nothing.

The final parameter to `BeginFigure` indicates whether the shape should be closed. The method uses the value of its `drawPolygon` parameter so this code closes the shape only if it is drawing a polygon.

After starting a new figure, the code calls the context's `PolyLineTo` method. Its first parameter is the array of points that should be connected. Unfortunately, if the first point in the array duplicates the point used in the call to BeginFigure, then the polyline includes that point twice and that messes up the connection between the first and last points.

For example, if the star used mitered instead of rounded corners, then the final corner between the first and last point would not be mitered. (To see the effect, pass the entire points array into the method here and change the main program so it doesn't use rounded corners. I'll leave that as a homework assignment.)

To work around this problem, the code uses the LINQ Skip extension method to skip the first point in the points array and pass only the rest of the array into the call to PolyLineTo.

The second parameter to PolyLineTo determines whether the line segments between the points in the polyline should be "stroked" (drawn). The example program sets this to true so the points are always drawn. If you don't want to draw the line segments, simply pass the method a null pen to make the method "draw" them with nothing. This is useful if you want to fill the shape but not draw its outline.

The final parameter to PolyLineTo indicates whether the shape should use rounded corners to connect its lines. If you set this to true, then segments are joined with rounded corners even if the pen used to draw the shape has a different LineJoin value. The example sets this final parameter to false.

Finally, after those short but somewhat confusing steps, the program calls the DrawingContext object's DrawGeometry method to draw the StreamGeometry containing the polygon or polyline.

The DrawPolygonOrPolyline method is declared private, so it is only visible inside the static DrawingContextExtensions class that defines it. You could make it public, but then the main program would need to use the same method to draw both polygons and polylines. While that wouldn't be the end of the world, it's usually better to make a method perform a single well-defined task instead of making one "super-method" that performs multiple unrelated chores.

Instead of making this method public, I created the following two public extension methods that call the private method.

```
// Draw a polygon.
public static void DrawPolygon(this DrawingContext drawingContext,
    Brush brush, Pen pen, Point[] points, FillRule fillRule)
{
    drawingContext.DrawPolygonOrPolyline(brush, pen, points, fillRule, true);
}

// Draw a polyline.
public static void DrawPolyline(this DrawingContext drawingContext,
    Brush brush, Pen pen, Point[] points, FillRule fillRule)
{
```

```
        drawingContext.DrawPolygonOrPolyline(brush, pen, points, fillRule, false);
}
```

Now using these methods from the main program is just easy as using the other methods provided by the `DrawingContext` class. The following code shows the program's full `OnRender` method.

```
// Draw some shapes.
protected override void OnRender(DrawingContext drawingContext)
{
    // Clear the background.
    Rect bgRect = new Rect(0, 0, this.ActualWidth, this.ActualHeight);
    drawingContext.DrawRectangle(Brushes.White, null, bgRect);

    // Define polygon points.
    const double lineThickness = 10;
    double centerX = mainGrid.ActualWidth / 2;
    double centerY = mainGrid.ActualHeight / 2;
    double radiusX = centerX - 2 * lineThickness;
    double radiusY = centerY - 2 * lineThickness;
    double theta = -Math.PI / 2;
    const double dtheta = Math.PI * 4 / 5;
    Point[] points = new Point[5];
    for (int i = 0; i < 5; i++)
    {
        points[i] = new Point(
            centerX + radiusX * Math.Cos(theta),
            centerY + radiusY * Math.Sin(theta));
        theta += dtheta;
    }

    // Draw the polygon.
    Pen pen = new Pen(Brushes.Green, lineThickness);
    pen.LineJoin = PenLineJoin.Round;
    drawingContext.DrawPolygon(Brushes.LightGreen,
        pen, points, FillRule.EvenOdd);

    // Make polyline points.
    theta = Math.PI / 2;
    radiusX *= 0.75;
    radiusY *= 0.75;
    for (int i = 0; i < 5; i++)
    {
        points[i] = new Point(
            centerX + radiusX * Math.Cos(theta),
            centerY + radiusY * Math.Sin(theta));
        theta += dtheta;
    }

    // Draw the polyline.
    pen = new Pen(Brushes.Blue, lineThickness / 2);
    drawingContext.DrawPolyline(null, pen,
        points, FillRule.EvenOdd);
}
```

The code first fills the window with a white background. It then creates some points to define the large star. It creates a green pen, sets its `LineJoin` property to `Round`, and calls the `DrawPolygon` extension method to draw the star.

The program then makes new points to define the smaller star. It creates a blue pen, leaves its `LineJoin` property with the default value `Bevel`, and calls the `DrawPolyline` extension method to draw the new star.

If you look back at the `DrawPolygonOrPolyline` method, you'll see that the code isn't really all that hard; it was just hard to figure out. I wonder why Microsoft didn't include simple methods such as this one in WPF to begin with. At least this extension method is as easy to use as the other `DrawingContext` methods.

33. USE LINEAR GRADIENT BRUSHES IN WINDOWS FORMS (91)

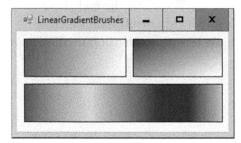

A `LinearGradientBrush` fills an area with a color gradient that blends smoothly from one color to another.

The `LinearGradientBrush` class has a `Dispose` method that you should call when you're done with the brush. To make that easier, place the brush in a `using` block so the program calls `Dispose` automatically when the block ends.

The example program demonstrates three of the `LinearGradientBrush` class's many different constructors. The following code uses one of the simpler ones, defining the brush by specifying a start point, endpoint, start color, and end color.

```
// Define a brush with two points and their colors.
using (LinearGradientBrush brush = new LinearGradientBrush(
    new Point(10, 10), new Point(155, 50), Color.Red, Color.White))
{
    e.Graphics.FillRectangle(brush, 10, 10, 140, 50);
    e.Graphics.DrawRectangle(Pens.Black, 10, 10, 140, 50);
}
```

This is somewhat awkward because you specify the brush using points but you specify the areas to draw with a point, width, and height.

The following code uses a `Rectangle` to specify both the brush's area and the area to be drawn. The final parameter to the brush's constructor gives the direction in which the colors should flow. This can be `BackwardDiagonal`, `ForwardDiagonal`, `Horizontal`, or `Vertical`. Alternatively, you can specify the angle in which the colors should flow.

```
// Define a brush with a Rectangle, colors, and gradient mode.
Rectangle rect = new Rectangle(160, 10, 125, 50);
using (LinearGradientBrush brush = new LinearGradientBrush(
    rect, Color.Blue, Color.White, LinearGradientMode.ForwardDiagonal))
{
    e.Graphics.FillRectangle(brush, rect);
    e.Graphics.DrawRectangle(Pens.Black, rect);
}
```

The final example in this program uses the following code to make a gradient that flows between more than two colors.

```
// Define a gradient with more than 2 colors.
rect = new Rectangle(10, 70, 275, 50);
using (LinearGradientBrush brush = new LinearGradientBrush(
    rect, Color.Blue, Color.White, 0f))
{
    // Create a ColorBlend object. Note that you
```

```
    // must initialize it before you save it in the
    // brush's InterpolationColors property.
    ColorBlend colorBlend = new ColorBlend();
    colorBlend.Colors = new Color[]
    {
        Color.Red, Color.Orange, Color.Yellow, Color.Lime,
        Color.Blue, Color.Indigo, Color.Violet,
    };
    colorBlend.Positions = new float[]
    {
        0f, 1/6f, 2/6f, 3/6f, 4/6f, 5/6f, 1f
    };
    brush.InterpolationColors = colorBlend;

    e.Graphics.FillRectangle(brush, rect);
    e.Graphics.DrawRectangle(Pens.Black, rect);
}
```

This code creates the brush specifying the `Rectangle` that it should cover, two colors, and the angle 0 degrees (so this is a horizontal gradient).

It then creates a `ColorBlend` object to represent the brush's colors. It initializes the object's `Colors` property to an array of `Color` values. It then sets the `Positions` property to an array of floats between 0 and 1 that indicate where inside the brush the different colors should appear.

Finally, the code sets the brush's `InterpolationColors` property to the `ColorBlend` object.

> **NOTE:** You must initialize the `ColorBlend` object before you set the `InterpolationColors` property equal to it or the program will crash.

Defining linear gradient brushes in this way is fairly easy, but it's even easier in WPF where you can give a control a background gradient at design time.

34. DRAW JUSTIFIED TEXT (97)

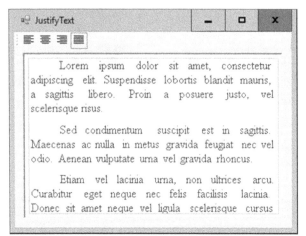

A Label control's TextAlign property lets you easily align a string horizontally and vertically. For example, you can set this property to BottomCenter to display text centered at the bottom of the Label.

Similarly if you use a Graphics object's DrawString method to draw text, the StringFormat class makes it fairly easy to left justify, right justify, or center a line of text.

Strangely, neither the Label control nor the StringFormat class gives you a method to fully justify a line of text so it extends all the way to both the left and right margins. This example shows how you can use the DrawString method to fully justify paragraphs of text.

The following DrawParagraphs method draws a string's paragraphs with the proper alignment.

```
// Draw justified text on the Graphics object in the indicated Rectangle.
private RectangleF DrawParagraphs(Graphics gr, RectangleF rect,
    Font font, Brush brush, string text,
    TextJustification justification, float lineSpacing,
    float indent, float paragraphSpacing)
{
    // Split the text into paragraphs.
    string[] paragraphs = text.Split('\n');

    // Draw each paragraph.
    foreach (string paragraph in paragraphs)
    {
        // Draw the paragraph keeping track of remaining space.
        rect = DrawParagraph(gr, rect, font, brush, paragraph,
            justification, lineSpacing, indent, paragraphSpacing);

        // See if there's any room left.
        if (rect.Height < font.Size) break;
    }

    return rect;
}
```

This code splits the text into paragraphs delimited by the newline character \n. It then loops through the paragraphs and calls the DrawParagraph method described next to draw them.

After it draws a paragraph, the code compares the height of the remaining rectangle to the font's size. If there's no room to draw any more text, the method returns.

The following code shows the `DrawParagraph` method, which draws a single paragraph.

```
// Draw a paragraph by lines inside the Rectangle. Return a RectangleF
// representing any unused space in the original RectangleF.
private RectangleF DrawParagraph(Graphics gr, RectangleF rect,
    Font font, Brush brush, string text,
    TextJustification justification, float lineSpacing,
    float indent, float extraParagraphSpacing)
{
    // Get the coordinates for the first line.
    float y = rect.Top;

    // Break the text into words.
    string[] words = text.Split(' ');
    int startWord = 0;

    // Repeat until we run out of text or room.
    for (;;)
    {
        // See how many words will fit.
        // Start with just the next word.
        string line = words[startWord];

        // Add more words until the line won't fit.
        int endWord = startWord + 1;
        while (endWord < words.Length)
        {
            // See if the next word fits.
            string testLine = line + " " + words[endWord];
            SizeF lineSize = gr.MeasureString(testLine, font);
            if (lineSize.Width + indent > rect.Width)
            {
                // The line is too wide. Don't use the last word.
                endWord--;
                break;
            }
            else
            {
                // The word fits. Save the test line.
                line = testLine;
            }

            // Try the next word.
            endWord++;
        }

        // See if this is the last line in the paragraph.
        if ((endWord == words.Length) &&
            (justification == TextJustification.Full))
        {
            // This is the last line. Don't justify it.
            DrawLine(gr, line, font, brush,
                rect.Left + indent,
                y,
                rect.Width - indent,
                TextJustification.Left);
        }
        else
        {
```

```
                    // This is not the last line. Justify it.
                    DrawLine(gr, line, font, brush,
                        rect.Left + indent,
                        y,
                        rect.Width - indent,
                        justification);
                }

                // Move down to draw the next line.
                y += font.Height * lineSpacing;

                // Make sure there's room for another line.
                if (font.Size > rect.Height) break;

                // Start the next line at the next word.
                startWord = endWord + 1;
                if (startWord >= words.Length) break;

                // Don't indent subsequent lines in this paragraph.
                indent = 0;
            }

            // Add a gap after the paragraph.
            y += font.Height * extraParagraphSpacing;

            // Return a RectangleF representing any unused
            // space in the original RectangleF.
            float height = rect.Bottom - y;
            if (height < 0) height = 0;
            return new RectangleF(rect.X, y, rect.Width, height);
        }
```

This method breaks the paragraph into words delimited by space characters and then loops through the words. The loop continues until the method runs out of words or it runs out of room to draw them.

Each time through the loop, the code builds a string, adding more words until the string no longer fits in the available width. It then removes the final word so the string fits. (If the first word is so long that it won't fit, the method draws only that word and it is truncated.)

If the string contains all of the remaining words, and if the program is fully justifying the text, then the code calls the DrawLine method to left justify this line. (Normally when you fully justify text, you don't justify the final line. Imagine how weird it would be if the last line contained only two words. You would have the first word on the far left, a huge space, and the second word on the far right.)

If this is not the end of the paragraph or the program isn't fully justifying the text, then the method calls the following DrawLine method to draw the line with the desired justification.

```
            // Draw a line of text.
            private void DrawLine(Graphics gr, string line, Font font,
                Brush brush, float x, float y, float width,
                TextJustification justification)
            {
```

```
    // Make a rectangle to hold the text.
    RectangleF rect = new RectangleF(x, y, width, font.Height);

    // See if we should use full justification.
    if (justification == TextJustification.Full)
    {
        // Justify the text.
        DrawJustifiedLine(gr, rect, font, brush, line);
    }
    else
    {
        // Make a StringFormat to align the text.
        using (StringFormat sf = new StringFormat())
        {
            // Use the appropriate alignment.
            switch (justification)
            {
                case TextJustification.Left:
                    sf.Alignment = StringAlignment.Near;
                    break;
                case TextJustification.Right:
                    sf.Alignment = StringAlignment.Far;
                    break;
                case TextJustification.Center:
                    sf.Alignment = StringAlignment.Center;
                    break;
            }

            gr.DrawString(line, font, brush, rect, sf);
        }
    }
}
```

This method first checks the justification parameter. If justification is `Full`, then the method calls the `DrawJustifiedLine` method described shortly to draw the text.

If justification is not `Full`, then the method makes a `StringFormat` object with the proper alignment and uses it to draw the text.

The following code shows the `DrawJustifiedLine` method tht actually performs the justification.

```
    // Draw justified text on the Graphics object in the indicated Rectangle.
    private void DrawJustifiedLine(Graphics gr, RectangleF rect,
        Font font, Brush brush, string text)
    {
        // Break the text into words.
        string[] words = text.Split(' ');

        // Add a space to each word and get their lengths.
        float[] wordWidth = new float[words.Length];
        float totalWidth = 0;
        for (int i = 0; i < words.Length; i++)
        {
            // See how wide this word is.
            SizeF size = gr.MeasureString(words[i], font);
            wordWidth[i] = size.Width;
            totalWidth += wordWidth[i];
```

```
        }

        // Get the additional spacing between words.
        float extraSpace = rect.Width - totalWidth;
        int numSpaces = words.Length - 1;
        if (words.Length > 1) extraSpace /= numSpaces;

        // Draw the words.
        float x = rect.Left;
        float y = rect.Top;
        for (int i = 0; i < words.Length; i++)
        {
            // Draw the word.
            gr.DrawString(words[i], font, brush, x, y);

            // Move right to draw the next word.
            x += wordWidth[i] + extraSpace;
        }
    }
}
```

This method splits the line into words delimited by spaces. It loops through the words and uses the Graphics object's MeasureString method to see how wide each word will be when drawn.

Next, the code subtracts the total of the word widths from the rectangle's available width. The result is the leftover space that must be inserted between the words. The program divides the leftover space by the number of gaps between the words to see how big those gaps should be.

The method then loops through the words again, drawing each and allowing room for the gap before the next word.

 NOTE: Full justification works best when the text contains words that are small compared to the width of the rectangle. A line with only a few very long words will have large gaps between them.

Download the example to see additional details.

Part VIII. Image Processing

The examples in the preceding part of the book deal with drawing shapes such as line segments, circles, and text. The examples in this part of the book deal with images. They show how you can get, set, and modify the individual pixels in an image. They also show how you can process the pixels in an image, for example to convert an image to grayscale. Finally they show how to save images in different file formats such as JPG or PNG, and how to adjust the compression level in JPG files.

35. OPTIMIZE JPG COMPRESSION LEVELS (19)

This example lets you check image quality and file size at different JPG compression levels. Use the File menu's Open command to load an image file. Then use the scroll bar to adjust the JPG Compression Index.

When you change the compression level, the program saves the loaded image into a temporary file at the selected compression level. It then displays the resulting image and the file's size.

This example demonstrates several useful techniques. The most important of those, at least as far as this program is concerned, is demonstrated by the following method, which saves an image in a JPG file with a desired compression index.

```
// Save the file with a specific compression level.
private void SaveJpg(Image image, string filename, long compression)
{
    try
    {
        EncoderParameters encoderParams = new EncoderParameters();
        encoderParams.Param[0] = new EncoderParameter(
            System.Drawing.Imaging.Encoder.Quality, compression);

        ImageCodecInfo codecInfo = GetEncoderInfo("image/jpeg");
        File.Delete(filename);
        image.Save(filename, codecInfo, encoderParams);
    }
    catch (Exception ex)
    {
        MessageBox.Show(ex.Message, "JPG Error",
            MessageBoxButtons.OK, MessageBoxIcon.Error);
    }
}
```

This method creates an `EncoderParameters` object to hold information to send to the encoder that will create the JPG file. It then fills in the object's compression index.

Next, the method calls the `GetEncoderInfo` method (described shortly) to get information about the encoder for JPG files. It deletes the previous temporary file if it exists and uses the encoder to save the image in the temporary file again with the new encoder parameters.

NOTE: You may have noticed that the code includes a complete namespace path in the class name `System.Drawing.Imaging.Encoder.Quality`. Unfortunately, the `System.Drawing.Imaging` namespace and the `System.Text` namespace both define an `Encoder` class.

If this statement just used `Encoder` without specifying the namespace, Visual Studio wouldn't know which `Encoder` class to use. This program uses the full path to the class so there's no ambiguity.

The following code shows the `GetEncoderInfo` method.

```
// Return an ImageCodecInfo object for this mime type.
private ImageCodecInfo GetEncoderInfo(string mimeType)
{
    ImageCodecInfo[] encoders = ImageCodecInfo.GetImageEncoders();
    for (int i = 0; i <= encoders.Length; i++)
    {
        if (encoders[i].MimeType == mimeType) return encoders[i];
    }
    return null;
}
```

This code loops through the available encoders until it finds one with the right mime type, in this case `image/jpeg`.

The program uses the following code to load an image file.

```
// The original uncompressed image.
private Image OriginalImage = null;

// Open an image file.
private void openMenuItem_Click(object sender, EventArgs e)
{
    if (pictureOpenFileDialog.ShowDialog() == DialogResult.OK)
    {
        try
        {
            // See how big the file is.
            originalSizeLabel.Text = FileSize(pictureOpenFileDialog.FileName);

            // Load the file.
            OriginalImage = LoadBitmapUnlocked(pictureOpenFileDialog.FileName);

            // Display a sample image at the current compression level.
            ShowSampleImage();

            // Enable the Save As command.
            saveAsMenuItem.Enabled = true;
        }
        catch (Exception ex)
        {
            MessageBox.Show(ex.Message, "Load Error",
                MessageBoxButtons.OK, MessageBoxIcon.Error);
```

```
            }
        }
    }
```

The variable `OriginalImage` will hold the image.

When you select the File menu's Open command, the `openMenuItem_Click` event handler displays an `OpenFileDialog`. If you select a file and click Open, the program calls the `FileSize` method (described shortly) to display the file's size. It then calls the `LoadBitmapUnlocked` method (also described shortly) to load the image and save it in the `OriginalImage` variable. Finally, the code calls the `ShowSampleImage` method (yet another method to be described shortly) and enables the Save As menu item.

The following code shows the `FileSize` method.

```
// Return a file's size.
private string FileSize(string filename)
{
    FileInfo fileinfo = new FileInfo(filename);
    return fileinfo.Length.ToFileSizeApi();
}
```

This method creates a `FileInfo` object for the file. The `FileInfo` class, which is defined in the `System.IO` namespace, provides properties and methods for working with files. For example, its properties tell you a file's creation and last access date and time, directory name, extension, and length.

The method calls the `ToFileSizeApi` extension method described in the example, "10. Format File Sizes (35)," to return the file size in KB, MB, or whatever unit makes sense. See that example earlier in this book for more information.

The following code shows the `LoadBitmapUnlocked` method.

```
// Load a bitmap without locking it.
private Bitmap LoadBitmapUnlocked(string filename)
{
    using (Bitmap bm = new Bitmap(filename))
    {
        return new Bitmap(bm);
    }
}
```

Normally when you use an image file to create a `Bitmap` object, that object keeps the image file open in case it needs to reconstruct the image later. In many programs that's rather annoying because it means you can't use some other application such as File Explorer to delete or rename the file while your program is running.

In this example, the problem is even more severe because this program deletes, rewrites, and redisplays its temporary file every time you change the compression level. If the file is locked, the program won't be able to delete the file so it will crash.

The LoadBitmapUnlocked method shows one way to avoid this problem. First, it uses the image file to create a Bitmap in a using block. It then creates and returns a new Bitmap copied from the original one. The new Bitmap is a copy made in memory so it doesn't need access to the image file.

When the using block ends, the program automatically calls the first Bitmap object's Dispose method and that frees the lock on the image file.

> **NOTE:** The LoadBitmapUnlocked method is a handy little tool to add to your programming toolkit.

The following code shows the ShowSampleImage method.

```
// Display a sample that uses the selected compression index.
private void ShowSampleImage()
{
    // Display the compression value.
    long compression = compressionScrollBar.Value;
    compressionLabel.Text = compression.ToString();

    // If no image is loaded, do nothing else.
    if (OriginalImage == null) return;

    // Save the image with the selected compression level.
    string filename = Application.StartupPath + "\\_temp.jpg";
    SaveJpg(OriginalImage, filename, compression);

    // Display the result without locking the file.
    imagePictureBox.Image = LoadBitmapUnlocked(filename);

    // See how big the file is.
    compressedSizeLabel.Text = FileSize(filename);
}
```

The method gets the compression level from the form's scroll bar and displays it in the form's label.

Next, it calls the SaveJpg method described earlier to save the image in a temporary file. It uses the LoadBitmapUnlocked method to display the image in a PictureBox, and it calls the FileSize method to display the file's size.

In the picture shown at the beginning of this post, the compression level is 38. It still produces a reasonable result and the compressed file's size is less than a quarter of the original file's size.

Your exact results will depend on the image. For example, images with large areas of solid colors don't compress well. Often you can get better results if you store them in lossless formats such as PNG.

36. Convert an Image to Grayscale (71)

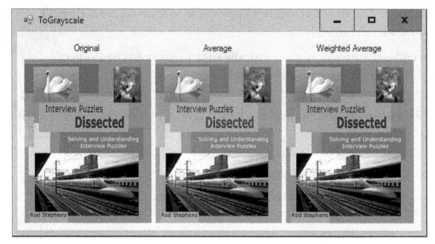

This book's cover shows a color version of the picture on the right. Unfortunately, the color is lost on this page because the book isn't printed in color. (That would be really expensive).

This example demonstrates two important techniques. The first allows you to manipulate the pixels in an image much more quickly than you normally can in a Windows Forms application. The second is the ostensible goal of this example: to convert an image to grayscale. The following two sections describe those two techniques.

Manipulating Pixels

This is an extremely important technique if you frequently need to manipulate an image's pixels because it makes pixel manipulation much faster. Large images contain a huge number of pixels, so any improvement in speed is important.

For example, my screen's resolution is currently 1,366 by 768 pixels, so an image that covers my screen would contain 1,366 × 768 or a bit more than a million pixels. If a program needs to manipulate the red, green, blue, and alpha components of every pixel, it needs to work with more than four million values.

> **NOTE:** A pixel's *alpha* component determines its opacity. Like the other color components, it has the byte data type. An alpha value of 0 means the pixel is completely transparent and a value of 255 means the pixels is completely opaque.

Many programs need to read the pixel values of an input image and then set the values of an output image's pixels. That doubles the number of values to manipulate to more than eight million.

As you can see, the number of values that an image processing application may need to manipulate can add up quickly. Even a fast computer can seem slow when it's processing so many values. For that reason, this is a pretty important example; more important than its 71 ranking may suggest.

That's enough motivation. Let's look at some programming details.

The .NET Framework's `Bitmap` class provides two methods that let you get and set individual pixel values: `GetPixel` and `SetPixel`.

The `GetPixel` method takes as parameters the X and Y coordinates of the pixel you want to examine and it returns a `Color` structure for that pixel. You can then use the structure's `R`, `G`, `B`, and `A` properties to get the pixel's red, green, blue, and alpha color components.

The `Bitmap` class's `SetPixel` method takes as parameters a pixel's X and Y coordinates and the `Color` value that you want to assign to the pixel.

You can use the `GetPixel` and `SetPixel` methods, together with `Color` values, to manipulate an image's pixels. Unfortunately, that's pretty slow. On my system, a test program I wrote took about 1.94 seconds to fill a 1,366 by 768 pixel bitmap with randomly colored pixels.

The `Bitmap32` class implemented by this example makes manipulating pixels much faster because it directly accesses an image's bytes. The following code shows the fields and properties that the class uses to store `Bitmap` data.

```
public class Bitmap32
{
    // Provide public access to the picture's byte data.
    public byte[] ImageBytes;
    public int RowSizeBytes;
    public const int PixelDataSize = 32;

    // A reference to the Bitmap.
    private Bitmap TheBitmap;

    // Save a reference to the bitmap.
    public Bitmap32(Bitmap bm)
    {
        TheBitmap = bm;
    }

    // Bitmap data.
    private BitmapData TheBitmapData;

    // Return the image's dimensions.
    public int Width
    {
        get
        {
            return TheBitmap.Width;
        }
    }
    public int Height
    {
        get
```

```
        {
            return TheBitmap.Height;
        }
    }
    ...
}
```

The `ImageBytes` array holds the pixels' color component values. The `RowSizeBytes` value holds the number of bytes per row of the image.

The constant `PixelDataSize` gives the number of bytes per pixel. This version of the class only works with 32-bit bitmaps. That kind of bitmap uses one byte for each of a pixel's red, green, blue, and alpha color components for a total number of 32 bits per pixel.

The value `TheBitmap` stores a reference to the `Bitmap` that a `Bitmap32` object represents. The class's only constructor simply stores a reference to the `Bitmap` in the variable `TheBitmap`.

The field named `TheBitmapData` stores information about the bitmap that the class needs to manipulate it. This data isn't very useful outside of this class, so it's declared `private`.

Finally, as you can probably guess, the read-only `Width` and `Height` properties return the bitmap's width and height in pixels.

Before a program can access a `Bitmap32` object's pixels, it must call the following `LockBitmap` method.

```
// Lock the bitmap's data.
public void LockBitmap()
{
    // Lock the bitmap data.
    Rectangle bounds = new Rectangle(
        0, 0, TheBitmap.Width, TheBitmap.Height);
    TheBitmapData = TheBitmap.LockBits(bounds,
        ImageLockMode.ReadWrite,
        PixelFormat.Format32bppArgb);
    RowSizeBytes = TheBitmapData.Stride;

    // Allocate room for the data.
    int totalSize = TheBitmapData.Stride * TheBitmapData.Height;
    ImageBytes = new byte[totalSize];

    // Copy the data into the ImageBytes array.
    Marshal.Copy(TheBitmapData.Scan0, ImageBytes, 0, totalSize);
}
```

Internally a `Bitmap` stores its pixel data in a one-dimensional array of bytes. Normally the system's memory manager can move those bytes around if it needs to rearrange memory. Before a C# program can directly access those bytes, they must be locked so they can't move.

The `LockBitmap` method creates a `Rectangle` that includes the entire image's pixels. It then calls the `Bitmap` object's `LockBits` method to lock the bytes for those pixels.

The method then calculates the amount of memory that those bytes occupy, allocates that much space in the ImageBytes array, and then uses Marshal.Copy to copy the byte data into the ImageBytes array.

Now the program can directly examine and modify the bytes in the ImageBytes array.

The ImageBytes array stores each pixel's blue, green, red, and alpha bytes *in that order*. For example, the blue component of the pixel in the image's upper left corner is in the first byte of the array. The next byte holds that pixel's green component, and so forth.

The Bitmap32 class provides several methods that make accessing particular bytes in the array easy. For example, the following GetPixel method returns a pixel's color components.

```
// Provide easy access to the color values.
public void GetPixel(int x, int y,
    out byte red, out byte green, out byte blue, out byte alpha)
{
    int i = y * TheBitmapData.Stride + x * 4;
    blue = ImageBytes[i++];
    green = ImageBytes[i++];
    red = ImageBytes[i++];
    alpha = ImageBytes[i];
}
```

This code multiplies the pixel's row number y by the number of bytes per row. It then adds the column number x multiplied by four. The result is the index in the array of the pixel's first byte.

The code then steps through the next four bytes and saves their values in the method's return parameters.

The Bitmap32 class provides a complementary SetPixel method that lets you set a pixel's color components. It also provides methods such as GetRed and SetBlue to get and set a pixel's color components individually.

After a program is finished manipulating an image's pixels, it must call the following method to unlock the Bitmap object's memory.

```
// Copy the data back into the Bitmap and release resources.
public void UnlockBitmap()
{
    // Copy the data back into the bitmap.
    int totalSize = TheBitmapData.Stride * TheBitmapData.Height;
    Marshal.Copy(ImageBytes, 0, TheBitmapData.Scan0, totalSize);

    // Unlock the bitmap.
    TheBitmap.UnlockBits(TheBitmapData);

    // Release resources.
    ImageBytes = null;
    TheBitmapData = null;
}
```

This method copies the data in the `ImageBytes` array back into the `Bitmap` and unlocks the `Bitmap` memory.

In one test, a program that created a 1,366 by 768 pixel image took about 1.94 seconds using the `Bitmap` class's `SetPixel` method but it took only 0.45 seconds using the `Bitmap32` class's `SetPixel` method and a mere 0.14 seconds when it directly accessed the `ImageBytes` array.

Converting to Grayscale

Using the `Bitmap32` class is relatively simple. First, create an instance of the class associated with a regular `Bitmap` object. Lock the `Bitmap32` and use it to manipulate the image's pixels. When you're done, unlock the object and the `Bitmap` is ready for use.

This example program uses the following method to convert a `Bitmap` to grayscale.

```
// Convert the Bitmap to grayscale.
private void BitmapToGrayscale(Bitmap bm, bool useAverage)
{
    // Make a Bitmap24 object.
    Bitmap32 bm32 = new Bitmap32(bm);

    // Lock the bitmap.
    bm32.LockBitmap();

    // Get color weights.
    float wr, wg, wb;
    if (useAverage)
    {
        wr = 1 / 3f;
        wg = 1 / 3f;
        wb = 1 / 3f;
    }
    else
    {
        wr = 0.3f;
        wg = 0.5f;
        wb = 0.2f;
    }

    // Process the pixels.
    for (int x = 0; x < bm.Width; x++)
    {
        for (int y = 0; y < bm.Height; y++)
        {
            byte r, g, b, a;
            bm32.GetPixel(x, y, out r, out g, out b, out a);
            byte gray = (byte)(wr * r + wg * g + wb * b);
            bm32.SetPixel(x, y, gray, gray, gray, a);
        }
    }

    // Unlock the bitmap.
    bm32.UnlockBitmap();
```

```
    }
```

The method creates a `Bitmap32` object associated with the `Bitmap` and locks the object.

Next, the code sets the weighting factors `wr`, `wg`, and `wb`. If the `useAverage` parameter is `true`, the code sets the values to $1/3$ to take a simple average of the pixels' color components. If `useAverage` is `false`, the code uses a non-uniform weighted average that gives more weight to the pixels' green components. The second method may produce a slightly better result, although it's often hard to tell the difference.

The code then loops through the image's pixels. It calculates the appropriate average of each pixel's red, green, and blue components and then sets all three of the components equal to that average.

After it sets all of the pixels' values, the code unlocks the `Bitmap32` object.

When the program starts, it uses the following code to display its grayscale images.

```
// Make the grayscale images.
private void Form1_Load(object sender, EventArgs e)
{
    BitmapToGrayscale(averagePictureBox.Image as Bitmap, true);
    BitmapToGrayscale(grayscalePictureBox.Image as Bitmap, false);
}
```

I gave all three of the program's `PictureBox` controls the same image at design time. This code gets the `averagePictureBox` control's image as a `Bitmap` and passes it to the `BitmapToGrayscale` method. The second parameter makes the method use a simple average. When the method returns, the `Bitmap` is still displayed in the `PictureBox` so the grayscale version appears automatically.

The code then repeats that step to make a weighted average grayscale image from the image in the `grayscalePictureBox` control.

37. COMPARE IMAGES TO FIND DIFFERENCES (36)

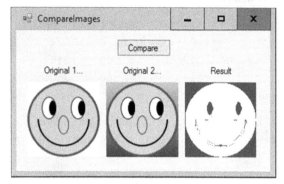

This example detects small differences in two images. Click the two labels on the left to load the two original images. Click the Compare button to make the program compare the images and show the pixels where they differ.

In the picture on the right, some of the differences have obvious explanations, such as the backgrounds outside of the smiley faces. Other differences, such as those around the smile and eyes, are much less obvious in the original images but they are easy to see in the result image.

The following code shows how the program compares the two original images.

```
// Compare the images.
private void compareButton_Click(object sender, EventArgs e)
{
    // Make copies of the original images.
    Bitmap bmA = original1PictureBox.Image as Bitmap;
    Bitmap bmB = original2PictureBox.Image as Bitmap;

    // Get the result dimensions.
    int width = Math.Min(bmA.Width, bmB.Width);
    int height = Math.Min(bmA.Height, bmB.Height);

    // Make result image.
    Bitmap bmC = new Bitmap(width, height);

    // Make Bitmap32 objects and lock them.
    Bitmap32 bm32a = new Bitmap32(bmA);
    Bitmap32 bm32b = new Bitmap32(bmB);
    Bitmap32 bm32c = new Bitmap32(bmC);
    bm32a.LockBitmap();
    bm32b.LockBitmap();
    bm32c.LockBitmap();

    // Process the images.
    for (int x = 0; x < width; x++)
    {
        for (int y = 0; y < height; y++)
        {
            byte ra, ga, ba, aa, rb, gb, bb, ab;
            bm32a.GetPixel(x, y, out ra, out ga, out ba, out aa);
            bm32b.GetPixel(x, y, out rb, out gb, out bb, out ab);

            // Make the result pixel red if the input pixels are different.
            if ((ra == rb) && (ga == gb) && (ba == bb))
                bm32c.SetPixel(x, y, 255, 255, 255, 255);
            else
                bm32c.SetPixel(x, y, 255, 0, 0, 255);
        }
    }
```

```
        }

        // Unlock and display the results.
        bm32a.UnlockBitmap();
        bm32b.UnlockBitmap();
        bm32c.UnlockBitmap();
        resultPictureBox.Image = bmC;
    }
```

The code gets the images stored in the two `PictureBox` controls on the form's left. It gets the smaller width and height of the images, and makes a result `Bitmap` with those dimensions.

The program then makes `Bitmap32` objects (described in the preceding example) for each of the three `Bitmap` objects and locks them.

Next, the program loops through the pixels that the original images have in common. If the red, green, and blue color components of the corresponding pixels in the two input images match, the program makes the corresponding result pixel white. (You could also compare the pixels' alpha values if you like.) If any of the color components are different, the program makes the corresponding result pixel red.

After it has processed all of the pixels, the code unlocks the `Bitmap32` objects and displays the result image in the `PictureBox` on the form's right.

Because this method makes small differences obvious, it works best with images that are almost identical. In the picture at the beginning of the post, the original images differ by just a few pixels.

In general, however, images are usually either identical or they have many differences. For example, if you save an image twice with slightly different JPG compression levels, most of the pixels in the two images will be slightly different and this example will produce a mostly red result.

38. SELECT AN AREA IN AN IMAGE (30)

This example lets the user click and drag to select a rectangular area in an image. It then displays the selected area to the right of the original image. You could modify it to do something else with the image such as saving it in a file or copying it to the clipboard.

The program starts by defining a couple of variables that it uses while selecting the area.

```
// The original image.
private Bitmap OriginalImage;

// The drags starting point.
private Point StartPoint;

// The area we are selecting.
private int X0, Y0, X1, Y1;
```

The variable `OriginalImage` holds a copy of the original, unmodified image. The value `IsSelecting` is `true` while the user is selecting an area. The value `StartPoint` holds the mouse's location when the user starts the drag.

When the program starts, the `Load` event handler saves a copy of the original image in the variable `OriginalImage`.

To let the user select an area, the example uses a `PictureBox` control's `MouseDown`, `MouseMove`, and `MouseUp` events. When the user presses the mouse down, the following `MouseDown` event handler starts the process.

```
// Start selecting the rectangle.
private void originalPictureBox_MouseDown(object sender, MouseEventArgs e)
{
    IsSelecting = true;
```

```
    // Copy the original image.
    OriginalImage = new Bitmap(originalPictureBox.Image);

    // Save the start point.
    StartPoint = e.Location;
}
```

This code sets IsSelecting to true to indicate that the user has started selecting an area. It makes a copy of the original, unmodified image, and finishes by saving the mouse's current position in variable StartPoint.

When the user moves the mouse, the following MouseMove event handler executes.

```
// Continue selecting.
private void originalPictureBox_MouseMove(object sender, MouseEventArgs e)
{
    // Do nothing it we're not selecting an area.
    if (!IsSelecting) return;

    // Make a Bitmap to display the selection rectangle.
    Bitmap bm = new Bitmap(OriginalImage);
    using (Graphics gr = Graphics.FromImage(bm))
    {
        // Draw the rectangle.
        Rectangle rect = GetRectangle(StartPoint, e.Location);
        using (Pen pen = new Pen(Color.Red, 3))
        {
            gr.DrawRectangle(pen, rect);
        }
    }

    // Display the temporary bitmap.
    originalPictureBox.Image = bm;
}
```

This code first checks IsSelecting and exits if no selection is in progress. It then creates a new copy of the original bitmap and makes a Graphics object associated with the copy.

Next, the code uses the GetRectangle method described shortly to get a Rectangle representing the area that the user has currently selected. It outlines that Rectangle on the temporary image with a thick, red pen.

The event handler finishes by displaying the temporary image.

The following MouseUp event handler finishes the selection process.

```
// Finish selecting the area.
private void originalPictureBox_MouseUp(object sender, MouseEventArgs e)
{
    // Do nothing it we're not selecting an area.
    if (!IsSelecting) return;
    IsSelecting = false;

    // Display the original image.
    originalPictureBox.Image = OriginalImage;

    // Copy the selected part of the image.
```

```
        Rectangle rect = GetRectangle(StartPoint, e.Location);
        Bitmap area = ImagePiece(OriginalImage, rect);

        // Display the result.
        resultPictureBox.Image = area;
        resultPictureBox.Show();
    }
```

Like the `MouseMove` event handler, this code first checks `IsSelecting` and exits if no selection is in progress. It then restores the original image to remove the previously drawn red rectangle.

Next, the code uses the `GetRectangle` method described next to get the final selection area. It uses the `ImagePiece` method (also described shortly) to get the selected part of the image and displays the result.

The following code shows the `GetRectangle` helper method.

```
        // Return a Rectangle with the two points as opposite corners.
        private Rectangle GetRectangle(Point point1, Point point2)
        {
            int x = Math.Min(point1.X, point2.X);
            int y = Math.Min(point1.Y, point2.Y);
            int width = Math.Abs(point2.X - point1.X);
            int height = Math.Abs(point2.Y - point1.Y);
            return new Rectangle(x, y, width, height);
        }
```

The `Graphics` class's `DrawRectangle` method requires a rectangle with a non-negative width and height. The `GetRectangle` helper method uses `Math.Min` and `Math.Abs` to make a `Rectangle` that represents the area between the two points and that has non-negative width and height.

The following code shows the `ImagePiece` helper method, which returns a `Bitmap` that holds a specified part of an image.

```
        // Return a piece of an image.
        private Bitmap ImagePiece(Bitmap bm, Rectangle sourceRect)
        {
            // Intersect the rectangle with the Bitmap's bounds.
            Rectangle bmRect = new Rectangle(0, 0, bm.Width, bm.Height);
            sourceRect.Intersect(bmRect);

            // Make sure the result has a positive size.
            if ((sourceRect.Width < 1) || (sourceRect.Height < 1)) return null;

            Bitmap piece = new Bitmap(sourceRect.Width, sourceRect.Height);
            using (Graphics gr = Graphics.FromImage(piece))
            {
                Rectangle destRect = new Rectangle(0, 0,
                    sourceRect.Width, sourceRect.Height);
                gr.DrawImage(OriginalImage, destRect,
                    sourceRect, GraphicsUnit.Pixel);
            }
            return piece;
        }
```

The method first finds the intersection of the `Bitmap` with the selection `Rectangle`. That way it doesn't return an image that includes areas inside the selection `Rectangle` but outside of the original `Bitmap`.

To find the intersection, the method makes a `Rectangle` representing the `Bitmap`. It then calls the selection `Rectangle` structure's `Intersect` method to make that `Rectangle` hold the intersection of the two rectangles.

The `DrawImage` method used later throws an exception if the area it is drawing has width or height less than one. To avoid that, the method returns `null` if the `Rectangle` is empty.

If the `Rectangle` is not empty, the method makes a `Bitmap` to fit it and an associated `Graphics` object. It copies the desired part of the input image into the new `Bitmap` and returns the result.

39. CROP A PICTURE (42)

This example doesn't really demonstrate any new and interesting techniques. It just uses the techniques described by the preceding example to let you crop an image and save the result into a file.

Like the preceding example, this one uses a PictureBox control's MouseDown, MouseMove, and MouseUp events to let the user select a rectangular area in the image. It then replaces the image displayed in the PictureBox with the area that the user selected.

This program even uses the GetRectangle and ImagePiece methods used by the preceding example.

For more information, download this example and look at its code, and review the description of the preceding example.

40. SELECT AN AREA IN A SCALED IMAGE (48)

The preceding example shows how to select a rectangular piece of an image in a `PictureBox` control.

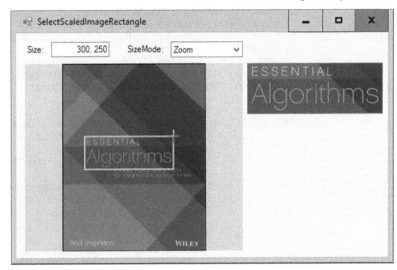

Unfortunately, that method only works if the `PictureBox` control's `SizeMode` property is set to `AutoSize` or `Normal`. If the `SizeMode` property has some other value, then the image is scaled or translated so the mouse's position over the control doesn't correspond exactly to the image's pixels.

This example solves that problem.

When you enter a size and select a `SizeMode` from the program's combo box, the program gives its `PictureBox` the size you entered and sets its `SizeMode` property accordingly. You can then click and drag to select part of the scaled image.

The code that lets you select an area on the `PictureBox` is almost exactly the same as the code used by the two preceding examples. If you haven't read those examples yet, you should do so to learn about the basic approach.

This example uses the following method to convert points from the `PictureBox` control's coordinate system into the image's scaled and translated coordinate system.

```
// Convert the coordinates for the image's SizeMode.
private Point ConvertPoint(PictureBox pic, Point point)
{
    int picHgt = pic.ClientSize.Height;
    int picWid = pic.ClientSize.Width;
    int imgHgt = pic.Image.Height;
    int imgWid = pic.Image.Width;

    int x = point.X;
    int y = point.Y;
    switch (pic.SizeMode)
    {
        case PictureBoxSizeMode.AutoSize:
        case PictureBoxSizeMode.Normal:
            // These are okay. Leave them alone.
            break;
        case PictureBoxSizeMode.CenterImage:
```

```
            x = point.X - (picWid - imgWid) / 2;
            y = point.Y - (picHgt - imgHgt) / 2;
            break;
        case PictureBoxSizeMode.StretchImage:
            x = (int)(imgWid * point.X / (float)picWid);
            y = (int)(imgHgt * point.Y / (float)picHgt);
            break;
        case PictureBoxSizeMode.Zoom:
            float picAspect = picWid / (float)picHgt;
            float imgAspect = imgWid / (float)imgHgt;
            if (picAspect > imgAspect)
            {
                // The PictureBox is wider/shorter than the image.
                y = (int)(imgHgt * point.Y / (float)picHgt);

                // The image fills the height of the PictureBox.
                // Get its width.
                float scaledWidth = imgWid * picHgt / imgHgt;
                float dx = (picWid - scaledWidth) / 2;
                x = (int)((point.X - dx) * imgHgt / (float)picHgt);
            }
            else
            {
                // The PictureBox is taller/thinner than the image.
                x = (int)(imgWid * point.X / (float)picWid);

                // The image fills the height of the PictureBox.
                // Get its height.
                float scaledHeight = imgHgt * picWid / imgWid;
                float dy = (picHgt - scaledHeight) / 2;
                y = (int)((point.Y - dy) * imgWid / picWid);
            }
            break;
    }

    return new Point(x, y);
}
```

First, the method creates some variables to hold the dimensions of the PictureBox and the image that it holds. It then uses a switch statement to handle the different SizeMode values.

If SizeMode is AutoSize or Normal, then the image isn't scaled or translated. That means the X and Y coordinates are correct, so the method leaves them unchanged.

If SizeMode is CenterImage, then the image is displayed at full scale and centered in the PictureBox. The code calculates the amount of empty space to the left and above the image in the PictureBox and subtracts it from the X and Y coordinates to get the corresponding position over the image. (If the PictureBox is smaller than the image, then the amounts of empty space are negative.)

If SizeMode is StretchImage, then the image is stretched to fill the PictureBox. The code simply scales the X and Y coordinates by the same factor used to scale the image.

Finally, if SizeMode is Zoom, the control stretches the image to be as large as possible without distorting it and then centers the result. For example, if the image is square and the PictureBox is tall and thin, then the image will fill the width of the PictureBox and there will be empty space above and below the image.

In this case, the code examines the aspect ratios (the ratio of width to height) of the PictureBox and the image. If the PictureBox is relatively short and wide compared to the image, the code scales the location's Y coordinate by the amount that the image is scaled vertically. It then calculates the scaled width of the image and uses that to find the amount of empty space to the image's left. The code subtracts that amount from the X coordinate and then scales the result by the scale factor used to set the image's resized width.

If the PictureBox is relatively tall and thin compared to the image, the code performs similar calculations switching the roles of the X and Y coordinates.

Now whenever this example uses a point, it uses the ConvertPoint method to convert from the PictureBox control's coordinate system into the image's adjusted coordinate system. For example, the following code shows the PictureBox control's MouseDown event handler.

```
// Start selecting the rectangle.
private void originalPictureBox_MouseDown(object sender, MouseEventArgs e)
{
    IsSelecting = true;

    // Copy the original image.
    OriginalImage = new Bitmap(originalPictureBox.Image);

    // Save the start point.
    StartPoint = ConvertPoint(originalPictureBox, e.Location);
}
```

This code is the same as the code used by the preceding example except it calls ConvertPoint before saving the mouse's current location.

41. DRAW A MANDELBROT SET FRACTAL (24)

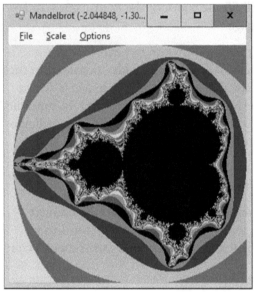

Mandelbrot (-2.044848, -1.30...

File   Scale   Options

This example draws one of the most famous fractals: the Mandelbrot set. The grayscale picture on the right can't begin to do it justice, so I've placed a full-color image on the book's cover.

This is a very complicated example so it would take up a huge amount of space if I covered every last detail. In order to save pages, I'm going to touch on the highlights here and let you download the example to see the rest of the details. I'll explain how to generate the Mandelbrot set but skip the details about how the program lets you change colors, zoom in on parts of the fractal, and set the maximum number of calculations.

The Mandelbrot set uses the following iterated equation to calculate colors for the points in a region.

$$Z(n+1) = Z(n)^2 + C$$

Here the $Z(n)$ and C are complex numbers. The program starts with values C and $Z(0)$. It uses those values to calculate $Z(1)$. It then uses C and $Z(1)$ to calculate $Z(2)$. It continues using C and the latest $Z(n)$ to calculate the next value $Z(n+1)$.

It can be shown that, if the magnitude of $Z(n)$ ever exceeds 2, then it eventually diverges towards infinity.

To find the color for the point (x, y), the Mandelbrot program sets $Z(0) = 0$ and $C = x + y$ * i. Here i is the imaginary number representing the square root of -1, not a program variable.

The program then generates values for $Z(n)$ until $Z(n)$'s magnitude exceeds 2 or it reaches some predetermined maximum number of iterations. At that point, the program uses the number of iterations it performed so far to assign the point's color. For example, if the program is using K colors and it performed I iterations, then it assigns the point color number I mod K.

The following code shows how the program draws the Mandelbrot set.

```
// Draw the Mandelbrot set.
private void DrawMandelbrot()
{
    // Work until the magnitude > 2.
    const int MaxMag = 2;
```

```
// Make a Bitmap to draw on.
int width = canvasPictureBox.ClientSize.Width;
int height = canvasPictureBox.ClientSize.Height;
TheBitmap = new Bitmap(width, height);
using (Graphics gr = Graphics.FromImage(TheBitmap))
{
    // Clear.
    gr.Clear(canvasPictureBox.BackColor);
    canvasPictureBox.Image = TheBitmap;
}
Application.DoEvents();

// Adjust the coordinate bounds to fit canvasPictureBox.
AdjustAspect();

// dReaC is the change in the real part
// (X value) for C. dImaC is the change in the
// imaginary part (Y value).
double dReaC = (Wxmax - Wxmin) / (width - 1);
double dImaC = (Wymax - Wymin) / (height - 1);

// Calculate the values.
int numColors = Colors.Count;
double reaC = Wxmin;
for (int x = 0; x < width; x++)
{
    double imaC = Wymin;
    for (int y = 0; y < height; y++)
    {
        Complex z = Z;
        Complex c = new Complex(reaC, imaC);
        int clr = 1;
        while ((clr < MaxIterations) && (z.Magnitude < MaxMag))
        {
            // Calculate Z(clr).
            z = z * z + c;
            clr++;
        }

        // Set the pixel's value.
        TheBitmap.SetPixel(x, y, Colors[clr % numColors]);

        imaC += dImaC;
    }
    reaC += dReaC;

    // Let the user know we//re not dead.
    if (x % 10 == 0) canvasPictureBox.Refresh();
}
canvasPictureBox.Refresh();

Text = "Mandelbrot (" +
    Wxmin.ToString("0.000000") + ", " +
    Wymin.ToString("0.000000") + ")-(" +
    Wxmax.ToString("0.000000") + ", " +
    Wymax.ToString("0.000000") + ")";
}
```

This method creates a `Bitmap` to fit the program's `PictureBox`, creates an associated `Graphics` object, and clears the `Bitmap`.

It then calls the `AdjustAspect` method. That method adjusts the world coordinate bounds `Wxmin`, `Wxmax`, `Wymin`, and `Wymax` so the area they represent has the same shape as the `Bitmap`. That prevents the fractal from be stretched out of shape. Download the example and take a look to see how that method works.

Next, the code calculates `dReaC` and `dImaC`. Those are the real and imaginary amounts by which the complex constant C changes as the program moves from pixel to pixel through the `Bitmap`.

Recall that the program iterates the equation $Z(n+1) = Z(n)^2 + C$ where $C = x + y * i$. The `dReaC` and `dImaC` values let the program update C for each new pixel.

The method then loops through the image's pixels. For each pixel, it creates the complex numbers $Z(0)$ and C, and performs the function's iteration. When the loop ends, the program uses the number of times it performed the iteration to set the pixel's color.

> **NOTE:** The `Complex` class is defined in the `System.Numerics` library. Use the Project menu's Add Reference command to add a reference to the library. To make using the class easier, you can include the following `using` directive.
>
> ```
> using System.Numerics;
> ```

After it sets the color for every 10th row of pixels, the method refreshes the `PictureBox` so you can see the program making progress.

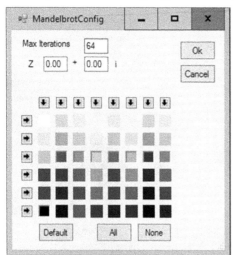

When it finishes, the method displays the current world coordinate bounds in the form's title bar so you know what part of the Mandelbrot set the program is displaying.

That's all there is to drawing the Mandelbrot set, but the example program has several other useful features. If you open the Options menu and select Set Options, the dialog on the left appears. The Max Iterations value determines the maximum number of times the program will iterate the complex equation for each pixel. Making this value larger means more pixels have different colors but it makes the program take longer.

The Z text boxes let you set the value of $Z(0)$ used in the equation's first iteration. For the "classic" Mandelbrot set, $Z(0)$ should be $0 + 0 * i$, but you can get some interesting results if you change this value. For example, try setting $Z(0)$ to $0.5 + 0.1 * i$ and zoom in on the result.

You can also use the dialog to set the colors used to draw the fractal. The dialog's color columns make the program use shades of a single color and can produce some pleasant results.

The program also lets you click and drag to zoom in on an area. The File menu's Save command lets you save the current image. The Scale menu lets you zoom out by a factor of 2, 4, or 8, or return to full scale. Download the example and explore its code to see how those features work.

The Mandelbrot set is fun and interesting to explore. If you make any particularly interesting images that you'd like to share, feel free to post them in comments on the book's web page.

42. Set an Image's Pixels in WPF (65)

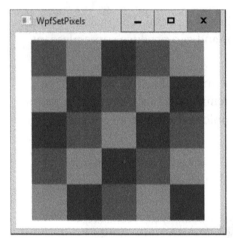

Modifying an image's pixels in a Windows Forms application is relatively simple. Just use a `Bitmap` object's `GetPixel` and `SetPixel` methods. For better performance, use the `Bitmap32` class described in earlier examples.

Unfortunately, manipulating an image's pixels is much harder in WPF.

To create a bitmapped image in WPF, you first create a `WriteableBitmap` object. Next, you create a one-dimensional array holding the raw pixel information for the image. Then you use the bitmap's `WritePixels` method to copy the pixel data into the image.

You can display the result by setting an **Image** control's **Source** property to the `WriteableBitmap` object.

The following code shows how this example creates its image.

```
private void Window_Loaded(object sender, RoutedEventArgs e)
{
    // Make a 3D array because that's easier to use.
    const int width = 240;
    const int height = 240;
    byte[,,] pixels = new byte[height, width, 4];

    // Color the pixels.
    for (int x = 0; x < width; x++)
    {
        for (int y = 0; y < height; y++)
        {
            int num = (int)(x / 48) + (int)(y / 48);
            switch (num % 3)
            {
                case 0:     // Red
                    pixels[x, y, 2] = 255;
                    break;
                case 1:     // Green
                    pixels[x, y, 1] = 255;
                    break;
                case 2:     // Blue
                    pixels[x, y, 0] = 255;
                    break;
            }
            pixels[x, y, 3] = 255;  // Alpha
        }
    }

    // Copy the data into a one-dimensional array.
    byte[] pixels1d = new byte[height * width * 4];
```

```
        Buffer.BlockCopy(pixels, 0, pixels1d, 0, pixels.Length);

        // Make the WriteableBitmap.
        WriteableBitmap wbitmap = new WriteableBitmap(
            width, height, 96, 96, PixelFormats.Bgra32, null);

        // Copy the color data into the WriteableBitmap.
        Int32Rect rect = new Int32Rect(0, 0, width, height);
        int stride = 4 * width;
        wbitmap.WritePixels(rect, pixels1d, stride, 0);

        // Create an Image to display the WriteableBitmap.
        Image image = new Image();
        image.Stretch = Stretch.None;
        image.Margin = new Thickness(0);
        grdMain.Children.Add(image);

        //Set the Image source.
        image.Source = wbitmap;
    }
```

The program first makes an array to hold the pixel byte data. Working in a one-dimensional array is annoying, so the program first creates a three-dimensional array. The first two dimensions represent a pixel's X and Y coordinates. The third dimension stores the pixel's blue, green, red, and alpha components in that order. For example, the entry pixels[10, 20, 1] holds the green component for the pixel at position (10, 20).

Initially the array's bytes are all 0. The program loops through the array making 48×48 pixel blocks of color. It also sets the pixels' alpha components to 255 so they are opaque.

After it finishes filling in the three-dimensional array, the program creates a one-dimensional array containing the same number of bytes. It uses Buffer.BlockCopy to copy the bytes from the first array into the second.

Next, the code creates a WriteableBitmap object. The parameters passed into the constructor give the bitmap's width, height, pixels per inch vertically (96) and horizontally (96), and pixel format (32 bits per pixel). The final null parameter indicates that the bitmap will not use a palette.

The code then makes an Int32Rect representing the part of the bitmap that the bytes will define. In this example, that's the entire bitmap.

The method also calculates the stride for the piece of the image being written. The *stride* is the number of bytes in a row of the pixel data. Because each pixel is represented by four bytes, this is the width of the byte data in pixels times four.

Now the program uses the WriteableBitmap object's WritePixels method to copy the byte data into the bitmap. It finishes by creating an Image control and displaying the WriteableBitmap in it.

43. SAVE A BITMAP INTO A FILE IN WPF (90)

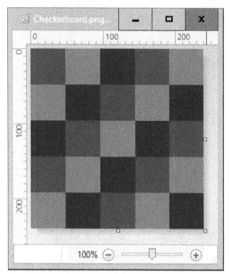

The preceding example shows how a WPF program can set the pixels in an image. This example shows how you can save that image into a file.

Like many other things in WPF, this isn't as easy as it is in Windows Forms. In a Windows Forms application, you simply call the `Bitmap` object's `Save` method and you're done.

To save a bitmap in WPF, you create a `BitmapEncoder` object for the file format that you want to use. You then use a `WriteableBitmap` object to create a `BitmapFrame` and you add it to the encoder's `Frames` list. You finish by opening a `FileStream` to the file that you want to write and calling the encoder's `Save` method to save it into the stream.

To make saving `WriteableBitmap` objects a bit easier, this example performs those steps in the following extension method.

```
// Save the WriteableBitmap into a PNG file.
public static void Save(this WriteableBitmap wbitmap, string filename)
{
    // Make the right kind of encoder depending on the file name's extension.
    BitmapEncoder encoder = null;
    string extension = Path.GetExtension(filename);
    switch (extension.ToLower())
    {
        case ".bmp":
            encoder = new BmpBitmapEncoder();
            break;
        //case ".exif":
        //    encoder = new ExifBitmapEncoder();
        //    break;
        case ".gif":
            encoder = new GifBitmapEncoder();
            break;
        case ".jpg":
        case ".jpeg":
            encoder = new JpegBitmapEncoder();
            break;
        case ".png":
            encoder = new PngBitmapEncoder();
            break;
        case ".tif":
        case ".tiff":
            encoder = new TiffBitmapEncoder();
            break;
        case ".wmp":    // Microsoft Window Media Photo
            encoder = new WmpBitmapEncoder();
```

```
                break;
            default:
                throw new NotSupportedException(
                    "Unknown file extension " + extension);
        }

        // Add the bitmap to the encoder's Frames collection.
        encoder.Frames.Add(BitmapFrame.Create(wbitmap));

        // Save the file.
        using (FileStream stream = new FileStream(filename, FileMode.Create))
        {
            encoder.Save(stream);
        }
    }
```

This method follows the steps described earlier. It creates the appropriate encoder, creates a frame for the bitmap and adds it to the encoder's Frames list, creates a FileStream, and makes the encoder save itself into the stream.

The rest of this example is similar to the preceding one. Like that example, it creates a WriteableBitmap and sets its pixels to draw a checkerboard. This example then finishes by calling the bitmap's Save extension method several times to save the image in various formats. For example, the following code shows how the program saves the image in the PNG format.

```
    wbitmap.Save("Checkerboard.png");
```

The code in the extension method is somewhat confusing, but using it is simple.

Part IX. Cryptography

Cryptography is a big deal these days. Many data breaches go unreported, but it is likely that at least a few important breaches occur every day.

There are many ways you can protect your data. For example, you can use a cloud service that encrypts data for you. Your programs can also use the .NET Framework's Cryptography library to encrypt your data.

This is a huge topic, so the few C# Helper examples that made the Top 100 list can only scratch the surface. For more information and examples, search the web.

For a more general discussion about how cryptographic algorithms work and their history, I highly recommend Bruce Schneier's book, *Applied Cryptography, Protocols, Algorithms, and Source Code in C* (Bruce Schneier, Wiley, 1996). Don't be afraid of the fact that the code is provided in C. If you can read C#, then you can read C.

44. ENCRYPT AND DECRYPT FILES (11)

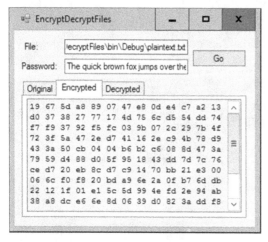

The algorithms behind encryption and decryption are complicated, but that doesn't mean the tools you use to perform encryption and decryption need to be complicated, too. Actually, those tools are complicated, too, but they're much simpler than the underlying cryptographic algorithms.

The .NET Framework's Cryptography library provides classes that help make cryptography a little simpler. Even with those classes, cryptography is somewhat confusing. Encrypting and decrypting files requires you to work with several different cryptographic objects that are more than a bit mystifying.

The following list gives a high-level summary of the steps that you need to follow to use .NET's encryption tools.

1. Create a *cryptographic service provider*, which provides access to its underlying encryption and decryption algorithms. Different providers use different algorithms.
2. Use the provider to create a *cryptographic transform* object. That object will either encrypt or decrypt the data.
3. Use the transform object to create a `CryptoStream` object. When you create this object, you give it a stream where it can output its results.
4. Write data into the `CryptoStream`. The stream encrypts or decrypts the data and spits the result into its output stream.

There's one other detail that I want to mention before I show you the code. A particular cryptographic service provider uses a complex algorithm to perform the actual encryption or decryption. Internally that algorithm needs to keep track of the state it is in while it works.

The state information is important and of necessity contains a large number of variables. It must be complicated to prevent an attacker from breaking into your encrypted data. For example, suppose the algorithm has only a few million possible internal states. Then an attacker could simply try initializing the provider with each of those states and then see which one decrypts your file.

The next logical question is, "How does the provider initialize its internal state?" The provider uses two values: a *key* and *initialization vector* (IV).

The key is basically your password. Unfortunately it needs to be a long string of randomish bits (or an array of bytes, if you prefer) and you probably don't want to have to memorize it.

The IV is also an array of bytes that the algorithm uses to initialize its internal state.

To avoid needing to memorize long arrays of bytes, you can use a more user-friendly password to generate the key and IV bytes. You then use those to initialize the provider when you make the cryptographic transform object.

Now let's look at some code. The following chunks of code work from the top down. First, I'll show you the highest level of code and then I'll show you the methods that perform the lower-level tasks.

The following EncryptFile and DecryptFile methods encrypt and decrypt files.

```
// Encrypt or decrypt a file, saving the results in another file.
public static void EncryptFile(string password, string inFile, string outFile)
{
    CryptFile(password, inFile, outFile, true);
}
public static void DecryptFile(string password, string inFile, string outFile)
{
    CryptFile(password, inFile, outFile, false);
}
```

Those methods just call the following CryptFile method, passing it a final parameter to indicate whether the method should encrypt or decrypt the file.

```
public static void CryptFile(string password, string inFile,
    string outFile, bool encrypt)
{
    // Create input and output file streams.
    using (FileStream inStream =
        new FileStream(inFile, FileMode.Open, FileAccess.Read))
    {
        using (FileStream outStream =
            new FileStream(outFile, FileMode.Create, FileAccess.Write))
        {
            // Encrypt/decrypt the input stream into the output stream.
            CryptStream(password, inStream, outStream, encrypt);
        }
    }
}
```

The CryptFile method makes two FileStream objects, one attached to the input file and one attached to the output file. It then calls the following CryptStream method, which does all of the interesting work.

```
// Encrypt the data in the input stream into the output stream.
public static void CryptStream(string password, Stream inStream,
    Stream outStream, bool encrypt)
{
    // Make an AES service provider.
    AesCryptoServiceProvider aesProvider = new AesCryptoServiceProvider();
```

```csharp
    // Find a valid key size for this provider.
    int keySizeBits = 0;
    for (int i = 1024; i > 1; i--)
    {
        if (aesProvider.ValidKeySize(i))
        {
            keySizeBits = i;
            break;
        }
    }
    Debug.Assert(keySizeBits > 0);
    Console.WriteLine("Key size: " + keySizeBits);

    // Get the block size for this provider.
    int blockSizeBits = aesProvider.BlockSize;

    // Generate the key and initialization vector.
    byte[] key = null;
    byte[] iv = null;
    byte[] salt = { 0x0, 0x0, 0x1, 0x2, 0x3, 0x4, 0x5, 0x6,
        0xF1, 0xF0, 0xEE, 0x21, 0x22, 0x45 };
    MakeKeyAndIV(password, salt, keySizeBits, blockSizeBits, out key, out iv);

    // Make the encryptor or decryptor.
    ICryptoTransform cryptoTransform;
    if (encrypt)
        cryptoTransform = aesProvider.CreateEncryptor(key, iv);
    else
        cryptoTransform = aesProvider.CreateDecryptor(key, iv);

    // Attach a CryptoStream to the output stream.
    // Closing the CryptoStream sometimes throws an exception if the
    // decryption didn't work (e.g. if we use the wrong password).
    try
    {
        using (CryptoStream cryptoStream = new CryptoStream(
            outStream, cryptoTransform, CryptoStreamMode.Write))
        {
            // Encrypt or decrypt the file.
            const int blockSize = 2048;
            byte[] buffer = new byte[blockSize];
            int bytesRead;
            while (true)
            {
                // Read some bytes.
                bytesRead = inStream.Read(buffer, 0, blockSize);
                if (bytesRead == 0) break;

                // Write the bytes into the CryptoStream.
                cryptoStream.Write(buffer, 0, bytesRead);
            }
        } // using cryptoStream
    }
    catch
    {
    }
    cryptoTransform.Dispose();
}
```

This method first creates an `AesService` provider. That provider implements the Advanced Encryption Standard (AES) algorithm.

> **NOTE:** The `System.Security.Cryptography` namespace includes several service providers that implement different encryption algorithms including AES, Data Encryption Standard (DES), RC2, Rijndael, and Triple DES (which basically applies DES three times in a row). Currently Microsoft recommends AES for encrypting data.
>
> For an overview of Microsoft's cryptography model and links to the provider classes, see the article ".NET Framework Cryptography Model" at `tinyurl.com/ybsvq44n`.

Next, the code needs to find a valid size for a key. The program starts with a size of 1,024 bits and then reduces the size until the AES provider's `ValidKeySize` method returns `true`. It then uses that key size. (My system can use 256-bit keys. Your results may vary.)

> **NOTE:** The key size that you get will depend on things such as which version of Windows you are using. If you will encrypt and decrypt files on different computers, they must be able to use the same key size. You may need to set this value yourself if one computer can use a larger key than the other one can.

The AES algorithm works by processing data in blocks. The program uses the provider's `BlockSize` property to find out how big those blocks are. (The blocks are 128 bits on my system.)

Next, the method generates the key and IV. To do that it uses an array of bytes called `salt`. The salt is a sequence of bytes that I picked "randomly" for this program. The idea is to add the salt to the password to make the number of possible combinations larger and therefore harder for an attacker to search. (For more information on salts, see the Wikipedia article `tinyurl.com/aat4l32`.)

You need to use the same salt to decrypt that you used to encrypt the data, but you should use a different salt for each set of programs that need to encrypt or decrypt the same data.

Having defined the `salt` array, the program calls the `MakeKeyAndIV` method described shortly to convert the password and salt into a key and IV.

Next, the program makes a `CryptoTransform` object. Depending on whether we are encrypting or decrypting, the code makes either an encryptor or a decryptor.

The program then creates a `CryptoStream` object. It passes the constructor the output stream and the cryptographic transform object.

Next, the code reads data from the input stream in blocks and writes the blocks out to the `CryptoStream`.

The method finishes by disposing of the transform object.

> **NOTE:** As the comment in the code mentions, closing the `CryptoStream` object sometimes throws an exception. In particular, if you try to decrypt some encrypted data and you use the wrong password, then when the program tries to close the `CryptoStream` it throws an exception with the following impressively uninformative error message.
>
> ```
> Padding is invalid and cannot be removed.
> ```
>
> This method just catches the error and ignores it, leaving the decrypted data full of gibberish. That's what you deserve for using the wrong password!

The following code shows the example's final piece: the `MakeKeyAndIV` method.

```
// Use the password to generate key bytes.
private static void MakeKeyAndIV(string password, byte[] salt,
    int keySizeBits, int blockSizeBits, out byte[] key, out byte[] iv)
{
    Rfc2898DeriveBytes deriveBytes =
        new Rfc2898DeriveBytes(password, salt, 1000);

    key = deriveBytes.GetBytes(keySizeBits / 8);
    iv = deriveBytes.GetBytes(blockSizeBits / 8);
}
```

This method uses a password string and salt to generate key and IV bytes.

First, it creates an `Rfc2898DeriveBytes` object. This object takes as inputs a password and a salt, and then returns a sequence of bytes generated by yet another cryptographic algorithm. (If you really want to know which algorithm it uses, look at `tinyurl.com/k9xgkn7` and follow the links that you find there.)

The final parameter to the object's constructor is the number of times the object iterates its algorithm to generate bytes. Microsoft recommends that this be at least 1,000. The iterations are very fast and you probably only need to do this once for a given password, so you can make this a big number without affecting performance too much.

After it has created the `Rfc2898DeriveBytes` object, the method calls that object's `GetBytes` method to fill the `key` and `iv` arrays.

That's the end of the code demonstrated by this example. The program also includes a static `CryptoStuff` class that provides these methods plus a few others that are not used by the example. The following list summarizes the class's methods that you might find useful in your programs.

- ➤ EncryptFile—Encrypts a file.
- ➤ DecryptFile—Decrypts a file.
- ➤ CryptBytes—Encrypts or decrypts a byte array.
- ➤ Encrypt—A string extension method that encrypts a string and returns a byte array.
- ➤ Decrypt—A byte array extension method that decrypts a byte array and returns a string.
- ➤ EncryptToHex—A string extension method that encrypts a string, converts the encrypted byte data into a hexadecimal string, and returns it.
- ➤ DecryptFromHex—A string extension method that takes a hexadecimal representation of a byte array, decrypts it, and returns the resulting string.

Download the example and see the code for additional details.

45. USE A CRYPTOGRAPHIC RANDOM NUMBER GENERATOR (38)

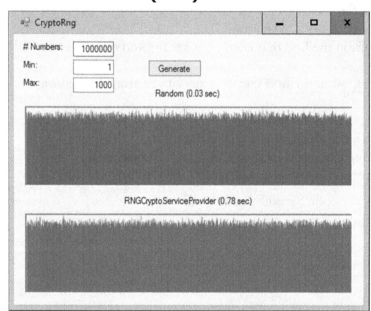

The Random class generates random numbers, but they aren't cryptographically secure. A random number generator is *cryptographically secure* if an attacker, after seeing a series of random numbers that you generate, cannot predict the next one with any success.

This example uses an RNGCryptoServiceProvider to generate random numbers. Here RNG stands for "random number generator."

Unfortunately, the RNGCryptoServiceProvider doesn't actually generate random numbers, it generates random bytes. It's up to you to convert those bytes into whatever values you need.

> **NOTE:** Technically no method can produce truly random values. The best a method can do is produce numbers that *appear* random. Those values are called *pseudorandom*.
>
> To get truly random values, you would need some sort of external origin for randomness such as a source of radioactive decay or the static in FM radio signals.
>
> To make this discussion simpler, the text uses the term "random" when it really means "pseudorandom."

The following RandomInteger method converts bytes provided by the RNGCryptoServiceProvider class into integers between upper and lower bounds.

```
// The random number provider.
private RNGCryptoServiceProvider Rand = new RNGCryptoServiceProvider();

// Return a random integer between a min and max value.
private int RandomInteger(int min, int max)
{
```

```
uint scale = uint.MaxValue;
while (scale == uint.MaxValue)
{
    // Get four random bytes.
    byte[] fourBytes = new byte[4];
    Rand.GetBytes(fourBytes);

    // Convert that into an uint.
    scale = BitConverter.ToUInt32(fourBytes, 0);
}

// Add min to the scaled difference between max and min.
return (int)(min + (max - min) * (scale / (double)uint.MaxValue));
}
```

The program creates the RNGCryptoServiceProvider object at the class level.

The RandomInteger method starts by setting the value scale to uint.MaxValue. It then enters a while loop that executes as long as scale is uint.MaxValue.

Inside the loop, the method uses the RNGCryptoServiceProvider to generate four bytes. It uses BitConverter.ToUInt32 to convert those four bytes into a four-byte unsigned integer (int) and sets scale equal to that value.

If scale is still uint.MaxValue, then the loop repeats until it gets a new value. It is extremely unlikely that scale will be uint.MaxValue and much less likely that this will happen twice in a row, so the loop shouldn't last long.

The code then divides scale by uint.MaxValue. This produces a floating-point value between 0.0 and 1.0, not including 1.0. The code multiplies this value by the difference between the maximum and minimum desired values and adds the result to the minimum value.

The result is a floating-point value between min and max, not including max. The code then casts the result into an int to truncate the value and get an integer. This matches the behavior provided by the Random class's Next method, which returns an integer between a lower bound (inclusive) and an upper bound (exclusive).

When you fill in the program's input values and click Generate, the program generates random numbers and displays histograms showing their distribution. The more numbers you generate, the closer the histograms' bars should be to the same height.

The program first uses the Random class to generate random numbers and displays their histogram on top. It then uses the RandomInteger method to generate a new set of numbers and displays their histogram on the bottom. Looking at the histograms, both seem pretty "random."

Cryptographic random number generators (CRNGs) may seem better than the Random class, but they do have a couple of disadvantages. First, they are relatively complicated and therefore slow. In one test, the `Random` class took 0.34 seconds to generate 10 million numbers but the `RNGCryptoServiceProvider` took 7.78 seconds, almost 23 times as long.

CRNGs also won't produce repeatable sequences. Sometimes it's useful to generate the same "random" sequence of numbers repeatedly so you can test a program. You can do that fairly easily with the `Random` class but not with a CRNG.

Download the example to see additional details such as how the program draws its histograms.

Part X. Dialogs

Windows Forms applications have easy access to several kinds of dialogs. For example, they can easily use the OpenFileDialog, PrintDialog, ColorDialog, FontDialog, and other dialogs to perform standard tasks.

The examples in this part of the book explain how to provide two kinds of dialogs that are notably missing: a full-featured folder selection dialog and a password dialog.

46. LET THE USER SELECT A FOLDER (12)

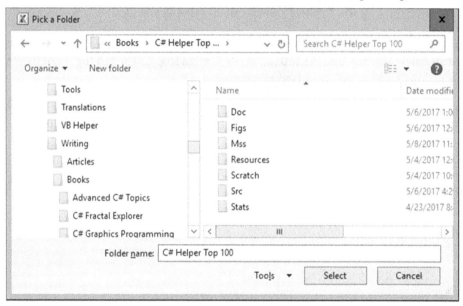

The .NET Framework's `OpenFileDialog` and `SaveFileDialog` components are reasonably full-featured. They're a lot like File Explorer with some added file selection capabilities thrown in.

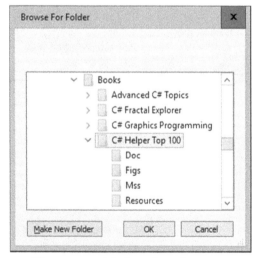

In contrast, the `FolderBrowserDialog` shown on the left is pretty pathetic. It only lets you use a hierarchical tree-like display, doesn't provide different views (such as Detail, List, and Large Icon), doesn't allow you to search, and doesn't let you type in parts of the folder's path if you know them so you can't copy and paste paths into the dialog.

Although Windows itself uses a much more powerful file and folder selection dialog, Microsoft has yet to give it to .NET developers.

In the past Microsoft provided the Windows API Code Pack for use in Windows Vista and later. That library provided tools to let you access the Windows API including a decent folder browser dialog.

Unfortunately, Microsoft dropped support for the Code Pack and it disappeared from Microsoft's web site.

The following sections describe a few ways that you can work around this problem and use a better folder browser.

Build Your Own

First, you can build your own folder browser dialog. This is a lot of work and means you need to debug and maintain your dialog.

This approach does give you a lot of flexibility, however. If there are special features that you would like to add to the dialog, you can do so as long as you're willing to spend the time and effort.

Third Party Software

Third-party software vendors make full-featured folder browsers. Some of them are open source and free. You can research and download these from the internet.

NuGet

Another approach is to install "Windows API Code Pack - Shell" from the package manager site NuGet (nuget.org). You can install the package from inside of recent versions of Visual Studio.

NOTE: NuGet is just a package repository and does not moderate the contents of the packages it holds. In particular, it doesn't guarantee that the packages are well-designed or safe.

To use this approach, start a new project. Then open the Tools menu, expand the NuGet Package Manager submenu, and select Manage NuGet Packages for Solution.

Next, use the search box to find the package that you want to install. For example, you could install WindowsAPICodePack-Shell by Aybe.

Check the box next to the package on the right and click Install. Then click through the various dialogs that appear. Note that one of the dialogs asks you to accept the package's licensing terms.

After you have installed the package, you can use the dialog in your program. Include the following using directive to make using the dialog easier.

```
using Microsoft.WindowsAPICodePack.Dialogs;
```

Then you can use the dialog as in the following code.

```
CommonOpenFileDialog dialog = new CommonOpenFileDialog();
dialog.InitialDirectory = folderTextBox.Text;
dialog.IsFolderPicker = true;
if (dialog.ShowDialog() == CommonFileDialogResult.Ok)
{
    folderTextBox.Text = dialog.FileName;
}
```

This code creates a `CommonOpenFileDialog` object and sets its initial directory. It then sets the dialog's `IsFolderPicker` property to `true` to indicate that the dialog should let the user select a folder.

The code displays the dialog and, if the user selects a folder and clicks OK, it displays the result.

Excel

Whenever possible, I prefer not to rely on third-party libraries. When I'm writing books or articles, I can't rely on you having installed any particular package, and I don't really want to have to review them all and make recommendations. There's also no guarantee that a particular package was well-written and safe, especially the free ones. They may also disappear at some later date, leaving my examples broken. (Like the Windows API Code Pack did.)

The final solution that I'll describe here, and the one used by the example program, takes advantage of a folder browser dialog that's included in some Microsoft Office programs such as Excel.

To use this dialog, start a project, open the Project menu, and select Add references. You'll use the Reference Manager to add two references.

First, open the Assemblies branch and click the Framework category. Find the `Microsoft.Office.Interop.Excel` library and check the box next to it. While you're there, note the library's version number. (On my system the most recent version is 14.0.0.0.)

Next, expand the dialog's COM branch and select the Type Libraries category. Find the `Microsoft Office XX Object Library` entry, where XX is the version used by the interop library. (My system has serval versions for both libraries and the program won't work if the versions don't match.)

Now your program can use Office automation to display Excel's dialog. Start by adding the following `using` directives to your program.

```
using Excel = Microsoft.Office.Interop.Excel;
using Core = Microsoft.Office.Core;
```

Now you can use the dialog. The following code shows how the example program displays the dialog and gets the result.

```
// Use the Excel folder browser.
private void excelFolderBrowserButton_Click(object sender, EventArgs e)
{
    Excel.Application excel = new Excel.Application();
    Core.FileDialog dialog = excel.FileDialog[
        Core.MsoFileDialogType.msoFileDialogFolderPicker];

    dialog.InitialFileName = folderTextBox.Text;
    dialog.ButtonName = "Select";
    dialog.Title = "Pick a Folder";

    const int ok = -1;
    const int cancel = 0;
    if (dialog.Show() == ok)
    {
        Core.FileDialogSelectedItems items = dialog.SelectedItems;
        folderTextBox.Text = items.Item(1);
    }
}
```

This method creates an Excel application object. It uses that object's `FileDialog` property to get a reference to the application's file dialog.

The `FileDialog` property is an indexed property that can return one of several different kinds of dialogs. The code uses the index `msoFileDialogFolderPicker` to obtain a reference to Excel's folder selection dialog.

The following list shows the constants that you can use to select different dialog types.

➢ `msoFileDialogOpen`–Selects a file for opening.
➢ `msoFileDialogSaveAs`–Selects a file to save in.
➢ `msoFileDialogFilePicker`–Selects a file for opening.
➢ `msoFileDialogFolderPicker`–Selects a folder.

Next, the code initializes the dialog. It sets the `InitialFileName` property to the directory where the dialog should start. The `ButtonName` property determines the text displayed on the OK button, and the `Title` property determines the dialog's title.

> **NOTE:** If you set the dialog's `InitialFileName` property to a location that doesn't exist, the dialog defaults to the `Document` directory.

The code then defines two constants, `ok = -1` and `cancel = 0`, to represent the values that that the dialog's `Show` method might return. The code displays the dialog and checks the returned result.

If the user selects a folder and clicks the OK button, the program displays the selected folder's name. The dialog's `SelectedItems` property is a collection of string values. If the program was using the dialog to select files instead of folders, then it could allow the user to select multiple files, and this collection might hold more than one result.

When you use the dialog to select a folder, however, this collection only holds one result. Because of the way the collection is implemented, its first item is in position 1 not 0 as is usual in C#. The program gets that item and displays it in the program's text box.

Excel's dialog has a few other properties such as `Filters` and `AllowMultiSelect` that you can use when you want to open files, but they don't apply when you're selecting a folder. The dialog won't let the user select multiple folders (it just can't) and filters don't really make sense for folders. (And why would you go to the trouble of using Excel's dialog to select files when the `OpenFileDialog` and `SaveFileDialog` do a reasonably good job?)

47. DISPLAY A PASSWORD DIALOG (62)

You might think that a program could start with a password dialog and then display its main form if the user enters a valid password. Unfortunately, by default when the initial password form closes, the whole application ends.

A better approach is to make the main form be the startup form. When it starts, the form's Load event handler displays the password form. If the user successfully enters the password, the program continues as normal. If the user fails to enter a valid password, the main form closes itself and the program ends.

The example program's main form uses the following Load event handler.

```
// Display the password dialog.
private void Form1_Load(object sender, EventArgs e)
{
    // Display the password form.
    PasswordDialog dialog = new PasswordDialog();
    if (dialog.ShowDialog() != DialogResult.OK)
    {
        // The user canceled.
        this.Close();
    }

    // Otherwise go on to show this form.
}
```

This code creates a PasswordForm and calls its ShowDialog method to display it. The ShowDialog call returns OK or Cancel depending on whether the user clicked the password form's OK button or the Cancel button.

The password dialog has a TextBox with PasswordChar set to X so no one can peek over the user's shoulder to see the password.

The form's CancelButton property is set to the Cancel button. If the user clicks that button, it automatically sets the form's DialogResult property to Cancel and hides the dialog.

If the user clicks the OK button, the following code executes.

```
// Validate the password.
private void okButton_Click(object sender, EventArgs e)
{
    if (passwordTextBox.Text == "Secret")
    {
        // The password is ok.
```

```
            this.DialogResult = DialogResult.OK;
        }
        else
        {
            // The password is invalid.
            MessageBox.Show("Invalid password.");
            passwordTextBox.Clear();
            passwordTextBox.Focus();
        }
    }
```

This code simply compares the password entered by the user to the string "Secret." If the password matches, the code sets the password form's `DialogResult` property to `OK`. That automatically hides the form and the main program's call to `ShowDialog` returns `OK`.

If the password is invalid, the program displays an error message and blanks the incorrect password. The password dialog's `DialogResult` property remains unset, so the dialog remains visible and the user can try again.

If the user presses the form's X button in the upper right corner, presses Alt-F4, or uses the form's system menu in the upper left corner to close the dialog, the `DialogResult` property is automatically set to `Cancel` so the program acts just as if the user had clicked the Cancel button.

Of course in a real application, you shouldn't put the correct password in the code. It would be easy for a hacker to look in the code and find the password.

You might also want to add a username text box to the dialog so the program can validate the username/password pair. For example, the program could try to use the username and password to open a password-protected database. If the database opens successfully, then the username/password pair is valid.

Part XI. Internet

The examples in this part of the book deal with the internet. They show how you can download information such as stock prices or weather forecasts from remote servers. They also show to access FTP servers to get file information.

These examples do not show how to use web services. Web services provide extra features such as input data validation, but they are also more complicated. The examples shown here use relatively simple techniques.

48. GET STOCK PRICES (13)

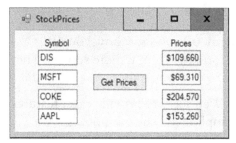

Many web sites can return stock prices to a program. This example uses a service provided by `download.finance.yahoo.com`.

When you enter stock ticker symbols in the text boxes on the left and click Get Prices, the program uses the symbols that you entered to build a URL similar to the following.

`http://download.finance.yahoo.com/d/quotes.csv?s=DIS+DIS.L+COKE+COKE.HK&f=sl1d1t1c1`

The end of the URL, which in this example is `&f=sl1d1t1c1`, tells the Yahoo server what data you want to download. The following table shows the tags that you can include in this part of the URL.

Tag	Meaning	Tag	Meaning	Tag	Meaning
a	Ask	a2	Average daily volume	a5	Ask size
b	Bid	b2	Ask (real-time)	b3	Bid (real-time)
b4	Book value	b6	Bid size	c	Change & percent change
c1	Change	c3	Commission	c6	Change (real-time)
c8	After hours change (real-time)	d	Dividends/share	d1	Last trade date
d2	Trade date	e	Earnings/share	e1	Error
e7	EPS estimate current year	e8	EPS estimate next year	e9	EPS estimate next quarter
f6	Float shares	g	Day's low	g1	Holdings gain percent
g3	Annualized gain	g4	Holdings gain	g5	Holdings gain percent (real-time)
g6	Holdings gain (real-time)	h	Day's high	i	More information
i5	Order book (real-time)	j	52-week low	j1	Market capitalization

Tag	Meaning	Tag	Meaning	Tag	Meaning
j3	Market cap (real-time)	j4	EBITDA	j5	Change from 52-week low
j6	Percent change from 52-week low	K	52-week high	k1	Last trade (real-time) with time
k2	Change percent (real-time)	k3	Last trade size	k4	Change from 52-week high
k5	Percent change from 52-week high	L	Last trade with time	l1	Last trade (price only)
l2	High limit	l3	Low limit	m	Day's range
m2	Day's range (real-time)	m3	50-day moving average	m4	200-day moving average
m5	Change from 200-day moving average	m6	Percent change from 200-day moving average	m7	Change from 50-day moving average
m8	Percent change from 50-day moving average	N	Name	n4	Notes
o	Open	P	Previous close	p1	Price paid
p2	Change in percent	p5	Price/sales	p6	Price/book
q	Ex-dividend date	r	P/E ratio	r1	Dividend pay date
r2	P/E ratio (real-time)	r5	PEG ratio	r6	Price/EPS estimate current year
r7	Price/EPS estimate next year	s	Symbol	s1	Shares owned
s7	Short ratio	t1	Last trade time	t6	Trade links
t7	Ticker trend	t8	1 year target price	v	Volume
v1	Holdings value	v7	Holdings value (real-time)	w	52-week range
w1	Day's value change	w4	Day's value change (real-time)	x	Stock exchange
y	Dividend yield				

This example uses the following tags.

Tag	Meaning
s	Symbol
11	Last trade (price only)
d1	Last trade date
t1	Last trade time
c1	Change

The service returns a single string containing the results. The stocks' entries are separated by newline \n characters. The values for each stock are separated by commas.

The following text shows a sample.

```
"DIS",109.66,"5/10/2017","4:02pm",-2.41
"MSFT",69.31,"5/10/2017","4:00pm",+0.27
"COKE",204.57,"5/10/2017","4:00pm",+1.42
"AAPL",153.26,"5/10/2017","4:00pm",-0.73
```

If a ticker symbol doesn't exist or if no data is available, the web site returns the string N/A for the values that don't exist.

The program uses the following GetWebResponse method to get a web response and return it in a string.

```
// Get a web response.
private string GetWebResponse(string url)
{
    // Make a WebClient.
    WebClient webClient = new WebClient();

    // Get the indicated URL.
    Stream response = webClient.OpenRead(url);

    // Read the result.
    using (StreamReader reader = new StreamReader(response))
    {
        return reader.ReadToEnd();
    }
}
```

This code creates a WebClient object and uses its OpenRead method to get a StreamReader that can read the result of the URL request. The code reads the stream to its end and returns the resulting string.

The following code shows how the program uses the GetWebResponse method.

```
// Get the stock prices.
private void getPricesButton_Click(object sender, EventArgs e)
{
    this.Cursor = Cursors.WaitCursor;
    Application.DoEvents();
```

```
// Build the URL.
string url = "";
if (symbol1TextBox.Text != "") url += symbol1TextBox.Text + "+";
if (symbol2TextBox.Text != "") url += symbol2TextBox.Text + "+";
if (symbol3TextBox.Text != "") url += symbol3TextBox.Text + "+";
if (symbol4TextBox.Text != "") url += symbol4TextBox.Text + "+";
if (url != "")
{
    // Remove the trailing plus sign.
    url = url.Substring(0, url.Length - 1);

    // Prepend the base URL.
    const string baseUrl =
        "http://download.finance.yahoo.com/d/quotes.csv?s=@&f=sl1d1t1c1";
    url = baseUrl.Replace("@", url);

    // Get the response.
    try
    {
        // Get the web response.
        string result = GetWebResponse(url);
        Console.WriteLine(result.Replace("\\r\\n", "\r\n"));

        // Pull out the current prices.
        string[] lines = result.Split(
            new char[] { '\r', '\n' },
            StringSplitOptions.RemoveEmptyEntries);
        price1TextBox.Text = FormatCurrency(lines[0].Split(',')[1]);
        price2TextBox.Text = FormatCurrency(lines[1].Split(',')[1]);
        price3TextBox.Text = FormatCurrency(lines[2].Split(',')[1]);
        price4TextBox.Text = FormatCurrency(lines[3].Split(',')[1]);
    }
    catch (Exception ex)
    {
        MessageBox.Show(ex.Message, "Read Error",
            MessageBoxButtons.OK, MessageBoxIcon.Exclamation);
    }
}

this.Cursor = Cursors.Default;
}
```

The code builds the URL from the symbols in the program's text boxes. It calls the
GetWebResponse method and parses the result to find the stock prices.

The code uses the following FormatCurrency method to display prices as currency values
with three digits after the decimal point.

```
// Return a number formatted as currency
// or a blank string if the text isn't a number.
private string FormatCurrency(string text)
{
    decimal value;
    if (decimal.TryParse(text, out value)) return value.ToString("C3");
    return "";
}
```

This method tries to convert the value into a decimal and, if it succeeds, the method returns the decimal value formatted as currency. If the original value isn't a valid decimal, for example if it is "N/A," the method returns a blank string.

This example only uses the second value, the stock price, so you really don't need the other tags in the URL. I've put them in here just to show how you can add more tags.

49. GENERATE AND DISPLAY HTML (43)

This example actually does two things: it makes a WebBrowser control navigate to the user's home page, and it shows how a program can generate and display HTML in the WebBrowser control at run time.

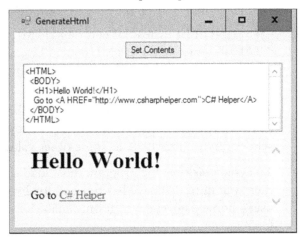

When the program starts, it uses the following code to navigate to the user's home page.

```
// Start at home.
private void Form1_Load(object sender, EventArgs e)
{
    displayWebBrowser.GoHome();
    //displayWebBrowser.Navigate("about:blank");
}
```

This code simply calls the WebBrowser control's GoHome method.

After the user's home page finishes loading, the WebBrowser control raises its DocumentCompleted event and the following code executes.

```
// Enable the button.
private void displayWebBrowser_DocumentCompleted(object sender,
WebBrowserDocumentCompletedEventArgs e)
{
    setContentsButton.Enabled = true;
}
```

This code simply enables the program's Set Contents button.

When you click the button, the program uses the following code to display the HTML code that's entered in the upper text box.

```
// Set the HTML contents.
private void setContentsButton_Click(object sender, EventArgs e)
{
    HtmlDocument doc = displayWebBrowser.Document;
    doc.Body.InnerHtml = htmlTextBox.Text;
}
```

This code simply gets the WebBrowser control's Document object (which represents the HTML document that is currently displayed) and sets its InnerHtml property to the text in the program's TextBox. That changes the document so it holds the HTML text and that makes the control display the HTML data.

> **NOTE:** Instead of entering HTML code in a text box, you could write code to generate the HTML code. For example, you could loop through some data and generate HTML code to display the data in a table.

The reason why the program starts by loading the user's home page is that the WebBrowser control's Document object initially has a Body property set to null. If the program tries to set doc.Body.InnerHtml to some other value, the program crashes.

To avoid crashing, the program must load something into the WebBrowser control and then wait until that page has finished loading. That's why this example starts by loading the user's home page and why it only enables its button after the home page has finished loading.

> **NOTE:** Instead of going to the user's home page, the program could make the browser control navigate to about:blank to display a blank document.

50. GET FILE SIZE AND MODIFICATION TIME ON AN FTP SERVER (50)

This example lets you query an FTP server to get information about a file. Enter the Uniform Resource Identifier (URI) for the file you're interested in. Be sure to use the `ftp` protocol not `http` or `https`.

Next, enter a username and password for the FTP site. If the file is available via anonymous FTP, enter "anonymous" for the user name and your email address for the password.

When you click the Get Info button, the program uses the following code to get the file's size and last modification time.

```
private void getInfoButton_Click(object sender, EventArgs e)
{
    try
    {
        this.Cursor = Cursors.WaitCursor;
        statusLabel.Text = "Working...";
        sizeTextBox.Clear();
        timeStampTextBox.Clear();
        Refresh();

        sizeTextBox.Text = FtpGetFileSize(uriTextBox.Text,
            usernameTextBox.Text, passwordTextBox.Text).ToString();
        timeStampTextBox.Text = FtpGetFileTimestamp(uriTextBox.Text,
            usernameTextBox.Text, passwordTextBox.Text).ToString();

        statusLabel.Text = "Done";
    }
    catch (Exception ex)
    {
        statusLabel.Text = "Error";
        MessageBox.Show(ex.Message);
    }
    finally
    {
        this.Cursor = Cursors.Default;
    }
}
```

This code displays a wait cursor and clears any previous results. It then calls the `FtpGetFileSize` and `FtpGetFileTimestamp` methods described shortly to get the desired information.

> **NOTE:** This example includes an unusually large amount of error handling because it has an unusually large number of ways it can fail.

The following code shows the `FtpGetFileSize` method.

```csharp
// Use FTP to get a remote file's size.
private long FtpGetFileSize(string uri, string user_name, string password)
{
    // Get the object used to communicate with the server.
    FtpWebRequest request = (FtpWebRequest)WebRequest.Create(uri);
    request.Method = WebRequestMethods.Ftp.GetFileSize;

    // Get network credentials.
    request.Credentials = new NetworkCredential(user_name, password);

    try
    {
        using (FtpWebResponse response = (FtpWebResponse)request.GetResponse())
        {
            // Return the size.
            return response.ContentLength;
        }
    }
    catch (Exception ex)
    {
        // If the file doesn't exist, return -1.
        // Otherwise rethrow the error.
        if (ex.Message.Contains("File unavailable")) return -1;
        throw;
    }
}
```

This code creates an `FtpWebRequest` object to work with the file. It sets the request's `Method` property to `GetFileSize` and gets a response. The only trick here is that the file's size is returned through the response's `ContentLength` property.

The `FtpGetFileTimestamp` method shown in the following code gets a file's creation date and time.

```csharp
// Use FTP to get a remote file's timestamp.
private DateTime FtpGetFileTimestamp(string uri, string user_name,
    string password)
{
    // Get the object used to communicate with the server.
    FtpWebRequest request = (FtpWebRequest)WebRequest.Create(uri);
    request.Method = WebRequestMethods.Ftp.GetDateTimestamp;

    // Get network credentials.
    request.Credentials = new NetworkCredential(user_name, password);

    try
    {
        using (FtpWebResponse response = (FtpWebResponse)request.GetResponse())
        {
            // Return the size.
```

```
                return response.LastModified;
            }
        }
        catch (Exception ex)
        {
            // If the file doesn't exist, return Jan 1, 3000.
            // Otherwise rethrow the error.
            if (ex.Message.Contains("File unavailable"))
                return new DateTime(3000, 1, 1);
            throw;
        }
    }
```

This code creates an FtpWebRequest object, sets its Method property to GetDateTimestamp, and gets a response. The trick here is that the file's timestamp is returned through the response's LastModified property.

51. GET WEATHER FORECASTS (61)

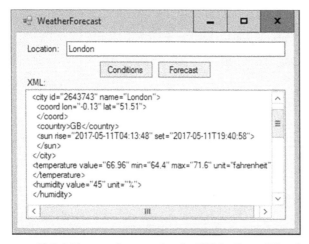

Many sites offer weather condition and forecast services. All of the ones I've found require you to have a developer key, although most of them have a free membership that works for a simple program like this one.

This example uses the OpenWeatherMap service available at openweathermap.org. I don't particularly recommend this site over the others, but it is fairly easy to use.

Some sites let you access remote functions by using Simple Object Access Protocol (SOAP) or other methods. With OpenWeatherMap you just navigate to a URL and it returns weather data.

For some (rather poorly written) information about the OpenWeatherMap API, go to openweathermap.org/api. The pages linked to that one provide information about the format of the URLs that you need to use and the types of data that they return.

This example uses two kinds of URL: one to return the current weather conditions and one to return a forecast.

The current conditions URL has the following format.

```
http://api.openweathermap.org/data/2.5/weather?q=London&mode=xml
    &units=imperial&APPID=APIKEY
```

Here:

➢ q=London is the location of interest. This can include values such as a place name, a city and country name, or a location code. The returned data includes the location code, so if you look up a city once by name, you can save the location code for later searches.
➢ mode=xml indicates that I want the returned results in an XML document.
➢ APPID=APIKEY specifies the developer key that you get when you sign up with OpenWeatherMap. Replace APIKEY with your key.
➢ units=imperial tells the server that I want imperial units such as degrees Fahrenheit instead of degrees Celsius or Kelvin.

The weather forecast URL has the following format.

```
http://api.openweathermap.org/data/2.5/forecast?q=London&mode=xml
    &units=imperial&APPID=APIKEY
```

The only difference is that the final part before the ? character is forecast instead of weather.

The following code shows how the program gets current conditions and forecasts.

```
// Enter your API key here.
// Get an API key by making a free account at:
//      http://home.openweathermap.org/users/sign_in
private const string APIKEY = "9749874xw2kfiq9029j092m0j9kfj07e";

// Query URLs. Replace @LOC@ with the location.
private const string CurrentUrl =
    "http://api.openweathermap.org/data/2.5/weather?" +
    "q=@LOC@&mode=xml&units=imperial&APPID=" + APIKEY;
private const string ForecastUrl =
    "http://api.openweathermap.org/data/2.5/forecast?" +
    "q=@LOC@&mode=xml&units=imperial&APPID=" + APIKEY;

// Get current conditions.
private void conditionsButton_Click(object sender, EventArgs e)
{
    // Compose the query URL.
    string url = CurrentUrl.Replace("@LOC@", locationTextBox.Text);
    xmlTextBox.Text = GetFormattedXml(url);
}

// Get a forecast.
private void forecastButton_Click(object sender, EventArgs e)
{
    // Compose the query URL.
    string url = ForecastUrl.Replace("@LOC@", locationTextBox.Text);
    xmlTextBox.Text = GetFormattedXml(url);
}
```

The APIKEY string holds your developer API key. The one shown here is just a random value and not a valid key. You can get your own key by regsitering for a free account at home.openweathermap.org/users/sign_in.

The strings CurrentUrl and ForecastUrl are the URLs to get current conditions and weather forecasts.

The Conditions button's Click event handler replaces the string @LOC@ in the conditions URL with the location entered in the program's text box. It then calls the GetFormattedXml method (described shortly) to get the returned XML data. It finishes by displaying the returned data in the result text box.

The Forecast button's Click event handler works similarly except it uses the weather forecast URL.

The following code shows the GetFormattedXml method.

```
// Return the XML result of the URL.
private string GetFormattedXml(string url)
{
    // Create a web client.
```

```
using (WebClient client = new WebClient())
{
    // Get the response string from the URL.
    string xml = client.DownloadString(url);

    // Load the response into an XML document.
    XmlDocument doc = new XmlDocument();
    doc.LoadXml(xml);

    // Format the XML.
    using (StringWriter stringWriter = new StringWriter())
    {
        XmlTextWriter xmlWriter = new XmlTextWriter(stringWriter);
        xmlWriter.Formatting = Formatting.Indented;
        doc.WriteTo(xmlWriter);

        // Return the result.
        return stringWriter.ToString();
    }
}
}
```

This method creates a WebClient object and calls its DownloadString method to visit the desired URL and fetch the result as a string. The string is XML data holding the result of the query defined by the URL.

Initially the XML data is unformatted so it's hard to read. To format the result, the method creates an XmlDocument object and loads it with the XML data.

The code then creates a StringWriter and an associated XmlTextWriter. It sets the XmlTextWriter object's Formatting property to Indented so the writer will add newlines and indentation when it rewrites the XML data.

Next, the code makes the XmlDocument write itself into the XmlTextWriter. The XmlTextWriter feeds its data into the StringWriter.

The method finishes by returning the StringWriter object's contents.

To see what kinds of information is contained in the returned XML data, look at the openweathermap.org/api pages or just run the example program (with your API key) and look at the results. Most of the data is pretty easy to understand. For example, the temperature value gives you a temperature.

Part XII. Miscellaneous Controls

This part of the book describes a couple of tricks for working with controls. These examples explain how to make a checked group box, search a control hierarchy for a control with a particular name, find `ListBox` entries that contain target values, and resize a `RichTextBox` control to fit its contents.

52. MAKE A CHECKED GROUP BOX (14)

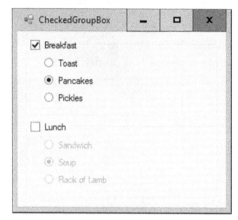

One useful control that's missing from Visual Studio's toolbox is a checked GroupBox. This control displays a CheckBox in its caption. When the user unchecks the CheckBox, all of the controls in the group are disabled.

While there is no such control in the .NET Framework, you can make a CheckBox and a GroupBox work together to provide a similar effect.

At design time, set the GroupBox control's Text property to an empty string. Position a CheckBox inside the GroupBox so it looks like it is the GroupBox control's caption. The result looks pretty good if you set the CheckBox control's Location property to 6, 0.

When the user unchecks the CheckBox, you can disable the GroupBox. Unfortunately, that also disables the CheckBox contained in it so the user cannot check it again.

You could place the CheckBox *on top of* the GroupBox rather than inside it, but the Form Designer tends to drop the CheckBox inside the GroupBox when you're not looking unless you're very careful.

This example uses the following ManageCheckGroupBox method to handle these problems relatively easily.

```
private void ManageCheckGroupBox(CheckBox chk, GroupBox grp)
{
    // Make sure the CheckBox isn't in the GroupBox.
    // This will only happen the first time.
    if (chk.Parent == grp)
    {
        // Reparent the CheckBox so it's not in the GroupBox.
        grp.Parent.Controls.Add(chk);

        // Adjust the CheckBox's location.
        chk.Location = new Point(
            chk.Left + grp.Left,
            chk.Top + grp.Top);

        // Move the CheckBox to the top of the stacking order.
        chk.BringToFront();
    }

    // Enable or disable the GroupBox.
    grp.Enabled = chk.Checked;
}
```

This method checks whether the CheckBox is inside the GroupBox and, if it is, the method moves it into the GroupBox control's parent. It then adjusts the CheckBox control's location so it has the same position on the form that it had originally. It also moves it to the front of the stacking order so it doesn't end up behind the GroupBox.

Finally, depending on the CheckBox state, the method enables or disables the GroupBox, which enables or disables all of the controls that it contains.

The following code shows how the program responds when the user checks or unchecks its CheckBox controls.

```
// Enable or disable the breakfast GroupBox.
private void breakfastCheckBox_CheckedChanged(object sender, EventArgs e)
{
    ManageCheckGroupBox(breakfastCheckBox, grpBreakfast);
}

// Enable or disable the lunch GroupBox.
private void lunchCheckBox_CheckedChanged(object sender, EventArgs e)
{
    ManageCheckGroupBox(lunchCheckBox, grpLunch);
}
```

These event handlers simply call the ManageCheckGroupBox method, passing it the appropriate CheckBox and its corresponding GroupBox.

53. FIND CONTROLS BY NAME (68)

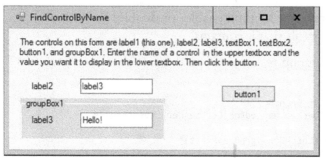

This example has an awkward user interface, largely because its controls refer to themselves. The program's goal is to search its control hierarchy to find controls by name.

When you click the button, the program finds the control whose name is in the upper `TextBox` and sets its `Text` property to the text entered in the lower `TextBox`.

Every control has a `Controls` property that is a collection of the child controls that it contains. You can use a child control's name as an index into that collection. For example, `groupBox1.Controls["label3"]` returns a reference to the `label3` control contained inside the `groupBox1` control.

Unfortunately, that only lets you search a single control's children. It doesn't search the whole hierarchy below that control. In other words, it doesn't search grandchildren, great grandchildren, and other descendants.

In particular, that means you can't use the form's `Controls` collection to search for controls that are inside containers. For example, the form's `Controls` collection won't find this example's `label3` control because that control is inside `groupBox1`.

This example uses the following `FindControl` extension method to search recursively through a control hierarchy to find a control by name.

```
// Recursively find the named control.
public static Control FindControl(this Control parent, string name)
{
    // Check the parent.
    if (parent.Name == name) return parent;

    // Recursively search the parent's children.
    foreach (Control ctl in parent.Controls)
    {
        Control found = FindControl(ctl, name);
        if (found != null) return found;
    }

    // If we still haven't found it, it's not here.
    return null;
}
```

The method starts by checking the parent to see if it has the target name. If it doesn't have the right name, the function calls itself recursively to check each of the parent's child controls. That call searches the children and any controls they contain.

If none of the recursive calls to FindControl finds the target control, then it's not within the parent's control hierarchy so the function returns null.

Note that this version of the method makes a case-sensitive search for the named control. You can change the code to perform a case-insensitive search if you like.

Also note that the form itself is a control, so you can search for it and search its control hierarchy. The program uses that fact in the following code, which executes when you click the form's button.

```
// Find the indicated control and set its text.
private void button1_Click(object sender, EventArgs e)
{
    // Find the control.
    Control control = this.FindControl(textBox1.Text);
    if (control == null)
    {
        MessageBox.Show("Could not find control '" + textBox1.Text + "'");
        return;
    }

    // Set its Text property.
    control.Text = textBox2.Text;
}
```

This code uses the FindControl extension method to search the form for the control with name stored in textBox1.Text. If it finds that control, the code sets its Text property to the value in textBox2.Text.

NOTE: The Control class defines the Controls and Text properties, so they exist even for controls where they don't make much sense. For example, a Label control has a Controls collection even though it cannot display child controls. Similarly, a PictureBox control has a Text property even though it doesn't display its value.

54. Select ListBox Values Containing Target Text (80)

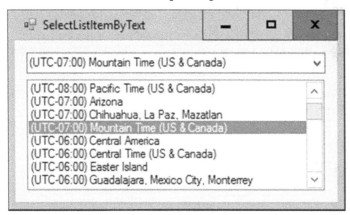

One of the examples on the C# Helper web site builds a list of time zones. I would like to select an initial value based on the text in the items, but I don't want to have to select the exact text, partly because that text may change depending on Daylight Savings. At different times during the year, a time zone may have different offsets from GMT depending on whether Daylight Savings is in effect. That means you won't know exactly what text the program will use to represent a particular time zone. Rather than selecting an exact ListBox entry, I want to find an entry that contains a particular substring such as my time zone's name.

It's not hard to loop through a ComboBox control's Items collection and examine each of the items to see if one of them contains a target string. That's straightforward, but it would be nice to use the same code to find items in ListBox controls, too.

The ComboBox and ListBox controls are practically the same, aside from their user interfaces, so you might think this would be trivial. Unfortunately, the two controls' Items collections are not the same kinds of objects. They are ComboBox.ObjectCollection and ListBox.ObjectCollection objects. That means you can't write a single method that explicitly takes either a ComboBox or a ListBox control's Items collection as a parameter.

Those two Items collections have different types, but they both implement the IEnumerable interface. That means you can loop through them and look at the objects they contain.

When it displays its items, a ComboBox or ListBox calls each item's ToString method to see what text it should display. Your code can use the same technique.

The following list summarizes the process for finding an item.

1. Iterate through the objects in the IEnumerable Items collection.
2. Use each item's ToString method to see what text the ComboBox or ListBox will display.
3. Use string methods to compare the value to the target value.
4. If you find the desired match, return the object that gave the match.

The `FindItemContaining` method shown in the following code follows those steps.

```
// Find an item containing the target string.
private static object FindItemContaining(IEnumerable items, string target)
{
    foreach (object item in items)
        if (item.ToString().Contains(target)) return item;
    return null;
}
```

To make using this method a bit easier, the example defines the following `ComboBox` and `ListBox` extension methods.

```
public static object FindItemContaining(this ComboBox cbo, string target)
{
    return FindItemContaining(cbo.Items, target);
}
public static object FindItemContaining(this ListBox lst, string target)
{
    return FindItemContaining(lst.Items, target);
}
```

These methods simply call the preceding `FindItemContaining` method.

The following code shows how the program builds its lists of time zones and then selects the entries for Mountain Time.

```
// Initialize the ComboBox and ListBox.
private void Form1_Load(object sender, EventArgs e)
{
    // list the time zones.
    timeZonesComboBox.DataSource = TimeZoneInfo.GetSystemTimeZones();
    timeZonesListBox.DataSource = TimeZoneInfo.GetSystemTimeZones();

    // Select Mountain Time.
    timeZonesComboBox.SelectedItem =
        timeZonesComboBox.FindItemContaining("Mountain Time");
    timeZonesListBox.SelectedItem =
        timeZonesListBox.FindItemContaining("Mountain Time");
}
```

The code uses `TimeZoneInfo.GetSystemTimeZones` to get a read-only collection holding information about the time zones defined on the local computer. It sets the `ComboBox` and `ListBox` controls' `DataSource` properties to the list so they display the time zones' names.

The program then uses the `FindItemContaining` extension methods to select the time zones containing the text, "Mountain Time."

55. FIT A RICHTEXTBOX TO ITS CONTENTS (100)

This is some text

Interview Puzzles
Dissected
Solving and Understanding
Interview Puzzles

Rod Stephens

Don't let the RichTextBox wrap long lines of text

Sometimes it's useful to make a `RichTextBox` control resize to fit its contents. For example, you might want to do that to display a Rich Text document containing a user agreement or help information.

In that scenario, you can set the control's `ReadOnly` property to `true` and set its `BackColor` property to white to make the control appear more like a white document. Alternatively, you can set its `ReadOnly` property to `true`, leave the `BackColor` property alone, and set `BorderStyle` to `None` to make the control look like a fancy label.

When this example starts, the following code executes to prepare the `RichTextBox`.

```
// Don't let the RichTextBox wrap long lines.
private void Form1_Load(object sender, EventArgs e)
{
    contentsRichTextBox.WordWrap = false;
    contentsRichTextBox.ScrollBars = RichTextBoxScrollBars.None;
}
```

This code sets the control's `WordWrap` property to `false` so the control doesn't try to wrap long lines of text to fit its current size. If you allow the control to wrap text while it's resizing itself, you get strange results where the control wraps text and then tries to make itself narrower. If you add a bunch of text, the control eventually makes itself extremely tall and thin. There may be a way to make that work, but it doesn't seem very useful.

Next, the code sets the control's `ScrollBars` property to `None`. If you don't do this, the control may display scroll bars when its size is too close to the size required by its contents. The scroll bars take up a lot of room (relatively speaking), so you can't see all of the contents. You can add some extra space to make sure the text fits (in fact, the code that follows does this to make things look nicer), but the scroll bars mess things up if they appear so you may as well turn them off.

When the contents of the control change and the new contents require a different amount of space than the old contents, the `RichTextBox` raises its `ContentsResized` event and the following event handler executes.

```
// Make the RichTextBox fit its contents.
private void contentsRichTextBox_ContentsResized(object sender,
ContentsResizedEventArgs e)
{
    const int margin = 5;
```

```
    RichTextBox rch = sender as RichTextBox;
    rch.ClientSize = new Size(
        e.NewRectangle.Width + margin,
        e.NewRectangle.Height + margin);
}
```

This code uses the e.NewRectangle parameter to see how much space the new contents need. It adds a margin so things don't look too crowded and then sets the control's ClientSize property appropriately.

Run the program and type some text into the RichTextBox. You can also copy and paste images or formatted text (such as the colored text displayed in Visual Studio's code editor) into the RichTextBox to see how it handles them.

Part XIII. Geometry

This part of the book contains several examples that deal with geometry. They work with geometric shapes such as points, lines, circles, and polygons.

This section is larger than most of the others because people seem to like these sorts of examples, probably because this kind of information is scarce.

I like these examples because they're interesting, mathematical, and somewhat challenging. They also give me an excuse to build graphics programs, which I thoroughly enjoy.

56. SEE WHERE TWO LINES INTERSECT (15)

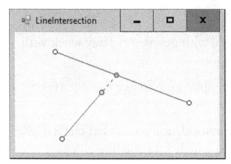

This example determines whether two line segments intersect and where the lines that contain them intersect.

There are several ways you can approach this problem. This example uses segments defined by parametric equations where $0 \leq t1 \leq 1$ and $0 \leq t2 \leq 1$.

If the first segment has endpoints (x11, y11) and (x12, y12), and the second segment has endpoints (x21, y21) and (x22, y22), then the line segments are defined by the following parametric functions.

```
X1(t) = x11 + dx1 * t1
Y1(t) = y11 + dy1 * t1
X2(t) = x21 + dx2 * t2
Y2(t) = y21 + dy2 * t2
```

In other words, as the value of t1 varies from 0 to 1, (X1(t), Y1(t)) give the points along the first line segment.

When the two segments intersect, the points (X1(t1), Y1(t1)) and (X2(t2), Y2(t2)) are the same. Setting the equations for the two points equal to each other gives the following equations.

```
x11 + dx1 * t1 = x21 + dx2 * t2
y11 + dy1 * t1 = y21 + dy2 * t2
```

You can rearrange those equations to get:

```
x11 - x21 + dx1 * t1 = dx2 * t2
y11 - y21 + dy1 * t1 = dy2 * t2
```

And then:

```
(x11 - x21 + dx1 * t1) *   dy2  = dx2 * t2 *   dy2
(y11 - y21 + dy1 * t1) * (-dx2) = dy2 * t2 * (-dx2)
```

Adding the equations gives:

```
(x11 - x21) * dy2 + ( dx1 * dy2) * t1 +
(y21 - y11) * dx2 + (-dy1 * dx2) * t1 = 0
```

Now solving for t1 gives:

```
t1 * (dy1 * dx2 - dx1 * dy2) = (x11 - x21) * dy2 + (y21 - y11) * dx2
```

So:

```
t1 = ((x11 - x21) * dy2 + (y21 - y11) * dx2) / (dy1 * dx2 - dx1 * dy2)
```

This may seem like a long, intimidating equation, but all of the values on the right hand side are just numbers, so you can plug them in to find t1. You can solve for t2 similarly.

The following list describes some useful properties of this result.

- If $0 \leq$ t1 $\leq$ 1, then the point lies on the first segment.
- If $0 \leq$ t2 $\leq$ 1, then the point lies on the second segment.
- If dy1 * dx2 - dx1 * dy2 = 0, then you can't calculate t1 or t2 because that would require dividing by 0. That happens if the lines are parallel.
- If the point of intersection is not on *both* segments, then this is probably *not* the point where the two segments are closest.

The FindIntersection method shown in the following code finds the intersection between the lines that contain the segments p1→p2 and p3→p4.

```
// Find the point of intersection between the lines p1 --> p2 and p3 --> p4.
private void FindIntersection(PointF p1, PointF p2, PointF p3, PointF p4,
    out bool linesIntersect, out bool segmentsIntersect,
    out PointF intersection, out PointF closeP1, out PointF closeP2)
{
    // Get the segments' parameters.
    float dx12 = p2.X - p1.X;
    float dy12 = p2.Y - p1.Y;
    float dx34 = p4.X - p3.X;
    float dy34 = p4.Y - p3.Y;

    // Solve for t1 and t2
    float denominator = (dy12 * dx34 - dx12 * dy34);
    float t1 = ((p1.X - p3.X) * dy34 + (p3.Y - p1.Y) * dx34) / denominator;
    if (float.IsInfinity(t1))
    {
        // The lines are parallel (or close enough to it).
        linesIntersect = false;
        segmentsIntersect = false;
        intersection = new PointF(float.NaN, float.NaN);
        closeP1 = new PointF(float.NaN, float.NaN);
        closeP2 = new PointF(float.NaN, float.NaN);
        return;
    }
    linesIntersect = true;

    float t2 = ((p3.X - p1.X) * dy12 + (p1.Y - p3.Y) * dx12) / -denominator;

    // Find the point of intersection.
    intersection = new PointF(p1.X + dx12 * t1, p1.Y + dy12 * t1);

    // The segments intersect if t1 and t2 are between 0 and 1.
    segmentsIntersect = ((t1 >= 0) && (t1 <= 1) && (t2 >= 0) && (t2 <= 1));

    // Find the closest points on the segments.
    if (t1 < 0) t1 = 0;
    else if (t1 > 1) t1 = 1;

    if (t2 < 0) t2 = 0;
    else if (t2 > 1) t2 = 1;

    closeP1 = new PointF(p1.X + dx12 * t1, p1.Y + dy12 * t1);
    closeP2 = new PointF(p3.X + dx34 * t2, p3.Y + dy34 * t2);
}
```

This method takes as parameters the points that define the segments. It uses the following output parameters to return results.

➢ linesIntersect—This is true if the lines containing the segments intersect
➢ segmentsIntersect—This is true if the segments intersect
➢ intersection—This is the point where the lines intersect
➢ closeP1—This is the point on the first segment that is closest to the point of intersection
➢ closeP2—This is the point on the second segment that is closest to the point of intersection

First the code calculates dx12, dy12, and the other values that define the lines. It then plugs the values and the points' coordinates into the equation shown earlier to calculate t1. If the result is infinity, then the denominator is 0 so the lines are parallel.

Next the code uses the values of t1 and t2 to find the points of intersection between the two lines.

If t1 and t2 are both between 0 and 1, then the line segments intersect.

The code then adjusts t1 and t2 so they are between 0 and 1. Those values generate the points on the two segments that are closest to the point of intersection. Finally the code uses the adjusted values of t1 and t2 to find those closest points.

To use the example program, click two points to define the first segment. Then click two more points to define the second segment.

The program then draws the segments. It highlights the point where the lines intersect, and the points on the segments that are closest to that point of intersection. In the figure at the beginning of this example, one of the "close" points is at the point of intersection so they are drawn on top of each other.

Finally the program draws a dashed line between the "close" points.

57. FIND THE DISTANCE BETWEEN A POINT AND A LINE SEGMENT (44)

This example treats the segment as parameterized vector where the parameter t varies from 0 to 1 much as the preceding example does. It finds the value of t that minimizes the distance from the point to the line segment's line.

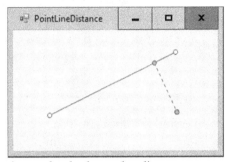

If t is between 0 and 1, then the point on the segment that is closest to the other point lies on the segment. Otherwise the closest point is one of the segment's endpoints. The program finds this closest point and calculates the distance between it and the target point.

The following code shows how the program finds the distance between the point pt and the segment p1→p2.

```
// Calculate the distance between point pt and the segment p1 --> p2.
private double FindDistanceToSegment(PointF pt,
    PointF p1, PointF p2, out PointF closest)
{
    float dx = p2.X - p1.X;
    float dy = p2.Y - p1.Y;
    if ((dx == 0) && (dy == 0))
    {
        // It's a point not a line segment.
        closest = p1;
        dx = pt.X - p1.X;
        dy = pt.Y - p1.Y;
        return Math.Sqrt(dx * dx + dy * dy);
    }

    // Calculate the t that minimizes the distance.
    float t = ((pt.X - p1.X) * dx + (pt.Y - p1.Y) * dy) / (dx * dx + dy * dy);

    // See if this represents one of the segment's
    // endpoints or a point in the middle.
    if (t < 0)
    {
        closest = new PointF(p1.X, p1.Y);
        dx = pt.X - p1.X;
        dy = pt.Y - p1.Y;
    }
    else if (t > 1)
    {
        closest = new PointF(p2.X, p2.Y);
        dx = pt.X - p2.X;
        dy = pt.Y - p2.Y;
    }
    else
    {
```

```
            closest = new PointF(p1.X + t * dx, p1.Y + t * dy);
            dx = pt.X - closest.X;
            dy = pt.Y - closest.Y;
        }

        return Math.Sqrt(dx * dx + dy * dy);
    }
```

The least obvious part of this code is the following statement.

```
    // Calculate the t that minimizes the distance.
    float t = ((pt.X - p1.X) * dx + (pt.Y - p1.Y) * dy) / (dx * dx + dy * dy);
```

So where does this formula come from?

To find the shortest distance between the point and the line segment, you need to know some relatively easy calculus and one clever fact. The clever fact is that if T minimizes an equation, then T also minimizes the equation squared. In this example, that means we can minimize the distance *squared* between the point and the line segment. The value t that we find will also minimize the non-squared distance.

A point on the line segment has coordinates (Pt1.X + t*dx, Pt1.Y + t*dy).

The distance squared between that point and the point Pt is:

$$[Pt.X - (Pt1.X + t*dx)]^2 + [Pt.Y - (Pt1.Y + t*dy)]^2$$

Taking the derivative with respect to t gives:

$$2*[Pt.X - (Pt1.X + t*dx)]*dx + 2*[Pt.Y - (Pt1.Y + t*dy)]*dy$$

To find the minimum, we set this equal to 0 and solve for t.

$$2*[Pt.X - (Pt1.X + t*dx)]*dx + 2*[Pt.Y - (Pt1.Y + t*dy)]*dy = 0$$

Now if you divide both sides by 2 and then combine the t terms you get:

$$-t*(dx2 + dy2) + dx*(Pt.X - Pt1.X) + dy*(Pt.Y - Pt1.Y) = 0$$

Subtracting the t term from both sides of the equation gives:

$$dx*(Pt.X - Pt1.X) + dy*(Pt.Y - Pt1.Y) = t*(dx2 + dy2)$$

Finally you can divide both sides by $(dx^2 + dy^2)$ to get:

$$t = [dx*(Pt.X - Pt1.X) + dy*(Pt.Y - Pt1.Y)] / (dx2 + dy2)$$

That's the equation used in the code.

The rest of the program is fairly straightforward. Download the example and look at the code to see additional details.

58. SEE WHERE TWO CIRCLES INTERSECT (18)

This example shows one method for finding where two circles intersect in C#. The following discussion is pretty mathy, so if you don't like math, skip down to the code.

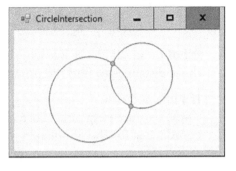

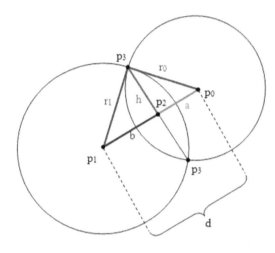

The Math

Consider the figure on the left showing two circles with radii r0 and r1. The points p0, p1, p2, and p3 have coordinates (x0, y0), (x1, y1) and so forth.

Let d = the distance between the circles' centers.

In that case:

$$d = \sqrt{(x_1 - x_0)^2 + (y_1 - y_0)^2} = a + b$$

Solving for a gives $a = d - b$. Now there are several cases.

- ➤ $d > r0 + r1$ The circles are too far apart to intersect.
- ➤ $d < |r0 - r1|$ One circle is inside the other so there is no intersection.
- ➤ $d = 0$ and $r0 = r1$ The circles are the same.
- ➤ $d = r0 + r1$ The circles touch at a single point.
- ➤ Otherwise   The circles intersect at two points.

The Pythagorean Theorem gives:

$$h^2 = r_0{}^2 - a^2 \text{ and } h^2 = r_1{}^2 - b^2$$

So:

$$r_0{}^2 - a^2 = r_1{}^2 - b^2$$

Substituting $a = d - b$ and multiplying this out gives:

$$r_0{}^2 - d^2 + 2 * d * b - b^2 = r_1{}^2 - b^2$$

The $-b^2$ terms on each side cancel each other out. You can then solve for b to get:

$$b = (r_1{}^2 - r_0{}^2 + d^2)/(2 * d)$$

Similarly:

$$a = (r_0{}^2 - r_1{}^2 + d^2)/(2 * d)$$

All of these values are known, so you can solve for a and b. All that remains is to use those distances to find the points of intersection p3.

If a line points in direction <dx, dy>, then lines that point in the directions <dy, –dx> and <–dy, dx> are perpendicular to the original line. Scaling the result gives the following coordinates for the points p3:

$$x_3 = x_2 \pm \frac{h(y_1 - y_0)}{d}$$

$$y_3 = y_2 \mp \frac{h(x_1 - x_0)}{d}$$

Be careful to notice the $\pm$ and $\mp$ symbols.

The Code

The following code shows the `FindCircleIntersections` method that the program uses to find intersections.

```
// Find the points where the two circles intersect.
private int FindCircleIntersections(
    float cx0, float cy0, float radius0,
    float cx1, float cy1, float radius1,
    out PointF intersection1, out PointF intersection2)
{
    // Find the distance between the centers.
    float dx = cx0 - cx1;
    float dy = cy0 - cy1;
    double dist = Math.Sqrt(dx * dx + dy * dy);

    // See how many solutions there are.
    if (dist > radius0 + radius1)
    {
        // No solutions, the circles are too far apart.
        intersection1 = new PointF(float.NaN, float.NaN);
        intersection2 = new PointF(float.NaN, float.NaN);
        return 0;
    }
    else if (dist < Math.Abs(radius0 - radius1))
    {
        // No solutions, one circle contains the other.
        intersection1 = new PointF(float.NaN, float.NaN);
        intersection2 = new PointF(float.NaN, float.NaN);
        return 0;
    }
    else if ((dist == 0) && (radius0 == radius1))
    {
```

```
        // No solutions, the circles coincide.
        intersection1 = new PointF(float.NaN, float.NaN);
        intersection2 = new PointF(float.NaN, float.NaN);
        return 0;
    }
    else
    {
        // Find a and h.
        double a = (radius0 * radius0 -
            radius1 * radius1 + dist * dist) / (2 * dist);
        double h = Math.Sqrt(radius0 * radius0 - a * a);

        // Find P2.
        double cx2 = cx0 + a * (cx1 - cx0) / dist;
        double cy2 = cy0 + a * (cy1 - cy0) / dist;

        // Get the points P3.
        intersection1 = new PointF(
            (float)(cx2 + h * (cy1 - cy0) / dist),
            (float)(cy2 - h * (cx1 - cx0) / dist));
        intersection2 = new PointF(
            (float)(cx2 - h * (cy1 - cy0) / dist),
            (float)(cy2 + h * (cx1 - cx0) / dist));

        // See if we have 1 or 2 solutions.
        if (dist == radius0 + radius1) return 1;
        return 2;
    }
}
```

This code follows the mathy explanation. The method calculates the distance between the circles' centers. It then determines which case applies so it knows how many solutions there are. The method plugs the values into the appropriate equations to find the correct solutions.

Download the example to see additional details.

Click and drag twice to define two circles. When you define the second circle, the program uses the FindCircleIntersections method to find the points where the circles intersect (if any). It then draws the circles and the intersections.

59. SEE WHERE A LINE AND CIRCLE INTERSECT (58)

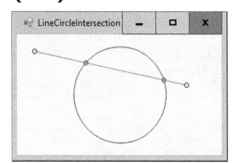

The `FindLineCircleIntersections` method shown shortly finds the points where a line intersects a circle. It takes as parameters a circle's center point and radius, and two points on the line. It uses out parameters to return the coordinates of the points of intersection. The method's return value indicates the number of points of intersection: 0, 1, or 2.

To find the points of intersection, the code considers the line as generated by the following equations.

```
X(t) = x1 + (x2 - x1) * t
Y(t) = y1 + (y2 - y1) * t
```

Here t ranges from 0 to 1 to generate the points on the line segment.

To find the points of intersection, plug those two equations into the following equation for a circle.

$$(X - Cx)^2 + (Y - Cy)^2 = radius^2$$

Then use the quadratic formula to solve for t. The result is 0, 1, or 2 real values for t depending on whether the line cuts through the circle, touches it tangentially, or misses it completely. After you find t, you can plug those its values back into the equations for the line to get the points of intersection.

Here's the `FindLineCircleIntersections` method.

```
// Find the points of intersection.
private int FindLineCircleIntersections(
    float cx, float cy, float radius,
    PointF point1, PointF point2,
    out PointF intersection1, out PointF intersection2)
{
    float dx = point2.X - point1.X;
    float dy = point2.Y - point1.Y;

    float A = dx * dx + dy * dy;
    float B = 2 * (dx * (point1.X - cx) + dy * (point1.Y - cy));
    float C = (point1.X - cx) * (point1.X - cx) + (point1.Y - cy) * (point1.Y - cy) -
radius * radius;

    float det = B * B - 4 * A * C;
    if ((A <= 0.0000001) || (det < 0))
    {
        // No real solutions.
        intersection1 = new PointF(float.NaN, float.NaN);
        intersection2 = new PointF(float.NaN, float.NaN);
```

```
        return 0;
    }
    else if (det == 0)
    {
        // One solution.
        float t = -B / (2 * A);
        intersection1 = new PointF(point1.X + t * dx, point1.Y + t * dy);
        intersection2 = new PointF(float.NaN, float.NaN);
        return 1;
    }
    else
    {
        // Two solutions.
        float t1 = (float)((-B + Math.Sqrt(det)) / (2 * A));
        intersection1 = new PointF(point1.X + t1 * dx, point1.Y + t1 * dy);
        float t2 = (float)((-B - Math.Sqrt(det)) / (2 * A));
        intersection2 = new PointF(point1.X + t2 * dx, point1.Y + t2 * dy);
        return 2;
    }
}
```

The program draws a large circle in the middle of its form. Click and drag to draw the line segment.

The main program uses the FindLineCircleIntersections method to find the points of intersection if there are any. It then draws the segment that you selected and the points of intersection.

60. See If A Point Lies Inside A Polygon (22)

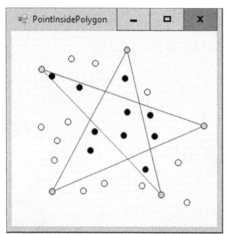

One way to determine whether a point lies within a polygon is to add up the angles between that point and adjacent pairs of points on the polygon taken in order. For example, if the point in question is P and points A and B are adjacent on the polygon, then you look at the angle ∠APB.

If the total of all of the angles is 2π or -2π, then the point is inside the polygon. If the total is zero, the point is outside. You can verify this intuitively with some simple examples using squares or triangles.

To use the example program, left-click to define the points that make up a polygon. Then right-click to define test points. If a test point is inside the polygon, the program draws it in black. If the point lies outside of the polygon, the program draws it in white.

The following code shows the `PointInPolygon` method that the program uses to determine whether a point lies inside the polygon.

```
// Return true if the point is in the polygon.
public bool PointInPolygon(List<Point> points, Point point)
{
    // Get the angle between the point and the first and last vertices.
    int max_point = points.Count - 1;
    float total_angle = GetAngle(
        points[max_point].X, points[max_point].Y,
        point.X, point.Y,
        points[0].X, points[0].Y);

    // Add the angles from the point
    // to each other pair of vertices.
    for (int i = 0; i < max_point; i++)
    {
        total_angle += GetAngle(
            points[i].X, points[i].Y,
            point.X, point.Y,
            points[i + 1].X, points[i + 1].Y);
    }

    // The total angle should be 2 * PI or -2 * PI if the point is in
    // the polygon and close to zero if the point is outside the polygon.
    return (Math.Abs(total_angle) > 0.000001);
}
```

This code first gets the angle made by the polygon's first and last points, plus the target point. It then loops through the polygon's other points calculating their angles and adding them up. When it finishes, the method returns `true` if the sum of the angles is close to 2π or -2π.

The following code shows the `GetAngle` method that the `PointInPolygon` method uses to find angles.

```
// Return the angle ABC between PI and -PI.
// Note that the value is the opposite of what you might
// expect because Y coordinates increase downward.
public static float GetAngle(float Ax, float Ay, float Bx, float By,
    float Cx, float Cy)
{
    // Get the dot product.
    float dot_product = DotProduct(Ax, Ay, Bx, By, Cx, Cy);

    // Get the cross product.
    float cross_product = CrossProductLength(Ax, Ay, Bx, By, Cx, Cy);

    // Calculate the angle.
    return (float)Math.Atan2(cross_product, dot_product);
}
```

This code uses the `DotProduct` and `CrossProductLength` methods to get the angle's dot product and cross product length.

> **NOTE:** If the angle's sides define the two vectors AB and BC, then the dot product is given by $|AB| * |BC| * Cos(\theta)$ and the length of the cross product is given by $|AB| * |BC| * Sin(\theta)$, where θ is the angle between the two vectors.

If you divide the length of the cross product by the length of the dot product, you get:

```
(|AB| * |BC| * Sin(theta)) / (|AB| * |BC| * Cos(theta)) =
Sin(theta)) / Cos(theta)) =
Tan(theta)
```

The `Math.ATan2` method takes opposite and adjacent side lengths for a right triangle and returns an angle with the corresponding tangent value. That fact plus the previous equations means `Math.Atan2(cross_product, dot_product)` returns the angle between the two vectors.

The code used to calculate dot products and cross products is straightforward and not very interesting (if you know how to calculate those things). For more details, download the example program and look at the code, or see Wikipedia (`en.wikipedia.org`) or Wolfram Mathworld (`mathworld.wolfram.com`).

61. CALCULATE A POLYGON'S AREA (40)

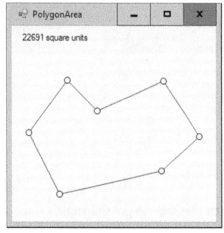

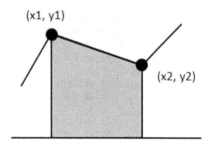

You can calculate the area of a polygon by adding the areas of the trapezoids that are defined by the polygon's edges when you drop them down to the X-axis. If two adjacent points along the polygon's edges have coordinates (x1, y1) and (x2, y2) as shown in the picture on the right above, then the shaded trapezoid below that edge has area given by the following equation.

    area = (x2 - x1) * (y2 + y1) / 2

If the points on the polygon are oriented clockwise, then the sides on the polygon's bottom give negative areas because x1 > x2. Those areas cancel out the parts of the other trapezoids that lie outside of the polygon as shown in the picture below.

Top areas   —   Bottom areas   =   Polygon area

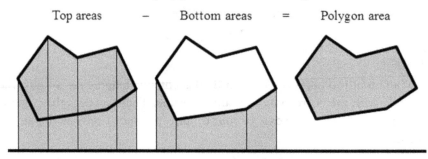

This method gives strange results for self-intersecting polygons, although it does work if the polygon intersects the X axis.

If you loop through the polygon's points and add up the trapezoid areas, the result is either the polygon's area or the negative off that area depending on the polygon's orientation. In the picture above, the result is positive if the polygon is oriented clockwise.

In C#, however, the point (0, 0) is in an image's upper left corner and the coordinates increase to the right and downward. Because Y increases downward, the pictures shown above are flipped upside down and the orientation is reversed.

That means the polygon's signed area is positive if the polygon is oriented counter clockwise and it's negative if the polygon is oriented clockwise, at least in device coordinates.

The following code shows how the example calculates a polygon's signed area.

```
// Return the polygon's area in "square units."
// Negative = clockwise, positive = clockwise.
private float SignedPolygonArea(List<Point> points)
{
    // Add the first point to the end.
    int numPoints = points.Count;

    // Get the areas.
    float area = 0;
    for (int i = 0; i < numPoints; i++)
    {
        int j = (i + 1) % numPoints;
        area +=
            (points[j].X - points[i].X) *
            (points[j].Y + points[i].Y) / 2;
    }

    // Return the result.
    return area;
}
```

The code gets the number of points in the polygon and then loops over the points' indices. For each index i, it calculates the index j = (i + 1) % numPoints for the polygon's next point. The mod operator % makes j wrap around to the first point when it reaches the end of the point list.

The code uses the formula shown earlier to calculate the area of each segment's trapezoid and adds it to the total area.

After it finishes processing all of the polygon's edges, the method returns the total area.

The following PolygonArea method simply returns the absolute value of the result given by the SignedPolygonArea method.

```
// Return the polygon's area in "square units."
public float PolygonArea(List<Point> points)
{
    // Return the absolute value of the signed area.
    return Math.Abs(SignedPolygonArea(points));
}
```

62. Find a Polygon's Centroid (55)

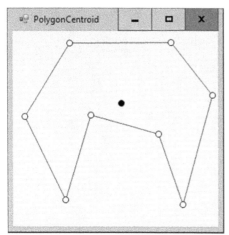

The centroid of a polygon is its "center of mass." If you were to cut the polygon out of cardboard or wood with uniform density, the centroid would be the point where you could balance the polygon on your finger.

Note that the centroid does not necessarily lie inside the polygon. For example, a donut-shaped polygon's centroid would be inside its central hole.

To account for situations such as that one, you might need to glue the wooden polygon to a piece of massless transparent plastic and place your finger on the plastic.

The centroid's coordinates (X, Y) are given by the following equations.

$$X = \frac{1}{6A} \sum (x_i + x_{i+1}) * (x_i * y_{i+1} - x_{i+1} * y_i)$$

$$Y = \frac{1}{6A} \sum (y_i + y_{i+1}) * (x_i * y_{i+1} - x_{i+1} * y_i)$$

Here A is the area of the polygon and Σ means to take the sum over all of the adjacent pairs of points in the polygon.

> **NOTE:** I've had trouble finding a good explanation of why these formulas work. I found a reasonable description online, but then the page disappeared. It reappeared in an archive but then it later disappeared again.
>
> For a reasonably understandable explanation, see the Math StackExchange post at `tinyurl.com/kd5v97a`. Hopefully that one will stick around.

Notice that the term inside the right pair of parentheses is the same in both the X and Y formulas. In the following code, which the program uses to find the polygon's centroid, that common value is saved in the variable `secondFactor`.

```
// Find the polygon's centroid.
private PointF FindCentroid(List<Point> points)
{
    int numPoints = points.Count;
    if (numPoints < 3) return new PointF(
        float.NegativeInfinity,
        float.NegativeInfinity);

    // Find the centroid.
    float X = 0;
```

```
        float Y = 0;
        float secondFactor;
        for (int i = 0; i < numPoints; i++)
        {
            int j = (i + 1) % numPoints;
            secondFactor =
                points[i].X * points[j].Y -
                points[j].X * points[i].Y;
            X += (points[i].X + points[j].X) * secondFactor;
            Y += (points[i].Y + points[j].Y) * secondFactor;
        }

        // Divide by -6 times the polygon's area.
        float polygon_area = SignedPolygonArea(points);
        X /= -(6 * polygon_area);
        Y /= -(6 * polygon_area);

        return new PointF(X, Y);
    }
```

The code first determines the number of points in the polygon. If the `points` list holds fewer than three points, then this isn't a polygon so the method simply returns.

The method then loops through the polygon's points adding the values shown in the equations above. The program saves the common value in variable `secondFactor` so it only needs to calculate it once. It also doesn't divide each term by 6A.

After the program finishes adding up all of the terms, the initial sums are positive if the polygon is oriented clockwise and negative if it's oriented counter clockwise.

The `SignedPolygonArea` method does the opposite: it returns a negative value if the polygon is oriented clockwise and a positive value if it's oriented counter clockwise.

That means if you divide the sums by 6A, the results are always negatives of the correct coordinates.

This is caused by the fact that Y coordinates increase downward in C# bitmaps but the formulas were designed by mathematicians who like Y to increase upward. To resolve this issue, the program divides the sums by -6A. (I considered modifying the formulas so the summations switched the sign, but decided to stick with the formulas you'll find elsewhere on the internet such as Wikipedia.)

As you click on the form to define the polygon's points, the program draws the points, the polygon, and the centroid.

63. SEE IF A POLYGON IS CONVEX (83)

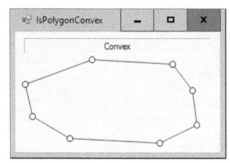

One way to see if a polygon is convex is to calculate the angles at each of the polygon's corners. If all of the angles have the same sign, either positive or negative depending on the orientation, then the polygon is convex.

Rather than actually finding the angles, you can simply find the cross products of the segments on either side of the angles. If the segments at point B are AB and BC, then the cross product written AB×BC has value |AB|*|BC|*Sin(θ) where |AB| means the length of segment AB and θ is the angle between the two segments.

Because lengths are always positive, the result is positive if Sin(θ) is positive, and that happens if θ is positive.

This example uses the following `IsConvex` method to determine whether a polygon is convex.

```
// Return true if the polygon is convex.
private bool IsConvex(List<Point> points)
{
    bool gotNegative = false;
    bool gotPositive = false;
    int numPoints = points.Count;
    for (int A = 0; A < numPoints; A++)
    {
        int B = (A + 1) % numPoints;
        int C = (B + 1) % numPoints;

        float crossProduct =
            CrossProductLength(
                points[A].X, points[A].Y,
                points[B].X, points[B].Y,
                points[C].X, points[C].Y);
        if (crossProduct < 0) gotNegative = true;
        else if (crossProduct > 0) gotPositive = true;

        if (gotNegative && gotPositive) return false;
    }

    // If we got this far, the polygon is convex.
    return true;
}
```

This method loops through the polygon's points. For each point A, it finds the indices of the following two points B and C. It then uses the `CrossProductLength` method described shortly to calculate AB×BC.

As it loops through the points, the code keeps track of whether it has found positive or negative cross products. If it has found both, then the method returns `false` to indicate that the polygon is not convex. If the code never finds both positive and negative cross products, it returns true to indicate that the polygon is convex.

The following code shows the CrossProductLength method.

```
// Return the cross product AB x BC.
public static float CrossProductLength(float Ax, float Ay,
    float Bx, float By, float Cx, float Cy)
{
    // Get the vectors' coordinates.
    float BAx = Ax - Bx;
    float BAy = Ay - By;
    float BCx = Cx - Bx;
    float BCy = Cy - By;

    // Calculate the Z coordinate of the cross product.
    return (BAx * BCy - BAy * BCx);
}
```

For more information on the cross product and how it is calculated, see the Math Is Fun web page tinyurl.com/oevtrts.

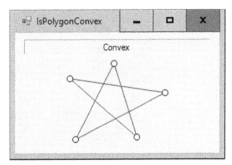

Note that the definition of convex for self-intersecting polygons is a bit fuzzy. If you interpret convex to mean that all angles have the same signs, then this example works just fine. That means, for example, that the star on the right is convex.

If you want convex to mean that the polygon has no "inner corners" like those that a star defines implicitly, then the method described here doesn't work for self-intersecting polygons. In that case, you should probably just check for self-intersection separately.

Part XIV. Algorithms

Algorithms are the recipes that make programs work. Some algorithms are relatively simple or do trivial things, but where's the fun in that? My favorite algorithms are complicated and perform difficult tasks. For example, I find it fascinating when you dump a bunch of numbers into a ray tracing algorithm and have a realistic three-dimensional scene pop out. Or when you click and drag to zoom in on the Mandelbrot set.

I've actually written several books about algorithms. The most recent is *Essential Algorithms: A Practical Approach to Computer Algorithms* (Rod Stephens, Wiley, 2013). You can learn more about it on its web page www.CSharpHelper.com/algorithms.html.

This part of this book describes a few of C# Helper's most popular algorithmic examples that didn't fit well in other parts of the book.

64. GENERATE PERMUTATIONS OF OBJECTS (16)

The permutations of a set of items include all of the possible arrangements of those items. For example, if the items are the letters A, B, and C, then their permutations are ABC, ACB, BAC, BCA, CAB, and CBA.

If you have N items, then there are N! possible permutations. (Here N! means "N factorial" and equals $N \times (N-1) \times (N-2) \times ... \times 2 \times 1$.

The basic idea behind this example is to use a recursive method to assign the next item in a permutation. The first call to the method assigns the permutation's first item, the next call assigns the second item, and so forth.

To assign an item, the method loops through all of the objects looking for those that have not already been assigned. When it finds such an item, the method performs the following steps.

➢ Adds the item to the current permutation.
➢ Marks the item as used in the current permutation.
➢ Recursively calls itself to assign the next item in the current permutation.
➢ When the recursive call returns, the method unmarks the item so it can be used again later.

The methods used by this program are generic, so they can find permutations for any kind of item. This example uses strings because strings are easy to enter on the form, but you can use the same methods to permute just about anything.

When you click the Go button, the program uses the following code to generate the items' permutations.

```
// Generate the permutations.
private void goButton_Click(object sender, EventArgs e)
{
    // Get the items.
    string[] items = itemsTextBox.Text.Split(' ');

    // Generate the permutations.
    List<List<string>> results =
        GeneratePermutations<string>(items.ToList());

    // Display the results.
    permutationsListBox.Items.Clear();
    foreach (List<string> combination in results)
    {
        permutationsListBox.Items.Add(string.Join(" ", combination.ToArray()));
    }
```

```
// Calculate the number of permutations.
long numPermutations = Factorial(items.Length);
numPermutationsTextBox.Text = numPermutations.ToString();

// Check the result.
Debug.Assert(permutationsListBox.Items.Count == numPermutations);
}
```

This code makes a list containing the words that you entered. It calls the
GeneratePermutations method to build the permutations and then displays the results.

The following GeneratePermutations method really just sets up and then calls the
PermuteItems method described shortly to do the real work.

```
// Generate permutations.
private List<List<T>> GeneratePermutations<T>(List<T> items)
{
    // Make an array to hold the permutation we are building.
    T[] currentPermutation = new T[items.Count];

    // Make an array to tell whether an item is in the current selection.
    bool[] inSelection = new bool[items.Count];

    // Make a result list.
    List<List<T>> results = new List<List<T>>();

    // Build the combinations recursively.
    PermuteItems<T>(items, inSelection,
        currentPermutation, results, 0);

    // Return the results.
    return results;
}
```

This method creates the currentPermutation array to hold the current permutation and
the inSelection array to indicate which items are in the current permutation. It then calls
the following PermuteItems method, telling it to assign the first item.

```
// Recursively permute the items that are not yet in the current selection.
private void PermuteItems<T>(List<T> items, bool[] inSelection,
    T[] currentPermutation, List<List<T>> results, int nextPosition)
{
    // See if all of the positions are filled.
    if (nextPosition == items.Count)
    {
        // All of the positioned are filled.
        // Save this permutation.
        results.Add(currentPermutation.ToList());
    }
    else
    {
        // Try options for the next position.
        for (int i = 0; i < items.Count; i++)
        {
            if (!inSelection[i])
            {
                // Add this item to the current permutation.
                inSelection[i] = true;
```

```
                currentPermutation[nextPosition] = items[i];

                // Recursively fill the remaining positions.
                PermuteItems<T>(items, inSelection,
                    currentPermutation, results, nextPosition + 1);

                // Remove the item from the current permutation.
                inSelection[i] = false;
            }
        }
    }
}
```

This method first checks whether the current permutation is full. If so, it adds the permutation to the results list and returns.

If the current permutation is not full, the code loops through the items. When it finds an item that is not yet in the permutation, the method adds that item to the permutation and then calls itself recursively to fill in the rest of the permutation.

When the recursive call returns, the method unmarks the item that it just added and continues looping through the remaining items.

65. GENERATE A ROUND ROBIN TOURNAMENT SCHEDULE (70)

In a round robin tournament, every team plays every other team. In large tournaments, teams are divided into pools and the teams in each pool play a round robin. Then the pool winners go on to single- or double-elimination playoffs.

Most tournament directors just go online and download a round robin schedule for the number of teams that are playing. If you're pressed for time, by all means do that, but if you have the time, writing your own program is more interesting and fun! (At least for a certain definition of "fun.")

This example uses an algorithm described at The Math Forum (tinyurl.com/kmf5n46). This algorithm assumes that there are enough fields (or courts or whatever) for every team to be able to play at the same time. For example, if you're scheduling a six team round robin volleyball pool, then you need at least three courts. If you don't have enough courts (which is typical at a volleyball tournament), then some teams will need to wait until a court becomes available.

The following GenerateRoundRobinOdd method returns an array where results[i, j] gives the opponent of team i in round j of the round robin tournament. This method only works if the number of teams is odd (hence the method's name). The Math Forum post mentioned above explains the algorithm.

```
// Return an array where results(i, j) gives the opponent of team i in round j.
// Note: numTeams must be odd.
private int[,] GenerateRoundRobinOdd(int numTeams)
{
    int n2 = (int)((numTeams - 1) / 2);
    int[,] results = new int[numTeams, numTeams];

    // Initialize the list of teams.
    int[] teams = new int[numTeams];
    for (int i = 0; i < numTeams; i++) teams[i] = i;

    // Start the rounds.
    for (int round = 0; round < numTeams; round++)
    {
        for (int i = 0; i < n2; i++)
        {
            int team1 = teams[n2 - i];
            int team2 = teams[n2 + i + 1];
            results[team1, round] = team2;
            results[team2, round] = team1;
```

```
        }

        // Set the team with the bye.
        results[teams[0], round] = Bye;

        // Rotate the array.
        RotateArray(teams);
    }

    return results;
}
```

Because this method assumes there are an odd number of teams, one team will have a bye (not play anyone) in each round.

The following `RotateArray` helper method rotates the items in the `team` array one position to the right. The algorithm calls this routine after each round.

```
// Rotate the entries one position.
private void RotateArray(int[] teams)
{
    int tmp = teams[teams.Length - 1];
    Array.Copy(teams, 0, teams, 1, teams.Length - 1);
    teams[0] = tmp;
}
```

This method saves the last item in the array, uses `Array.Copy` to copy the other array entries one position to the right, and then inserts the saved item at the beginning of the array.

The following `GenerateRoundRobinEven` method builds an array holding the pairings for an even number of teams.

```
// Return an array where results(i, j) gives opponent of team i in round j.
// Note: numTeams must be even.
private int[,] GenerateRoundRobinEven(int numTeams)
{
    // Generate the result for one fewer teams.
    int[,] results = GenerateRoundRobinOdd(numTeams - 1);

    // Copy the results into a bigger array,
    // replacing the byes with the extra team.
    int[,] results2 = new int[numTeams, numTeams - 1];
    for (int team = 0; team < numTeams - 1; team++)
    {
        for (int round = 0; round < numTeams - 1; round++)
        {
            if (results[team, round] == Bye)
            {
                // Change the bye to the new team.
                results2[team, round] = numTeams - 1;
                results2[numTeams - 1, round] = team;
            }
            else
            {
                results2[team, round] = results[team, round];
            }
```

```
            }
        }

        return results2;
    }
```

This method calls GenerateRoundRobinOdd to make a schedule for a tournament with one fewer team than is actually present. It then expands the result array and replaces the byes with the additional team. See the Math Forum post for a more complete explanation.

Finally, the GenerateRoundRobin method simply calls the GenerateRoundRobinOdd or GenerateRoundRobinEven methods depending on whether the number of teams is odd or even.

```
// Return an array where results(i, j) gives the opponent of team i in round j.
private int[,] GenerateRoundRobin(int numTeams)
{
    if (numTeams % 2 == 0)
        return GenerateRoundRobinEven(numTeams);
    else
        return GenerateRoundRobinOdd(numTeams);
}
```

The rest of this example simply displays the results and isn't very interesting. Download the example if you want to see the details.

66. DRAW A FAMILY TREE (82)

The original C# Helper post for this example was the end of a series of posts that explained how to draw a tree containing arbitrary objects such as text or pictures. Here I'll describe all of the key techniques explained in those posts and that are used by this example. This is a big example, so I'll describe it in pieces.

Classes

The DrawableTree class represents a tree. It provides top-level methods for arranging the the objects that it contains. The class is generic, so it can draw all sorts of objects, but those objects must provide a few features that a DrawableTree needs to arrange the objects. The IDrawable interface defines those features.

The DrawableTreeNode class represents an object in the tree. It is also generic and holds the IDrawable objects that the tree will draw.

The DrawablePerson class is the specific kind of object that this example arranges in the tree. This class holds a person's name and picture.

The following sections describe these classes in greater detail.

IDrawable

The following `IDrawable` interface defines the features that the objects must provide for the tree.

```
// Represents something that a DrawableTreeNode can draw.
public interface IDrawable
{
    // Set the object's required size.
    void SetSize(Graphics gr, Font font);

    // Return the object's required size.
    SizeF Size { get; }

    // Return true if the node is above this point.
    bool IsAtPoint(PointF center, PointF point);

    // Draw the object.
    void Draw(PointF center, Graphics gr,
        Pen pen, Brush bgBrush, Brush textBrush, Font font);
}
```

The `SetSize` method should figure out how much room the object needs. The read-only `Size` property returns the size calculated by `SetSize`.

The `IsAtPoint` method should return `true` if the object is at a particular point. The point `center` tells the object where it will be positioned.

The `Draw` method should draw the object centered at the indicated point.

This example passes the `Draw` method pens and brushes for the object to use, but you could modify the program to allow each object to use its own pen and brush.

DrawablePerson

The `DrawablePerson` class draws the picture of a person for the family tree. It also defines a `Description` field that holds a person's name.

If you modify the example to draw something else, such as a paragraph of text, you would replace `DrawablePerson` with your own class to represent whatever you want to draw.

The class is fairly long so I'll only touch on the highlights instead of showing you every line of code.

The following `FitRectangle` method returns the largest rectangle that fits within a bounding rectangle and that has the same aspect ratio as the picture.

```
// Return the biggest rectangle that fits within bounds
// and that has the same aspect ratio as the picture.
private RectangleF FitRectangle(Image picture, RectangleF bounds)
{
    // Get the X and Y scales.
```

```
float picWid = picture.Width;
float picHgt = picture.Height;
float picAspect = picWid / picHgt;
float rectAspect = bounds.Width / bounds.Height;
float scale = 1;
if (picAspect > rectAspect)
    scale = bounds.Width / picWid;
else
    scale = bounds.Height / picHgt;

// See where we need to draw.
picWid *= scale;
picHgt *= scale;
RectangleF drawingRect = new RectangleF(
    bounds.X + (bounds.Width - picWid) / 2,
    bounds.Y + (bounds.Height - picHgt) / 2,
    picWid, picHgt);
return drawingRect;
}
```

The DrawablePerson class uses the following code to calculate its size.

```
// The size of the drawn rectangles.
public SizeF NodeSize = new SizeF(100, 100);

// Set the object's required size.
public void SetSize(Graphics gr, Font font)
{
    // Pick a size at most 100x100 with the same aspect ratio as the picture.
    RectangleF rect = FitRectangle(Picture, new RectangleF(0, 0, 100, 100));
    NodeSize = rect.Size;
}
```

The NodeSize field stores the person's size. In this example, each person's entry must fit within a 100×100 pixel rectangle.

The SetSize method calls the FitRectangle method to find a rectangle that fits the picture and that is no more than 100 pixels on a side. It saves that rectangle's size in the NodeSize field.

The following code shows how the DrawablePerson class implements its IsAtPoint method.

```
// Return a RectangleF giving the node's location.
private RectangleF Location(PointF center)
{
    return new RectangleF(
        center.X - NodeSize.Width / 2,
        center.Y - NodeSize.Height / 2,
        NodeSize.Width, NodeSize.Height);
}

// Return True if the target is under this node.
public bool IsAtPoint(PointF center, PointF point)
{
    RectangleF rect = Location(center);
    return rect.Contains(point);
}
```

The `Location` helper method makes a rectangle for the object at a given location. The `IsAtPoint` method calls `Location` to get that rectangle. It then calls the rectangle's `Contains` method to determine whether the point lies inside the rectangle and returns the result.

The following code shows the `DrawablePerson` class's last interesting piece of code, the `Draw` method.

```
// Draw the person.
public void Draw(PointF center, Graphics gr,
    Pen pen, Brush bgBrush, Brush textBrush, Font font)
{
    // Draw a border.
    RectangleF rectf = Location(center);
    Rectangle rect = Rectangle.Round(rectf);
    if (Selected)
    {
        gr.FillRectangle(Brushes.White, rect);
        ControlPaint.DrawBorder3D(gr, rect,
            Border3DStyle.Sunken);
    }
    else
    {
        gr.FillRectangle(Brushes.LightGray, rect);
        ControlPaint.DrawBorder3D(gr, rect,
            Border3DStyle.Raised);
    }

    // Draw the picture.
    rectf.Inflate(-5, -5);
    rectf = FitRectangle(Picture, rectf);
    gr.DrawImage(Picture, rectf);
}
```

The `Draw` method creates a rectangle at the node's location. Depending on whether the object is selected, it fills the rectangle with either white or light gray. It then uses the `ControlPaint` class's static `DrawBorder3D` method to draw a three-dimensional border.

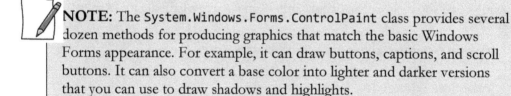

NOTE: The `System.Windows.Forms.ControlPaint` class provides several dozen methods for producing graphics that match the basic Windows Forms appearance. For example, it can draw buttons, captions, and scroll buttons. It can also convert a base color into lighter and darker versions that you can use to draw shadows and highlights.

The code then shrinks the rectangle by five pixels and draws the object's picture in it.

DrawableTreeNode

A `DrawableTreeNode` object represents a node in the tree. It contains the `IDrawable` object that it should draw. In this example, that's a `DrawablePerson` object.

This class is even longer than the `DrawablePerson` class so again I'll just cover the highlights.

The class performs three main tasks: sizing nodes, arranging nodes, and drawing nodes. Each of those tasks is performed recursively. For example, if the program calls the `Arrange` method for a node, that method also recursively arranges the descendant nodes in the node's subtree.

The following code shows the class's `SetSizes` method.

```
// Set the node's size and the size of its children.
public void SetSizes(Graphics gr, Font font)
{
    // Set the node's size.
    Data.SetSize(gr, font);

    // Set the children's sizes.
    foreach (DrawableTreeNode<T> child in Children)
        child.SetSizes(gr, font);
}
```

This method calls the `SetSize` method for the `IDrawable` object that this node represents. It then loops through its child nodes and recursively calls their `SetSizes` methods. When the method returns, all of the `SetSize` methods for the node's descendants will have been called.

The `Arrange` method is fairly long and involved so I won't include its code here. However, the idea isn't too complicated so I'll at least give you an overview.

The method takes as parameters two coordinates x and y passed by reference. Initially those values give the coordinates of the upper left corner of the area where the subtree will be drawn.

The method arranges the subtree below the `DrawableTreeNode` to the right and below the position (x, y).

When it returns, the method leaves x holding the rightmost coordinate needed by this node and its subtree. For example, if x is initially 100 and this node's subtree is 250 pixels wide, then x is 350 when the method returns.

The method also updates y. When it returns, y holds the largest Y coordinate needed by this subtree.

The `Arrange` method for a node first gets the size required by its own data object, which in this example is a `DrawablePerson`. The code then loops through the node's children and recursively calls their Arrange methods to make them arrange themselves. The method simply adds the child subtree widths to the variable x.

If a child's subtree is taller than the tallest subtree seen so far, the Arrange method updates the y variable.

After the Arrange method has finished recursively arranging the node's subtree, it calculates the position where the original node must be placed to center it over its subtree. It saves that value in a PointF variable named Center.

The DrawTree method shown in the following code draws a node and its subtree.

```
// Draw the subtree rooted at this node.
public void DrawTree(Graphics gr, Pen pen, Brush bgBrush,
    Brush textBrush, Font font)
{
    // Draw the links.
    DrawSubtreeLinks(gr, pen);

    // Draw the nodes.
    DrawSubtreeNodes(gr, pen, bgBrush, textBrush, font);
}
```

This method calls the DrawSubtreeLinks method to draw the links that connect the nodes in this subtree. It then calls DrawSubtreeNodes to draw the subtree nodes.

The DrawSubtreeLinks and DrawSubtreeNodes methods are long but fairly straightforward so I won't show them here. They just recursively crawl over the subtree and draw the links or nodes.

Notice that the DrawTree method is not recursive. It just calls the DrawSubtreeLinks and DrawSubtreeNodes methods (which *are* recursive) and doesn't call itself. The main program calls the root node's DrawTree method to draw the whole tree.

The final interesting piece to the DrawableTreeNode class is the following NodeAtPoint method.

```
// Return the DrawableTreeNode at this point (or null if there isn't one there).
public DrawableTreeNode<T> NodeAtPoint(PointF point)
{
    // See if the point is under this node.
    if (Data.IsAtPoint(Center, point)) return this;

    // See if the point is under a node in the subtree.
    foreach (DrawableTreeNode<T> child in Children)
    {
        DrawableTreeNode<T> hitNode = child.NodeAtPoint(point);
        if (hitNode != null) return hitNode;
    }

    return null;
}
```

This method calls its `Data` object's `IsNodeAt` method. If the data object's position includes the target point, the code returns the node object that is currently executing the method.

If the target point is not at the current node's position, the method loops through the node's children and recursively calls their `NodeAtPoint` methods. If any of those calls finds a node at the target point, then this method returns that node.

If none of the calls to `NodeAtPoint` returns a node, then the point is not under any of the nodes in this node's subtree, so the method returns `null`.

Main Program

The main program uses the following code to declare and initialize the tree's root node.

```
// The root node.
private DrawableTreeNode<DrawablePerson> root =
    new DrawableTreeNode<DrawablePerson>(
        new DrawablePerson(
            "Queen Elizabeth II && Prince Philip Duke of Edinburgh",
            Properties.Resources.Elizabeth_Philip));
```

This code creates a new `DrawableTreeNode<DrawablePerson>` object. This is a `DrawableTreeNode` that can hold a `DrawablePerson`. It initializes the node to hold the picture and names of Queen Elizabeth II & Prince Philip.

The form's `Load` event handler creates the other nodes similarly. It then uses the following code to build the tree's structure.

```
root.AddChild(charles);
charles.AddChild(william);
charles.AddChild(harry);
root.AddChild(anne);
anne.AddChild(peter);
anne.AddChild(zara);
root.AddChild(andrew);
andrew.AddChild(beatrice);
andrew.AddChild(eugenie);
...
ArrangeTree();
```

This code just calls the nodes' `AddChild` methods to add child nodes to their parent nodes' `Children` collections. The code finishes by calling the following `ArrangeTree` method.

```
private void ArrangeTree()
{
    using (Graphics gr = treePictureBox.CreateGraphics())
    {
        // Size the tree's nodes.
        root.SetSizes(gr, Font);

        // Arrange the tree once to see how big it is.
        float xmin = 0, ymin = 0;
        root.Arrange(ref xmin, ref ymin);
```

```
            // Arrange the tree again to center it horizontally.
            xmin = (this.ClientSize.Width - xmin) / 2;
            ymin = 10;
            root.Arrange(ref xmin, ref ymin);
        }

        treePictureBox.Refresh();
    }
```

This method first calls the root node's `SetSize` method to recursively set all of the nodes' sizes.

Next it sets variables x and y to 0 to indicate the upper left corner of the form's `PictureBox` and passes them by reference into the root node's `Arrange` method. That method recursively arranges the tree's nodes and leaves x and y holding the largest X and Y coordinates that the tree needs to use, assuming its upper left corner is at position (0, 0).

The method then calculates the X coordinate that it needs to use to center the tree on the form's `PictureBox` and calls the root node's `Arrange` method again to put the nodes in their final positions.

The following code shows the `Paint` event handler used by the program's `PictureBox`.

```
    // Draw the tree.
    private void treePictureBox_Paint(object sender, PaintEventArgs e)
    {
        e.Graphics.SmoothingMode = SmoothingMode.AntiAlias;
        e.Graphics.TextRenderingHint = TextRenderingHint.AntiAliasGridFit;
        using (Font font = new Font("Times New Roman", 10))
        {
            root.DrawTree(e.Graphics, Pens.Black, Brushes.White,
                Brushes.Black, font);
        }
    }
```

This code sets some `Graphics` object properties to produce smooth graphics. It then creates a font and calls the root node's `DrawTree` method.

When the user clicks on the tree, the following code selects the clicked node.

```
    // The currently selected node.
    private DrawableTreeNode<DrawablePerson> SelectedNode;

    private void picTree_MouseClick(object sender, MouseEventArgs e)
    {
        FindNodeUnderMouse(e.Location);
    }

    // Set SelectedNode to the node under the mouse.
    private void FindNodeUnderMouse(PointF pt)
    {
        // Deselect the previously selected node.
        if (SelectedNode != null)
        {
            SelectedNode.Data.Selected = false;
            nodeTextLabel.Text = "";
```

```
    }

    // Find the node at this position (if any).
    SelectedNode = root.NodeAtPoint(pt);

    // Select the node.
    if (SelectedNode != null)
    {
        SelectedNode.Data.Selected = true;
        nodeTextLabel.Text = SelectedNode.Data.Description;
    }

    // Redraw.
    treePictureBox.Refresh();
}
```

The `SelectedNode` variable keeps track of the currently selected node, if one is selected.

The `PictureBox` control's `MouseClick` event handler calls the `FindNodeUnderMouse` method, which does all of the interesting work.

The `FindNodeUnderMouse` method deselects the previously selected node if there is such a node. It then calls the root node's `NodeAtPoint` method to find the point, if any, at the mouse's current position. If there is a node at this point, the code selects it and displays that node's description.

The method finishes by refreshing the program's `PictureBox` to redraw the tree.

Summary

This is a long example, but it demonstrates some useful techniques. It uses recursive methods in several places to traverse the tree's nodes.

It also calls related methods in a particular order to avoid unwanted effects. For example, it draws links between nodes before it draws the nodes so the links don't appear on top of the nodes.

Similarly, it sizes nodes before arranging them. By making sizing and arranging two separate steps, the program reduces the number of times it must size its nodes.

Real family tree software provides many extra features to handle things such as couples, divorces, remarriages, stepchildren, and more. The example shown here simply draws a tree.

Download the example to see additional details.

Part XV. Three-Dimensional Programs

Three-dimensional programs are a lot of fun to write and play with, but they come with a moderately steep learning curve. This is one place where WPF actually helps. It doesn't make the mathematics any easier, it uses some extremely verbose XAML code, and you still need a good understanding of how to orient shapes in three dimensions, but at least WPF provides a framework that helps get you started.

The examples in this part of the book introduce three-dimensional programming with WPF and C#. They show how to build simple shapes, apply textures, draw surfaces, and display wireframes.

67. ROTATE A THREE-DIMENSIONAL CUBE WITH WPF (27)

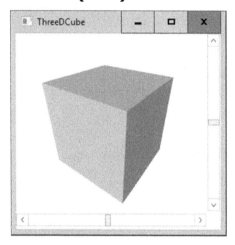

This example shows how you can write a WPF program that displays and rotates a three-dimensional cube using only XAML. It displays a yellow cube and scroll bars that you can use to rotate the cube and view it from different directions.

The program uses XAML code to do everything. The XAML code defines the cube's data, creates the scrollbars, and rotates the cube when you adjust the scrollbars.

The XAML code is pretty long so I'll describe only the most important sections of the code and I'll describe them in pieces.

The program's window contains a `Grid` control with two rows and two columns. The vertical scrollbar occupies the right column's first row. The horizontal scrollbar sits in the bottom row's first column.

The grid's upper left cell contains a `Viewport3D` object, and that's where things get interesting. A `Viewport3D` provides a surface where the program can display three-dimensional objects. You can think of it as a window or viewport on a spaceship that lets you peek through your computer's monitor into a three-dimensional world.

The following code shows how the program defines the `Viewport3D` object and its contents.

```
<Viewport3D Margin="4,4,4,4" Grid.Row="0" Grid.Column="0">
    <Viewport3D.Camera>
        <PerspectiveCamera
            Position = "0, 2, 3"
            LookDirection = "0, -2, -3"
            UpDirection = "0, 1, 0"
            FieldOfView = "60">
        </PerspectiveCamera>
    </Viewport3D.Camera>

    <ModelVisual3D>
        <ModelVisual3D.Content>
            <Model3DGroup>
                <!-- Lights -->
                <AmbientLight Color="Gray" />
                <DirectionalLight Color="Gray" Direction="1,-2,-3" />
                <DirectionalLight Color="Gray" Direction="-1,2,3" />

                <GeometryModel3D>
```

```
                    <GeometryModel3D.Transform>
                        <Transform3DGroup>
                            <RotateTransform3D>
                                <RotateTransform3D.Rotation>
                                    <AxisAngleRotation3D
                                        Axis="0 1 0"
            Angle="{Binding ElementName=hscroll, Path=Value}" />
                                </RotateTransform3D.Rotation>
                            </RotateTransform3D>
                            <RotateTransform3D>
                                <RotateTransform3D.Rotation>
                                    <AxisAngleRotation3D
                                        Axis="1 0 0"
            Angle="{Binding ElementName=vscroll, Path=Value}" />
                                </RotateTransform3D.Rotation>
                            </RotateTransform3D>
                        </Transform3DGroup>
                    </GeometryModel3D.Transform>

                    <GeometryModel3D.Geometry>
                        <!-- Cube -->
                        <MeshGeometry3D
                            Positions="
                                -1,-1,-1    1,-1,-1    1,-1, 1  -1,-1, 1
                                -1,-1, 1    1,-1, 1    1, 1, 1  -1, 1, 1
                                 1,-1, 1    1,-1,-1    1, 1,-1   1, 1, 1
                                 1, 1, 1    1, 1,-1   -1, 1,-1  -1, 1, 1
                                -1,-1, 1   -1, 1, 1   -1, 1,-1  -1,-1,-1
                                -1,-1,-1   -1, 1,-1    1, 1,-1   1,-1,-1
                                "

                            TriangleIndices="
                                0   1  2     2  3  0
                                4   5  6     6  7  4
                                8   9 10    10 11  8
                                12 13 14    14 15 12
                                16 17 18    18 19 16
                                20 21 22    22 23 20
                                " />
                    </GeometryModel3D.Geometry>

                    <GeometryModel3D.Material>
                        <DiffuseMaterial Brush="Yellow" />
                    </GeometryModel3D.Material>
                </GeometryModel3D>
            </Model3DGroup>
        </ModelVisual3D.Content>
    </ModelVisual3D>
</Viewport3D>
```

The viewport determines where you are looking in the three-dimensional scene. To extend the spaceship analogy, it determines where the spaceship's window is and the direction it is facing.

The viewport's Camera property determines the position and direction in which you're looking. (Perhaps you should stop thinking about a spaceship viewport and think of a camera attached to the side of the spaceship.)

This example uses a `PerspectiveCamera`. That object represents a perspective projection so objects farther away from the camera's position appear smaller than objects that are closer.

> **NOTE:** WPF also has an `OrthographicCamera` class that does not provide perspective. In an orthographic projection, objects that are the same size appear at the same size regardless of their distances from the camera.

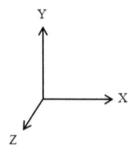

The `PerspectiveCamera` object uses several properties to determine its position and orientation. The `Position` property gives the camera's X, Y, and Z coordinates. In this example, the camera is at position (0, 2, 3).

Like many other graphics systems, WPF use a coordinate system with the axes orientated as shown in the picture on the left. The Y axis points up, the X axis points to the right, and the Z axis points out of the page toward you.

The camera's `LookDirection` property determines the camera's direction. The value <0, -2, -3> used by this example means the camera is pointed from its position back toward the origin.

The `UpDirection` property determines the direction that is "up" for the camera. (Imagine holding a camera tilted at an angle so the resulting photo looks tilted.)

The picture on the left shows how the `LookDirection` and `UpDirection` properties determine the camera's orientation.

The camera's `FieldOfView` property determines the camera's horizontal field of view in degrees.

After it defines the camera, the viewport defines its contents, which in this example is a `ModelVisual3D` object. That object contains a `Model3DGroup`.

The group first defines some lights. The `AmbientLight` represents a directionless light that fills the entire scene. Ambient light is basically what lets you see under your desk even though no light actually shines directly under there.

The next two lights are directional. They represent light starting from a source such as the sun that's infinitely faraway and shining in a particular direction.

The lights are all gray. That means that they have neutral colors (as opposed to a red or yellow tint) and medium intensity.

NOTE: In most scenes you need to use multiple light sources to produce a result that looks good. Their colors add when they shine on the same surface, so you usually cannot give the lights full intensity without making the scene appear too bright and washed out.

Next, the `ModelVisual3D` object defines a `GeometryModel3D`. This is a model that can render a three-dimensional object with a material. I'll get to the example's material shortly, but in general materials determine an object's color, texture, reflectivity, and other surface characteristics.

NOTE: A `GeometryModel3D` can define only one geometry and only one material. If you want to make multiple objects with different materials, such as red and blue cubes or a single cube with differently colored sides, then you need to use more than one `GeometryModel3D` object.

The `GeometryModel3D` object begins with a transformation group that contains two rotation transformations. The first rotates the geometric model around the Y axis. The second rotates it around the X axis.

The rotations' `Angle` properties are bound to the program's two scroll bars' `Value` properties. When you adjust a scrollbar's value, the rotations automatically update.

After the transform, the geometry model sets its actual `Geometry` property to a `MeshGeometry3D` object. A `MeshGeometry3D` object defines the triangles that make up a three-dimensional shape.

NOTE: A three-dimensional scene is always made up of triangles. Any other shape, such as a rectangle, circle, or sphere, is made up of triangles.

The `Positions` collection holds the coordinates of the points that make up the triangles.

The `Triangles` collection contains the indices of the points that make up the triangles. For example, the collection starts with the indices 0, 1, and 2. That means points 0, 1, and 2 in the `Positions` collection make up a triangle.

Note that the points that define a triangle must be *outwardly oriented*. That means if you look at the triangle from outside of the cube, its points must be ordered in the counterclockwise direction.

The three-dimensional drawing system uses that outward orientation to *cull* triangles that are hidden by the body of an object. For example, if a triangle is on the side of the cube opposite the camera, then its points seem to be oriented in a clockwise direction when seen from the camera. Because the points don't seem to be outwardly oriented, the drawing system concludes that this is a *backface* and doesn't bother to draw it.

 NOTE: If a triangle's orientation is backwards, then it will not be visible when it should be. In this example, pieces of the cube would be missing.

If you look closely at the `Positions` collection in the code, you'll find that each point appears three times. The drawing system uses shared points to make the edges between adjacent triangles smoother. For example, suppose you're drawing a sphere. If adjacent triangles share points, then their edges are drawn smoothly and the resulting sphere looks smooth.

In contrast, the edges of a cube's sides should be sharp. To ensure that the faces of the cube are not blurred together, they must not share vertices. This example gives each face of the cube its own copy of its vertices so they are not shared and the drawing system doesn't try to smooth their boundaries. (The cube looks pretty strange if the sides share points.)

The last piece of XAML code defines the `GeometryModel3D` object's material. This example uses a simple yellow diffuse material.

If this all seems rather complicated, that's because it is. Some of the nesting of objects within other objects seems unnecessary, but the objects that have non-trivial properties such as the `GeometryModel3D` and the lights are complicated because they do complicated things.

Download the example and take some time to study it before you move on to more complicated three-dimensional examples. Try some experiments. For example, try adding a second cube with a different color.

When you're satisfied that you understand how the pieces fit together, you can move on the following examples.

68. APPLY TEXTURES TO A THREE-DIMENSIONAL CUBE (78)

This example demonstrates several important techniques. First, it shows how to use C# code to build three-dimensional scenes. As part of that, the example shows how to write a method that creates a rectangle. Next, it shows how to respond to keyboard events to adjust the viewing position.

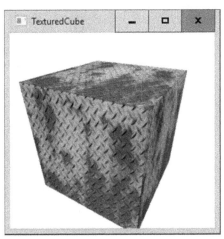

Finally, the example shows how to add textures to a scene's triangles. In this context a *texture* is an image that is mapped onto a scene's surfaces to create a more realistic result than you get from shapes with single colors.

Getting Started

The preceding example used XAML code to build its scene. That works for a simple scene such as a cube, but if you're creating thousands of triangles to define a landscape or mathematical surface, then you probably don't want to create them all by hand in XAML code.

Fortunately, anything you can do in XAML code you can also do in C# code behind. It's often much easier to write code to generate complex scenes than it is to create the scene entirely in XAML code. This example builds a simple cube and, as the preceding example shows, you can certainly do that in XAML code. However, you'll need the technique shown here to build the more complex examples that follow.

This example uses roughly the same objects as the previous one, it just creates many of them in code. The following shows this example's XAML code.

```xml
<Window x:Class="howto_wpf_textures.Window1"
    xmlns="http://schemas.microsoft.com/winfx/2006/xaml/presentation"
    xmlns:x="http://schemas.microsoft.com/winfx/2006/xaml"
    Title="howto_wpf_textures"
    Height="500" Width="500"
    Loaded="Window_Loaded"
    KeyDown="Window_KeyDown">
    <Grid>
        <Viewport3D Grid.Row="0" Grid.Column="0" Name="MainViewport" />
    </Grid>
</Window>
```

All this code does is define two event handlers, `Window_Loaded` and `Window_KeyDown`, and create a `Viewport3D` object named `MainViewport`.

The example's C# code creates the rest of the objects. Those objects' classes are defined in the System.Windows.Media.Media3D namespace, so the program includes the following using directive.

```
using System.Windows.Media.Media3D;
```

The following code shows how the program gets started.

```
// The main object model group.
private Model3DGroup MainModel3Dgroup = new Model3DGroup();

// The camera.
private PerspectiveCamera TheCamera;

// The camera's current location.
private double CameraPhi = Math.PI / 6.0;        // 30 degrees
private double CameraTheta = Math.PI / 3.0;      // 60 degrees
private double CameraR = 5.0;

// The change in CameraPhi when you press the up and down arrows.
private const double CameraDPhi = 0.1;

// The change in CameraTheta when you press the left and right arrows.
private const double CameraDTheta = 0.1;

// The change in CameraR when you press + or -.
private const double CameraDR = 0.1;

// Create the scene.
private void Window_Loaded(object sender, RoutedEventArgs e)
{
    // Give the camera its initial position.
    TheCamera = new PerspectiveCamera();
    TheCamera.FieldOfView = 60;
    MainViewport.Camera = TheCamera;
    PositionCamera();

    // Define lights.
    DefineLights();

    // Create the model.
    DefineModel(MainModel3Dgroup);

    // Add the group of models to a ModelVisual3D.
    ModelVisual3D modelVisual = new ModelVisual3D();
    modelVisual.Content = MainModel3Dgroup;

    // Display the main visual to the viewport.
    MainViewport.Children.Add(modelVisual);
}
```

The code begins by defining some variables. It creates a Model3DGroup to hold everything and a PerspectiveCamera to view the model.

The program represents the camera's position in spherical coordinates with the camera's position stored in variables CameraPhi, CameraTheta, and CameraR. (If you don't remember how spherical coordinates work, see Wikipedia's page about them at tinyurl.com/c6qccu3).

The constants `CameraDPhi`, `CameraDTheta`, and `CameraDR` indicate the amounts by which the camera coordinates are modified when you press the arrow keys, +, and -.

The `Window_Loaded` event handler gets everything ready to go. It creates the camera and calls the `PositionCamera` method to set its location, look direction, and up direction. It then calls `DefineLights` to define the scene's lights, and the `DefineModel` method to define the model.

Next, the event handler creates a `ModelVisual3D` object and sets its content to the object `MainModel3Dgroup` that contains the model and lights. It finishes by adding the `ModelVisual3D` to the `Viewport3D` object that was defined by the XAML code.

The `PositionCamera` and `DefineLights` methods are relatively straightforward so I won't include them here. Instead, I want to focus on the code that defines the model.

Defining the Model

The `DefineModel` method shown in the following code simply calls the `MakeMesh` method.

```
// Add the model to the Model3DGroup.
private void DefineModel(Model3DGroup modelGroup)
{
    MakeMesh(modelGroup);
}
```

This may seem like an unnecessary step (in this example it probably is), but I've found it useful. The `DefineModel` method can call several methods to make an assortment of meshes. All of the objects in a mesh share the same material so they can only use one color or texture. That means for more complex scenes the `DefineModel` method may call many other methods to define meshes that use different materials.

The following code shows the `MakeMesh` method that this example uses.

```
// Make a textured cube.
private void MakeMesh(Model3DGroup modelGroup)
{
    // Make a mesh to hold the surface.
    MeshGeometry3D mesh = new MeshGeometry3D();

    // Create the cube's sides.
    Vector3D vx = new Vector3D(2, 0, 0);
    Vector3D vy = new Vector3D(0, 2, 0);
    Vector3D vz = new Vector3D(0, 0, 2);
    AddRectangle(mesh, new Point3D(-1, -1, 1), vx, vy);      // Front.
    AddRectangle(mesh, new Point3D(-1, -1, -1), vz, vy);     // Left.
    AddRectangle(mesh, new Point3D(1, -1, 1), -vz, vy);      // Right.
    AddRectangle(mesh, new Point3D(1, -1, -1), -vx, vy);     // Back.
    AddRectangle(mesh, new Point3D(-1, 1, 1), vx, -vz);      // Top.
```

```
                AddRectangle(mesh, new Point3D(-1, -1, 1), -vz, vx);     // Bottom.

                // Make the surface's material using an image brush.
                ImageBrush metalBrush = new ImageBrush();
                metalBrush.ImageSource =
                    new BitmapImage(new Uri("metal.jpg", UriKind.Relative));
                DiffuseMaterial metalMaterial = new DiffuseMaterial(metalBrush);

                // Make the mesh's model.
                GeometryModel3D surfaceModel = new GeometryModel3D(mesh, metalMaterial);

                // Make the surface visible from both sides.
                //surfaceModel.BackMaterial = metalMaterial;

                // Add the model to the model groups.
                modelGroup.Children.Add(surfaceModel);
            }
```

The method starts by creating a `MeshGeometry3D` object. It then creates the cube's sides.

At some level, everything in the scene is defined by triangles, but it's often useful to make methods to build the model in bigger pieces. To make building the cube easier, I defined an `AddRectangle` method that adds two triangles to make up a rectangle for the model.

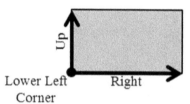

I'll describe the `AddRectangle` method shortly. For now, you need to know that it takes as parameters a point representing the rectangle's lower left corner, and two vectors pointing to the right and up along the rectangle's edges. The picture on the left shows how the lower left corner point and the two vectors define the rectangle.

To make calling `AddRectangle` easier, the `MakeMesh` method defines vectors parallel to the X, Y, and Z axes. It then uses them to create the cube's rectangles.

NOTE: If you need to, you can draw a picture of the scene to figure out how define the rectangles. A quick sketch often makes it much easier to visualize a scene.

After it defines the rectangles, the method creates an `ImageBrush` and sets its source to the picture file `metal.jpg` stored in the project's output directory. It then uses the brush to create a new material.

Next, the method creates a `GeometryModel3D` object holding the mesh and the material.

The next statement, which is commented out, makes the model use the same material for it `BackMaterial` property.

Recall that if the camera sees a triangle's vertices oriented clockwise, then the triangle is a backface, so the drawing system culls the triangle and doesn't draw it. If you give a model a BackMaterial, then the drawing system uses it to draw backfaces instead of culling them.

The BackMaterial is useful if you are drawing a flat surface that has no thickness. Then it lets the camera view the surface from either side. However, a BackMaterial makes the drawing system consider every triangle from both sides, essentially doubling the amount of work that it needs to do. That won't matter in this example because it holds only 12 triangles, but it could limit performance on a big scene containing thousands of triangles. For that reason, it's better if you don't set the BackMaterial property unless you must.

The method finishes by adding the model to the model group.

Creating Rectangles

The following code shows the AddRectangle method.

```
// Add a rectangle to the mesh.
private void AddRectangle(MeshGeometry3D mesh,
    Point3D llCorner, Vector3D right, Vector3D up)
{
    // Get the index of the first point.
    int i = mesh.Positions.Count;

    // Add the points.
    mesh.Positions.Add(llCorner);                    // A = lower left corner.
    mesh.Positions.Add(llCorner + right);            // B = lower right corner.
    mesh.Positions.Add(llCorner + right + up);   // C = upper right corner.
    mesh.Positions.Add(llCorner + up);               // D = upper left corner.

    // Set texture coordinates.
    mesh.TextureCoordinates.Add(new Point(0, 1));    // A
    mesh.TextureCoordinates.Add(new Point(1, 1));    // B
    mesh.TextureCoordinates.Add(new Point(1, 0));    // C
    mesh.TextureCoordinates.Add(new Point(0, 0));    // D

    // Define triangle ABC.
    mesh.TriangleIndices.Add(i);
    mesh.TriangleIndices.Add(i + 1);
    mesh.TriangleIndices.Add(i + 2);

    // Define triangle ACD.
    mesh.TriangleIndices.Add(i);
    mesh.TriangleIndices.Add(i + 2);
    mesh.TriangleIndices.Add(i + 3);
}
```

To add a triangle to a mesh, you first add its vertices to the mesh's Positions collection. You then add the indices of the vertices that define the triangles to the mesh's TriangleVertices collection. This is the same thing the preceding example did in XAML code.

The `AddRectangle` method first records the number of vertices already in the mesh. That number will be the index of the next point added to the `Positions` collection.

Next, the method adds the rectangle's corners to the collection. Notice how the code adds vectors to the rectangle's lower left corner to define the rectangle's corners. A point plus a vector gives the point where you would end up if you started at the original point and then walked down the vector.

> **NOTE:** The `AddRectangle` method lets the rectangle's two triangles share their common vertices. That saves some space and makes the drawing system smooth the triangles' shared edge. The triangles lie in the same plane, so you shouldn't see that edge anyway.

After it defines the rectangle's points, the method sets their texture coordinates. I'll explain that in the next section.

The method finishes by adding the `TriangleIndices` entries that define the rectangle's two triangles.

Defining Texture Coordinates

(0, 0)   (1, 0)

(0, 1)   (1, 1)

The `AddRectangle` method shown in the preceding section sets each vertex's texture coordinates. Those coordinates are measured in the same way that C# measures coordinates in an image with (0, 0) in the upper left corner and coordinates increasing to the right and down. The coordinates are usually referred to as U and V coordinates instead of X and Y coordinates.

The picture on the left shows an image's texture coordinates.

You can look at the `AddRectangle` method again to see how it assigns the texture coordinates for each of the rectangle's vertices.

Due to a weird feature of the way the drawing system colors triangles, it seems to scale the texture coordinates that are *actually used*, so a program uses the entire width and height of the texture. If your triangles use texture coordinates that cover the entire U and V ranges 0 to 1, then the texture isn't scaled (or it's scaled by a factor of 1) so everything is as you would expect.

But suppose you have a single triangle in a mesh and its texture coordinates only span the range $0 \leq U \leq 0.5$ and $0 \leq V \leq 0.5$. In that case, the drawing system "helpfully" scales the coordinates so they use the texture's entire area. Instead of using the image's upper left area, the triangle uses the image's whole surface. (I don't really know why it's doing this. I've messed with the `ImageBrush` object's viewport parameters and haven't been able to find a reasonable solution. If you find one, please post a comment on the book's web page.)

One workaround is to make sure the triangles in the mesh cover the ranges $0 \leq U \leq 1$ and $0 \leq V \leq 1$. Another solution is to crop the texture image so it only includes the parts of the texture that you actually want to use.

Handling Keyboard Events

The following code handles the program's KeyDown events.

```
// Adjust the camera's position.
private void Window_KeyDown(object sender, KeyEventArgs e)
{
    switch (e.Key)
    {
        case Key.Up:
            CameraPhi += CameraDPhi;
            if (CameraPhi > Math.PI / 2.0) CameraPhi = Math.PI / 2.0;
            break;
        case Key.Down:
            CameraPhi -= CameraDPhi;
            if (CameraPhi < -Math.PI / 2.0) CameraPhi = -Math.PI / 2.0;
            break;
        case Key.Left:
            CameraTheta += CameraDTheta;
            break;
        case Key.Right:
            CameraTheta -= CameraDTheta;
            break;
        case Key.Add:
        case Key.OemPlus:
            CameraR -= CameraDR;
            if (CameraR < CameraDR) CameraR = CameraDR;
            break;
        case Key.Subtract:
        case Key.OemMinus:
            CameraR += CameraDR;
            break;
    }

    // Update the camera's position.
    PositionCamera();
}
```

This code checks the key that was pressed and then updates the spherical coordinates that define the camera's position. If you press the up or down arrow, the code changes the camera's phi value. If you press the left or right arrow, the code changes the camera's theta value. If you press + or -, the code adjusts the camera's distance from the origin to zoom in or out.

The method finishes by calling the PositionCamera method described earlier to set the camera's new position and look direction.

Summary

This seems like a complicated program and it is. However, once you understand it, you can use most of it unchanged in future projects. Often you only need to make a few changes to the DefineModel and MakeMesh methods. If you want to modify the lighting, you can also change the DefineLights method.

The AddRectangle method makes creating rectangles easy. Similarly, you can define other methods to build other shapes if you need them. For example, you could turn the MakeMesh method used in this example into an AddBox method. With a bit of work, you can make all sorts of methods to create meshes representing spheres, cylinders, cones, and other useful shapes.

69. Draw a Smooth Surface (47)

The C# Helper web site contains several examples that show how to draw surfaces in various ways. This example is a combination of the most advanced techniques described by those posts.

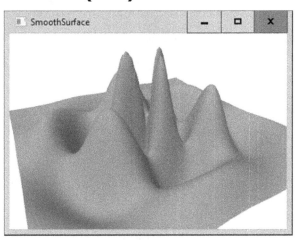

The basic idea behind this example is to use a function $Z(x, y)$ to generate points on the surface over an area in the X-Z plane. The program uses those values to create triangles representing the surface.

The example "67. Rotate a Three-Dimensional Cube With WPF (27)" explained that when two triangles share vertices, the drawing system smooths the edge between those triangles. To make the surface appear smooth, this program reuses the triangles' points whenever possible.

One way to do that is to very carefully design the way you build the triangles so you remember which previously created vertices should be reused in new triangles. That works well but can be tricky. It's also not a reusable technique. For example, if you later want to draw a smooth sphere, cylinder, or torus, you need to use a different scheme for reusing vertices.

This example makes vertex reuse much simpler by storing the vertices in a dictionary. When the program needs to find a vertex, it simply looks it up in the dictionary.

Most of the program is similar to the preceding one that draws a textured cube. It uses XAML code to create a `Viewport3D` and then creates the rest of the program's objects in C# code. The program's C# code also manages user interactions as before, allowing you to adjust the scene by pressing the arrow keys and the + and - keys.

The following `MakeMesh` method creates the triangles that make up this example's surface.

```
// Make the smooth surface.
private void MakeMesh(Model3DGroup modelGroup)
{
    // Make a mesh to hold the surface.
    MeshGeometry3D mesh = new MeshGeometry3D();

    // Define the area where we will draw the surface.
    const double xmin = -1.5;
    const double xmax = 1.5;
    const double dx = 0.03;
    const double zmin = -1.5;
    const double zmax = 1.5;
```

```
        const double dz = 0.03;

        // Create the surface's triangles.
        for (double x = xmin; x <= xmax - dx; x += dx)
        {
            for (double z = zmin; z <= zmax - dz; z += dx)
            {
                // Make points at the corners of the surface
                // over (x, z) - (x + dx, z + dz).
                Point3D p00 = new Point3D(x, F(x, z), z);
                Point3D p10 = new Point3D(x + dx, F(x + dx, z), z);
                Point3D p01 = new Point3D(x, F(x, z + dz), z + dz);
                Point3D p11 = new Point3D(x + dx, F(x + dx, z + dz), z + dz);

                // Add the triangles.
                AddTriangle(mesh, p00, p01, p11);
                AddTriangle(mesh, p00, p11, p10);
            }
        }

        // Make the surface's material.
        DiffuseMaterial material = new DiffuseMaterial(Brushes.Orange);

        // Make the mesh's model.
        GeometryModel3D surfaceModel = new GeometryModel3D(mesh, material);

        // Make the surface visible from both sides.
        surfaceModel.BackMaterial = material;

        // Add the model to the model groups.
        modelGroup.Children.Add(surfaceModel);
    }
```

This method works much as the version used by the preceding example does. The main difference is in how it creates the mesh's objects.

This version loops over an area in the X-Z plane. It uses the function F (described shortly) to calculate the Y coordinate of the surface over the positions (x, z). It makes points to define an area on the surface and then calls the AddTriangle method (also described shortly) to create the triangle.

The method finishes as the previous version did by creating a material, making a model for the mesh and material, and adding the model to the main model group.

The following code shows the function that generates the surface.

```
        // The function that defines the surface we are drawing.
        private double F(double x, double z)
        {
            const double two_pi = 2 * 3.14159265;
            double r2 = x * x + z * z;
            double r = Math.Sqrt(r2);
            double theta = Math.Atan2(z, x);
            return Math.Exp(-r2) * Math.Sin(two_pi * r) * Math.Cos(3 * theta);
        }
```

This method simply calculates the following somewhat intimidating function.

$$z = e^{-r^2} Sin(2\pi r) Cos(3\theta)$$

Here r and θ come from the spherical coordinates for the point $(x, 0, z)$.

The following code shows the AddTriangle method.

```
// Add a triangle to the indicated mesh reusing existing points.
private void AddTriangle(MeshGeometry3D mesh,
    Point3D point1, Point3D point2, Point3D point3)
{
    // Get the points' indices.
    int index1 = AddPoint(mesh.Positions, point1);
    int index2 = AddPoint(mesh.Positions, point2);
    int index3 = AddPoint(mesh.Positions, point3);

    // Create the triangle.
    mesh.TriangleIndices.Add(index1);
    mesh.TriangleIndices.Add(index2);
    mesh.TriangleIndices.Add(index3);
}
```

This method uses the AddPoint method described shortly to add the triangle's points to the mesh. It then adds indices to define the triangle.

Note that the method assumes the points are outwardly oriented. The code that calls AddTriangle must generate the points in counterclockwise order to avoid creating holes in the surface.

The following code shows how the AddPoint method works.

```
// A dictionary to hold points for fast lookup.
private Dictionary<Point3D, int> PointDictionary =
    new Dictionary<Point3D, int>();

// If the point already exists, return its index.
// Otherwise create the point and return its new index.
private int AddPoint(Point3DCollection points, Point3D point)
{
    // If the point is in the point dictionary,
    // return its saved index.
    if (PointDictionary.ContainsKey(point))
        return PointDictionary[point];

    // We didn't find the point. Create it.
    points.Add(point);
    PointDictionary.Add(point, points.Count - 1);
    return points.Count - 1;
}
```

This code first defines a class-level dictionary to hold points. The dictionary's keys are Point3D objects and its values are the points' indices in the mesh's Positions collection.

The method starts by checking the dictionary to see if the indicated point is already present in the dictionary. If it is, the method returns the point's index, which is stored in the dictionary.

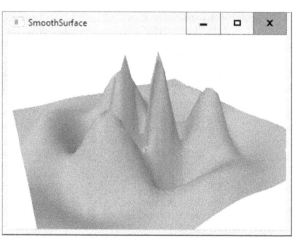

If the point isn't in the dictionary, the method adds the point to the mesh, adds the point and its index to the dictionary, and returns the point's index.

The dictionary means the `Addtriangle` method doesn't need to worry about whether a point already exists. The `AddPoint` method figures that out and then returns the correct index.

If you want to see what the surface looks like without smoothing, comment out the code that checks to see if the point already exists in the dictionary and the statement that adds points to the dictionary.

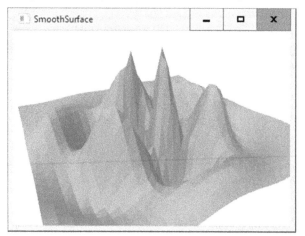

The two pictures on this page show the surface with and without shared points. I've decreased the number of triangles used by the program and lightened the pictures to make the difference more obvious.

70. Draw a Data Surface That Has an Altitude Map (94)

This example is similar to the preceding one with two modifications. First, it uses an array of data instead of a mathematical function. The data could represent sales figures over time, production quotas, rainfall, or just about anything else that it makes sense to view as a three-dimensional surface.

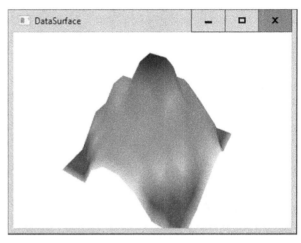

The second change is that the program shades the surface with an altitude map. Points with high Y values are blue and those with low values are red. Unfortunately, all of the colors appear gray on this page. You can see a full-color image of the program on the book's back cover.

The program uses a simple two-dimensional array named `values` to hold the data. For example, `values[1, 3]` holds the data value (Y coordinate) where x = 1 and z = 3.

The `MakeData` method initializes the array. It's not a very interesting method, so I won't reproduce it here.

A more interesting piece of code is the following `CreateAltitudeMap` method, which creates a `WriteableBitmap` holding the altitude map image.

```
// Create the altitude map texture bitmap.
private WriteableBitmap CreateAltitudeMap(double[,] values)
{
    // Calculate the function's value over the area.
    int xwidth = values.GetUpperBound(0) + 1;
    int zwidth = values.GetUpperBound(1) + 1;

    // Get the upper and lower bounds on the values.
    var valueQuery =
        from double value in values
        select value;
    double ymin = valueQuery.Min();
    double ymax = valueQuery.Max();

    // Make the BitmapMaker.
    BitmapMaker bmMaker = new BitmapMaker(xwidth, zwidth);

    // Set the pixel colors.
    for (int ix = 0; ix < xwidth; ix++)
    {
        for (int iz = 0; iz < zwidth; iz++)
```

```
        {
            byte red, green, blue;
            MapRainbowColor(values[ix, iz], ymin, ymax,
                out red, out green, out blue);
            bmMaker.SetPixel(ix, iz, red, green, blue, 255);
        }
    }

    // Convert the BitmapMaker into a WriteableBitmap and return it.
    return bmMaker.MakeBitmap(96, 96);
}
```

This method gets the dimensions of the data values. It then uses LINQ to find the largest and smallest values in the data array.

Next, the code makes a `BitmapMaker` object to fit the data. The `BitmapMaker` class is a wrapper for the code described in the earlier example 40, "Set an Image's Pixels in WPF." It provides methods to let you get and set the red, green, blue, and alpha components of an image's pixels. Its `MakeBitmap` method uses the pixel data to create and return a `WriteableBitmap` object holding the image.

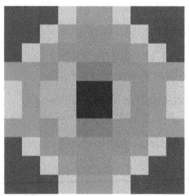

After it creates the `BitmapMaker` object, the `CreateAltitudeMap` method loops over the data in the `values` array. It calls the `MapRainbowColor` method described shortly to map each Y value to a color. It then uses the `BitmapMaker` object's `SetPixel` method to save the pixel's color.

After it has colored all of the image's pixels, the code calls the `BitmapMaker` object's `MakeBitmap` method to get the `WriteableBitmap`. The picture on the left shows the color map greatly enlarged (and unfortunately in grayscale instead of color).

The `MapRainbowColor` method shown in the following code maps a value to a color in the rainbow depending on the value's position between a minimum and maximum value.

```
// Map a value to a rainbow color.
private void MapRainbowColor(double value, double minValue, double maxValue,
    out byte red, out byte green, out byte blue)
{
    // Convert into a value between 0 and 1023.
    int intValue = (int)(1023 * (value - minValue) / (maxValue - minValue));

    // Map different color bands.
    if (intValue < 256)
    {
        // Red to yellow. (255, 0, 0) to (255, 255, 0).
        red = 255;
        green = (byte)intValue;
        blue = 0;
    }
```

```
    else if (intValue < 512)
    {
        // Yellow to green. (255, 255, 0) to (0, 255, 0).
        intValue -= 256;
        red = (byte)(255 - intValue);
        green = 255;
        blue = 0;
    }
    else if (intValue < 768)
    {
        // Green to aqua. (0, 255, 0) to (0, 255, 255).
        intValue -= 512;
        red = 0;
        green = 255;
        blue = (byte)intValue;
    }
    else
    {
        // Aqua to blue. (0, 255, 255) to (0, 0, 255).
        intValue -= 768;
        red = 0;
        green = (byte)(255 - intValue);
        blue = 255;
    }
}
```

The method first maps the value into the range 0 to 1,023. It divides that range into four pieces represented by shades of red, yellow, green, and blue and calculates the components needed to create the appropriate color.

The last piece of the example that I want to discuss is the way it uses the altitude map to make a texture. The `CreateAltitudeMap` method makes a `WriteableBitmap` that is later passed into the methods that define the surface's triangles.

Eventually the program calls an `AddPoint` method similar to the one used by the preceding example. The following code shows this example's version of that method.

```
// If the point already exists, return its index.
// Otherwise create the point and return its new index.
private int AddPoint(Point3DCollection points,
    PointCollection positions, Point3D point)
{
    // If the point is in the point dictionary,
    // return its saved index.
    if (PointDictionary.ContainsKey(point))
        return PointDictionary[point];

    // We didn't find the point. Create it.
    points.Add(point);
    PointDictionary.Add(point, points.Count - 1);

    // Set the point's texture coordinates.
    positions.Add(
        new Point(
            (point.X - xmin) * textureXscale,
            (point.Z - zmin) * textureZscale));
```

```
        // Return the new point's index.
        return points.Count - 1;
    }
```

This method looks for the indicated point in the **PointDictionary** and returns its index if it is present. If the point isn't in the dictionary, the code adds it to the mesh and to the dictionary.

The method also sets the point's texture coordinate so the X and Z values included in the data use textures ranging from 0 to 1.

The following code shows the part of the MakeMesh method that creates the surface's texture.

```
        // Make the texture brush.
        ImageBrush textureBrush = new ImageBrush(wbm);

        // Make the material.
        DiffuseMaterial surfaceMaterial = new DiffuseMaterial(textureBrush);

        // Make the mesh's model.
        GeometryModel3D surfaceModel = new GeometryModel3D(mesh, surfaceMaterial);

        // Make the surface visible from both sides.
        surfaceModel.BackMaterial = surfaceMaterial;

        // Add the model to the model groups.
        modelGroup.Children.Add(surfaceModel);
```

This code takes the **WriteableBitmap** named wbm and uses it to create a new **ImageBrush**. It uses the brush to create a **DiffuseMaterial** and then uses that to make the surface's model.

The code sets the model's **BackMaterial** to the same material so you can view the surface from both sides. It then adds the new model to the main model group.

To see additional details, download the example and look at its code. I know I've skipped a *lot* of details, but I think the description given here, plus the explanations in previous examples, should be enough to let you understand what the program is doing if you review the code.

71. DRAW THREE-DIMENSIONAL LINE SEGMENTS (81)

The previous few examples showed how to draw various three-dimensional scenes. They let you draw triangles that are either shaded or textured. Unfortunately, the drawing system doesn't provide a simple way to show a wireframe of a model.

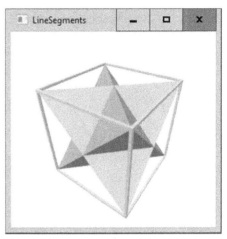

One workaround is to make long, skinny, three-dimensional boxes to represent line segments.

This example is the end of a short sequence of examples on the C# Helper web site. It shows how to draw long, skinny boxes that extend themselves if desired to make them line up neatly where they meet.

The following AddPrism method uses the AddRectangle method described by the example, "68. Apply Textures to a Three-Dimensional Cube (78)," to draw a three-dimensional box.

```
// Make a prism.
private void AddPrism(MeshGeometry3D mesh,
    Point3D corner, Vector3D v1, Vector3D v2, Vector3D v3)
{
    // Make the prism.
    Point3D A = corner;
    Point3D B = A + v1;
    Point3D C = B + v3;
    Point3D D = C - v1;
    Point3D E = A + v2;
    Point3D F = B + v2;
    Point3D G = C + v2;
    Point3D H = D + v2;

    AddRectangle(mesh, D, v1, v2);      // Front.
    AddRectangle(mesh, A, v3, v2);      // Left.
    AddRectangle(mesh, C, -v3, v2);     // Right.
    AddRectangle(mesh, B, -v1, v2);     // Back.
    AddRectangle(mesh, G, -v3, -v1);    // Top.
    AddRectangle(mesh, A, v1, v3);      // Bottom.
}
```

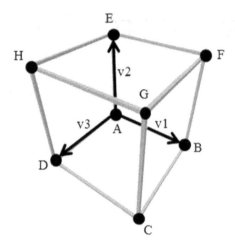

This method takes as parameters a mesh, corner point, and three vectors that define the prism as shown on the left. In the picture, the corner point is A and the vectors are v1, v2, and v3.

The code uses the point and the vectors to define the prism's vertices. It then uses the `AddRectangle` method to create the prism's sides.

To work properly, the vectors must be oriented according to the right-hand rule. To use the rule, hold up your right hand and point your fingers in the direction of vector v1. Next, curl your fingers toward v2. (You may need to turn your hand over to make them curl in the right direction.) If you do this, your thumb should point in the direction of vector v3.

You should be able to try this to verify that v1, v2, and v3 satisfy the right-hand rule in the picture above.

In this example, the vectors are mutually perpendicular and have the same lengths. As a result, the prism's sides are squares and the prism is a cube.

In general, the vectors don't need to meet at right angles and they could have different lengths. If the vectors are perpendicular but have different lengths, the result is a box like the one shown on the right.

If the vectors are not mutually perpendicular, the result is a skewed prism.

NOTE: More precisely the solid is a *parallelepiped*, a solid where each face is a parallelogram, but "`AddPrism`" is easier to type than "`AddParallelepiped`."

To draw three-dimensional line segments, the program uses the following `AddSegment` method. This method uses `AddPrism` to draw long, skinny prisms connecting two points.

```
// Make a segment between two points.
private void AddSegment(MeshGeometry3D mesh, double thickness,
    Point3D point1, Point3D point2, bool extend = false)
{
    // Get the segment's vector.
    Vector3D v = point2 - point1;

    // Extend the vector if desired.
    if (extend)
    {
        // Increase the segment's length on both ends by thickness / 2.
```

```
        Vector3D n = ScaleVector(v, thickness / 2.0);
        point1 -= n;
        point2 += n;
        v = point2 - point1;
    }

    // Get an up vector.
    Vector3D up = new Vector3D(0, 1, 0);      // Y axis.

    // See if up and v are more or less parallel.
    Vector3D vn = v;
    vn.Normalize();
    if (Vector3D.CrossProduct(up, vn).Length < 0.1)
    {
        // Use the X axis instead.
        up = new Vector3D(1, 0, 0);
    }

    // Get the scaled up vector.
    Vector3D n1 = ScaleVector(up, thickness);

    // Get another scaled perpendicular vector.
    Vector3D n2 = Vector3D.CrossProduct(v, n1);
    n2 = ScaleVector(n2, thickness);

    // Make a skinny box.
    AddPrism(mesh, point1 - n1 / 2.0 - n2 / 2.0, n1, v, n2);
}
```

This method first finds the vector between the two points. I'll call this the "main vector" in the following discussion.

If the extend parameter is true, the method extends the main vector's length by half of the segment's desired thickness in each direction. Don't worry about *why* it does that for now. I'll say more about it later.

However, it's worth understanding *how* the code extends the main vector. The ScaleVector helper method shown in the following code makes a vector in the same direction as an original vector but with a given length.

```
    // Set the vector's length.
    private Vector3D ScaleVector(Vector3D vector, double length)
    {
        return vector / vector.Length * length;
    }
```

This method divides the vector by its current length, multiplies it by the desired length, and returns the resulting vector. When you multiply or divide a vector by a number, the overloaded / and * operators perform those actions on each of the vector's X, Y, and Z, components. The result is a vector pointing in the same direction but with length scaled by the number that you multiplied or divided by.

The AddSegment method uses ScaleVector to turn the main vector into a vector pointing in the same direction but having a length equal to half of the segment's thickness. It then adds that vector to the segment's end points so they are a bit farther apart.

> **NOTE:** If you don't understand this operation, you may want to study the code some more. The rest of the code uses this kind of vector arithmetic a lot.

Next, the AddSegment method needs to find two vectors that are perpendicular to the main vector. A vector cross product can find a vector perpendicular to two other vectors. The cross product of two vectors v1 and v2 is a third vector v3 perpendicular v1 and v2 and with length |v3| = |v1|*|v2|*Sin(θ), where θ is the angle between v1 and v2. The direction of the new vector is determined by the right-hand rule. (For more information on cross products, see the Math Is Fun post tinyurl.com/oevtrts.)

To find a vector perpendicular to the main vector, the AddSegment method can use the Vector3D class's CrossProduct method. It takes the cross product of the main vector and any other vector up. Unfortunately, that only works if up isn't parallel to the main vector, and initially the AddSegment method has no up vector defined. It needs to build one.

The method first tries setting up to a vector parallel to the Y axis. If the two vectors are close to parallel, the cross product's length is small. In that case, the code sets up to a vector parallel to the X axis.

Next, the method takes the cross product of up and the main vector. The result is a vector n1 that is perpendicular to the main vector. The method scales the result so it has length equal to the desired segment thickness.

The code then takes the cross product of n1 and the main vector to get a second vector n2 perpendicular to both n1 and the main vector. The method scales this vector so it has the same length as n1.

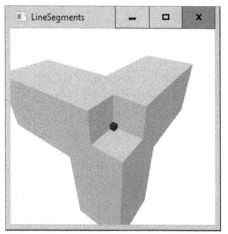

At this point, the method has the main vector and two short perpendicular vectors. It passes them to the AddPrism method to make the skinny prism representing the segment.

Now back to the issue of extending the segment. The prism that represents the segment is not infinitely thin. That means if multiple prisms meet at a common point, there is a void in the corner that they make.

In the picture on the left, a little dark cube sits at the corner where three thick segments meet. Extending the segments makes them fill in the corner, as shown in the picture on the right.

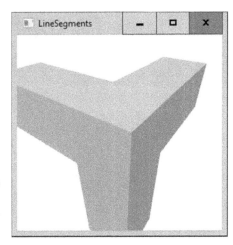

The rest of the program is just a matter of using the AddTriangle and AddSegment methods to produce the three-dimensional scene.

If you look at the picture at the beginning of this example, you'll see that the program draws two interlocking tetrahedrons surrounded by a wireframe. The MakeTetrahedrons method defines a light blue mesh and a light green mesh. It calls AddTriangle four times for each to create the two interlocking tetrahedrons.

The MakeCage method calls AddSegment 12 times to create a cage of thin pink prisms surrounding the tetrahedrons.

The MakeTetrahedron and MakeCage methods are relatively straightforward so I won't describe them here. Download the example to see their code.

Between them, this example and "68. Apply Textures to a Three-Dimensional Cube (78)," demonstrate most of the techniques that you need to use to make complex three-dimensional scenes.

72. DRAW A WIREFRAME (17)

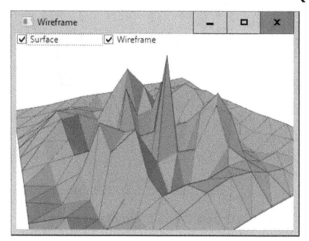

The preceding example showed how to make three-dimensional line segments. That technique makes it relatively easy to create a wireframe. I'll explain how that works shortly.

To make the example a bit more useful, I also moved the drawing primitive methods so they are now `MeshGeometry3D` extension methods defined in the `MeshExtensions` class. That makes them easier to reuse and keeps them from cluttering up the main program's code.

The following list summarizes the `MeshGeometry3D` extension methods.

- ➤ `AddPoint`–Adds a point to the mesh, optionally reusing existing points
- ➤ `AddTriangle`–Adds a triangle to the mesh, optionally reusing existing points
- ➤ `AddRectangle`–Adds a rectangle to the mesh, optionally reusing existing points
- ➤ `AddPrism`–Adds a prism to the mesh
- ➤ `AddSegment`–Adds a segment to the mesh, optionally extending it
- ➤ `AddUniqueSegment`–Similar to `AddSegment` but won't add duplicate segments
- ➤ `ToWireframe`–Returns a new mesh containing segments for the source mesh's wireframe

The methods that allow shared points take an optional parameter of type `Dictionary<Point3D, int>`. If that parameter is not `null`, the method checks it to see if a particular point is already in the mesh and reuses it if possible. If you omit this parameter, the method creates a new point so the points are not shared.

For example, the following code shows the `AddPoint` extension method.

```
// Add the point. If pointDictionary is not null, reuse points.
public static int AddPoint(this MeshGeometry3D mesh, Point3D point,
    Dictionary<Point3D, int> pointDictionary = null)
{
    if (pointDictionary != null)
    {
        // If the point is in the dictionary, reuse it.
        if (pointDictionary.ContainsKey(point))
            return pointDictionary[point];

        // It doesn't exit. Save its new index.
        pointDictionary.Add(point, mesh.Positions.Count);
    }
```

```
        // Create the point.
        mesh.Positions.Add(point);
        return mesh.Positions.Count - 1;
    }
```

If the `pointDict` parameter is not `null`, the method uses it to try to reuse existing points. If `pointDict` is `null`, the method always creates a new point.

The following `AddUniqueSegment` method uses a similar technique to add a segment to a mesh without adding duplicate segments.

```
    // Add a segment if it is not already in the dictionary.
    public static void AddUniqueSegment(this MeshGeometry3D mesh,
        Dictionary<int, int> segmentDict,
        int index1, int index2, Point3D point1, Point3D point2,
        double thickness, bool extend = false)
    {
        // Get a unique ID for a segment connecting the two points.
        if (index1 > index2)
        {
            int temp = index1;
            index1 = index2;
            index2 = temp;
        }
        int segment_id = index1 * 10000 + index2;

        // If we've already added this segment, do nothing.
        if (segmentDict.ContainsKey(segment_id)) return;
        segmentDict.Add(segment_id, segment_id);

        // Create the segment.
        AddSegment(mesh, thickness, point1, point2, extend);
    }
```

The method takes as a parameter a `Dictionary<int, int>` that it uses to keep track of existing segments. The code starts by calculating an ID for the new segment. The ID consists of the smaller point index multiplied by 10,000 plus the larger point index. For example, if the points have indices 42 and 17, then the segment ID is 170,042.

Next, the method uses the dictionary to see if it has already added a segment with that ID. If the dictionary contains that ID, the method returns.

NOTE: The whole point of this method is to avoid creating reversed segments, for example between points 17 and 42 and then later between points 42 and 17.

This method may not work properly if a mesh's triangles don't share points. If two points appear twice with different indices, then the method would allow two different segments to connect the copies. This method works well for this example, however, because the surface uses shared points.

If the dictionary does not contain the new segment ID, the method adds it and creates the new segment.

The other extension methods are straightforward, except for the following `ToWireframe` method.

```csharp
// Return a MeshGeometry3D representing this mesh's wireframe.
public static MeshGeometry3D ToWireframe(this MeshGeometry3D sourceMesh,
    double thickness)
{
    // Make a mesh to hold the wireframe.
    MeshGeometry3D wireframe = new MeshGeometry3D();

    // Make a dictionary for segment sharing.
    Dictionary<int, int> segmentDict = new Dictionary<int, int>();

    // Loop through the mesh's triangles.
    for (int triangle = 0; triangle < sourceMesh.TriangleIndices.Count;
        triangle += 3)
    {
        // Get the source triangle's point indices.
        int index1 = sourceMesh.TriangleIndices[triangle];
        int index2 = sourceMesh.TriangleIndices[triangle + 1];
        int index3 = sourceMesh.TriangleIndices[triangle + 2];

        // Get the source triangle's corner points.
        Point3D point1 = sourceMesh.Positions[index1];
        Point3D point2 = sourceMesh.Positions[index2];
        Point3D point3 = sourceMesh.Positions[index3];

        // Make the triangle's three segments.
        wireframe.AddUniqueSegment(segmentDict,
            index1, index2, point1, point2, thickness, true);
        wireframe.AddUniqueSegment(segmentDict,
            index2, index3, point2, point3, thickness, true);
        wireframe.AddUniqueSegment(segmentDict,
            index3, index1, point3, point1, thickness, true);
    }

    return wireframe;
}
```

This method creates a new mesh. It then makes a `Dictionary<int, int>` to keep track of the segments it creates.

Next, the code loops through the triangles defined by the source mesh. It gets each triangle's corner indices and points. It then calls the `AddUniqueSegment` method to add segments connecting the three corners.

Notice that the method uses the indices of the points in the source mesh to define the segment IDs. Those points probably don't exist in the new mesh so they won't have indices there.

The method finishes by returning the new mesh. The main program can then create a material for it and use it to create a `GeometryModel3D`.

To make the example a bit more interesting, I also added checkboxes that let you show or hide the surface and wireframe. The code that generates the surface and wireframe models saves their GeometryModel3D objects in two form-level variables SurfaceModel and WireframeModel.

When you check or uncheck one of the checkboxes, the following event handler shows and hides the appropriate models.

```
// Show and hide the appropriate GeometryModel3Ds.
private void chkContents_Click(object sender, RoutedEventArgs e)
{
    // Remove the GeometryModel3Ds.
    for (int i = MainModel3Dgroup.Children.Count - 1; i >= 0; i--)
    {
        if (MainModel3Dgroup.Children[i] is GeometryModel3D)
            MainModel3Dgroup.Children.RemoveAt(i);
    }

    // Add the selected GeometryModel3Ds.
    if ((SurfaceModel != null) && ((bool)chkSurface.IsChecked))
        MainModel3Dgroup.Children.Add(SurfaceModel);
    if ((WireframeModel != null) && ((bool)chkWireframe.IsChecked))
        MainModel3Dgroup.Children.Add(WireframeModel);
}
```

This method loops through the MainModel3Dgroup object's Children collection and removes any GeometryModel3D objects. That removes the two models without removing the MainModel3Dgroup object's lights.

The code finishes by adding the selected models back into the Children collection.

Download the example program, examine its code, and experiment with it. The mesh extension methods make it relatively easy to create new three-dimensional scenes.

Part XVI. ListView and TreeView

The examples in this part of the book work with two powerful controls: ListView and TreeView.

The ListView control displays items that have sub-items in several different views. The following list summarizes the views.

- ➤ Details–Displays small icons, the items, and their sub-items in rows and columns
- ➤ LargeIcon–Displays large icons with the items below them
- ➤ List–Displays small icons and the items
- ➤ SmallIcon–Displays small icons and the items
- ➤ Tile–Displays large icons, the items, and their sub-items

The TreeView control displays hierarchical data in a tree similar to the one used on the left side of File Explorer.

73. DISPLAY ICONS IN A LISTVIEW CONTROL (72)

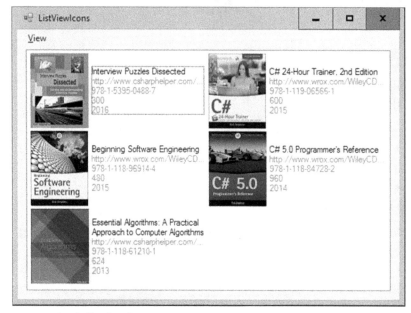

The `ListView` control displays two sizes of icons for its items. When its `View` property is `LargeIcon` or `Tile`, the control displays large icons. When the `View` property is `SmallIcon`, `List`, or `Details`, the control displays small icons.

The control gets its icons from two `ImageList` components.

Take the following steps to make a `ListView` control display icons.

> ➤ Add two `ImageList` components to the form.
> ➤ Set the components' `ImageSize` properties to the sizes of the images they will contain. All of the images in a given `ImageList` should have the same size. In this example, one `ImageList` contains 31×32 pixel images and the other contains 80×100 pixel images.
> ➤ Set the `ImageList` components' `ColorDepth` properties to the color depth used by the images. In this example, all of the images use 32-bit color, so the `ColorDepth` properties are set to `Depth32bit`.
> ➤ Add the images to the `ImageList` controls.
> ➤ Set the `ListView` control's `SmallImageList` and `LargeImageList` properties to the two `ImageList` components.
> ➤ When you add an item to the `ListView` control, set its `ImageIndex` property to the index of the item's image in the `ImageLists`. Each item has a single `ImageIndex` property, so its small and large images must have the same indices in the two `ImageList` controls.
> ➤ Make the program set the `ListView` control's `View` property as desired.

The example's menu items let you set the `ListView` control's `View` property. For example, the following code executes when you select the Tile menu item.

```
private void tileMenuItem_Click(object sender, EventArgs e)
{
```

```
    booksListView.View = View.Tile;
    CheckMenuItem(viewMenu, sender as ToolStripMenuItem);
}
```

This code sets the `ListView` control's `View` property and calls the `CheckMenuItem` method. That method loops through the View menu and unchecks all of the menu items except the one passed in as a parameter. That method is reasonably straightforward so I won't show it here. Download the example to see how it works.

That's all there is to setting up the `ListView` to display icons. This example also defines two extension methods that make working with `ListView` controls a bit easier.

The following `MakeColumnHeaders` extension method sets a `ListView` control's column headers.

```
// Make the ListView's column headers.
// The ParamArray entries should alternate between
// strings and HorizontalAlignment values.
public static void MakeColumnHeaders(this ListView lvw,
    params object[] headerInfo)
{
    // Remove any existing headers.
    lvw.Columns.Clear();

    // Make the column headers.
    for (int i = headerInfo.GetLowerBound(0);
        i <= headerInfo.GetUpperBound(0);
        i += 3)
    {
        lvw.Columns.Add(
            (string)headerInfo[i],
            (int)headerInfo[i + 1],
            (HorizontalAlignment)headerInfo[i + 2]);
    }
}
```

This method's parameter uses the `params` keyword so the calling code can pass any number of values into it. Those values should be triples consisting of a column's header text, width, and alignment.

The method clears the control's `Columns` collection. It then loops through the `headerInfo` values and uses them to define the columns.

The following code shows how the example program uses this extension method to define its `ListView` columns.

```
// Make the column headers.
booksListView.MakeColumnHeaders(
    "Title", 230, HorizontalAlignment.Left,
    "URL", 220, HorizontalAlignment.Left,
    "ISBN", 130, HorizontalAlignment.Left,
    "Pages", 50, HorizontalAlignment.Right,
    "Year", 60, HorizontalAlignment.Right);
```

Normally to create a `ListView` row, you add an item and then add its sub-items one at a time. The second extension method, which is shown in the following code, lets you add an item and its sub-items in a single step.

```
// Add a row to the ListView.
public static ListViewItem AddRow(this ListView lvw, int imageIndex,
    params string[] values)
{
    // Make the item.
    ListViewItem newItem = new ListViewItem(values, imageIndex);
    lvw.Items.Add(newItem);
    return newItem;
}
```

This method creates a new `ListViewItem` object, adds it to the `ListView` control's `Items` collection, and returns the item in case the main program needs to use it.

The following code shows how the example creates one of its book entries.

```
booksListView.AddRow(0, "Interview Puzzles Dissected",
    "http://www.csharphelper.com/puzzles.htm",
    "978-1-5395-0488-7", "300", "2016");
```

Download the example to see additional details.

Title	URL	ISBN	Pages	Year
Interview Puzzles Dissected	http://www.csharphelper.com/puzzles.htm	978-1-5395-0488-7	300	2016
C# 24-Hour Trainer, 2nd Edition	http://www.wrox.com/WileyCDA/WroxTit...	978-1-119-06566-1	600	2015
Beginning Software Engineering	http://www.wrox.com/WileyCDA/WroxTit...	978-1-118-96914-4	480	2015
C# 5.0 Programmer's Reference	http://www.wrox.com/WileyCDA/WroxTit...	978-1-118-84728-2	960	2014
Essential Algorithms: A Practical Approach to Computer Algorithms	http://www.csharphelper.com/algorithms...	978-1-118-61210-1	624	2013

74. Use ListView Groups (23)

One of the less known features of the `ListView` control is that it can group items. The control in the picture above defines two groups: C# Books and Software Books. Any item not placed in a defined group goes in the Default group.

You can create `ListView` groups at either design or run time. This example uses the following code to create two groups at run time.

```
// Make some groups.
ListViewGroup csharpGroup = new ListViewGroup("C# Books");
ListViewGroup softwareGroup = new ListViewGroup("Software Books");
booksListView.Groups.Add(csharpGroup);
booksListView.Groups.Add(softwareGroup);
```

The following extension method creates a new `ListView` item and assigns it to a group.

```
// Add a row to a group in the ListView.
public static ListViewItem AddRow(this ListView lvw, ListViewGroup group,
    int imageIndex, params string[] values)
{
    ListViewItem newItem = lvw.AddRow(imageIndex, values);
    newItem.Group = group;
    return newItem;
}
```

This method uses the `AddRow` extension method described in the preceding example to create the new `ListViewItem`. It then sets the item's group and returns it.

The following code shows how the main program creates one of the `ListView` entries.

```
booksListView.AddRow(softwareGroup, 2, "Beginning Software Engineering",
    "http://www.wrox.com/WileyCDA/WroxTitle/... ",
    "978-1-118-96914-4", "480", "2015");
```

To place an entry in the Default group, pass the method null for the group parameter.

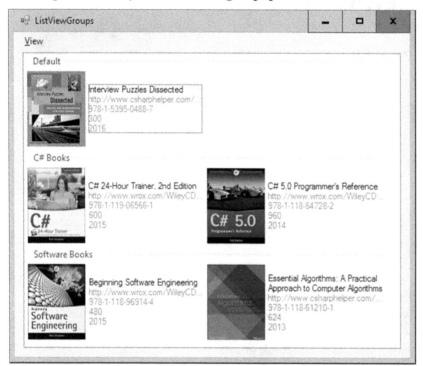

The ListView control groups its entries in all of its views except List. For example, the picture on the left shows the example program displaying its Tile view.

75. Sort a ListView Control on the Column Clicked (39)

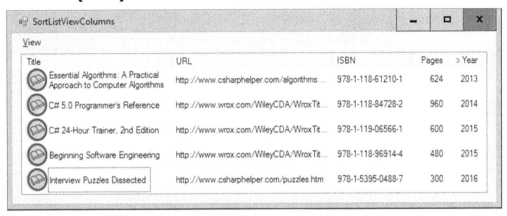

If a `ListView` is displaying its Details view, then you can make it sort on the column you click, but it's a lot more work than simply sorting the `ListView` control's items.

To sort using the items, you can simply set the control's `Sorting` property to `Ascending` or `Descending`. Unfortunately, that only makes the control sort on its items and not their sub-items. It won't even use the sub-items to break ties when two items have the same text.

To modify the control's sorting behavior, you must create a helper class that implements the `IComparer` interface. The key to this class is the `Compare` method. That method takes as parameters two `ListViewItem` objects that it should compare. The method should return -1 if the first should come before the second in the sort order, 0 if the items are equal, and 1 if the first item should come after the second.

The following code shows the `ListViewComparer` class used by this example.

```
// Compares two ListView items based on a selected column.
public class ListViewComparer : IComparer
{
    private int ColumnNumber;
    private SortOrder SortOrder;

    public ListViewComparer(int columnNumber, SortOrder sortOrder)
    {
        ColumnNumber = columnNumber;
        SortOrder = sortOrder;
    }

    // Compare two ListViewItems.
    public int Compare(object x, object y)
    {
        // Get the ListViewItems.
        ListViewItem xitem = x as ListViewItem;
```

```
        ListViewItem yitem = y as ListViewItem;

        // Get the corresponding sub-item values.
        string xstring;
        if (xitem.SubItems.Count <= ColumnNumber) xstring = "";
        else xstring = xitem.SubItems[ColumnNumber].Text;

        string ystring;
        if (yitem.SubItems.Count <= ColumnNumber) ystring = "";
        else ystring = yitem.SubItems[ColumnNumber].Text;

        // Compare them.
        int result;

        // See if the values look like numbers.
        double xdouble, ydouble;
        if (double.TryParse(xstring, out xdouble) &&
            double.TryParse(ystring, out ydouble))
        {
            // Treat as a number.
            result = xdouble.CompareTo(ydouble);
        }
        else
        {
            // See if the values look like dates.
            DateTime xdate, ydate;
            if (DateTime.TryParse(xstring, out xdate) &&
                DateTime.TryParse(ystring, out ydate))
            {
                // Treat as a date.
                result = xdate.CompareTo(ydate);
            }
            else
            {
                // Treat as a string.
                result = xstring.CompareTo(ystring);
            }
        }

        // Return the result depending on sort order.
        if (SortOrder == SortOrder.Ascending) return result;
        return -result;
    }
}
```

The class uses private fields `ColumnNumber` and `SortOrder` to keep track of the column on which the object should sort and whether it should sort ascending or descending. The class's constructor initializes those values.

The `Compare` method, which is required by the `IComparer` interface, is the key to the class. It compares sub-items to determine how two items should be ordered.

The method needs to do a little checking to guard against the case when either of the items doesn't have a sub-item in the column clicked. For example, if you're comparing the items' fourth sub-item but one of the items only has two sub-items, then the method shouldn't try to look at that item's fourth sub-item.

The code also tries to convert the values into doubles and dates to see if it should sort the values using those data types. For example, as strings "9" comes after "100" but as numbers 9 comes before 100. Similarly as strings "10/10/2010" comes before "1/1/2020" but as dates 10/10/2010 comes after 1/1/2020. Comparing values as numbers or dates makes more sense to users.

The example program uses the following code to sort when you click on a ListView column.

```
// The current sorting column.
private ColumnHeader SortingColumn = null;

// Sort on this column.
private void booksListView_ColumnClick(object sender, ColumnClickEventArgs e)
{
    // Get the new sorting column.
    ColumnHeader newColumn = booksListView.Columns[e.Column];

    // Figure out the new sorting order.
    SortOrder sortOrder;
    if (SortingColumn == null)
    {
        // New column. Sort ascending.
        sortOrder = SortOrder.Ascending;
    }
    else
    {
        // See if this is the same column.
        if (newColumn == SortingColumn)
        {
            // Same column. Switch the sort order.
            if (SortingColumn.Text.StartsWith("> "))
                sortOrder = SortOrder.Descending;
            else
                sortOrder = SortOrder.Ascending;
        }
        else
        {
            // New column. Sort ascending.
            sortOrder = SortOrder.Ascending;
        }

        // Remove the old sort indicator.
        SortingColumn.Text = SortingColumn.Text.Substring(2);
    }

    // Display the new sort order.
    SortingColumn = newColumn;
    if (sortOrder == SortOrder.Ascending)
        SortingColumn.Text = "> " + SortingColumn.Text;
    else
        SortingColumn.Text = "< " + SortingColumn.Text;

    // Create a comparer.
    booksListView.ListViewItemSorter =
        new ListViewComparer(e.Column, sortOrder);
```

```
        // Sort.
        booksListView.Sort();
    }
```

The `SortingColumn` variable keeps track of the column that the program is currently using for sorting.

When the user clicks a column header, the program determines which column was clicked. It then determines the new sorting order that it should use. If the new column is the same as the old one, the program switches the sort order. If the new column is different from the previous column, it sorts in ascending order.

The program adds "> " to the column header when it sorts ascending and "< " when it sorts descending. It uses these characters to determine the current sort order and to show the user the sort order.

After it decides on the new sort order, the program removes the sorting indicator ("> " or "< ") from the current sort column and adds it to the new sort column.

Finally, the program creates a new `ListViewItemSorter` object, passing its constructor the appropriate column number and sort order. The code finishes by calling the `ListView` control's `Sort` method to make it resort its data.

That's about all there is to the program's code, although the `ListView` control has a couple of additional features that are relevant. For example, if the control's `AllowColumnReorder` property is `true`, the user can drag the control's column headers into new positions. Even if the columns are rearranged, the control still works with their original indices. For example, if you drag column 3 into position 0, it is still column 3 as far as the `ListView` control is concerned. That means the example program still works even if the user rearranges the columns.

The `ListView` control's `Details` view is the only one with columns that you can click, but the control keeps the items in sorted order when you switch to another view. For example, if you use the Details view to sort book entries by number of pages, then when you switch to Tile view the books are still sorted by number of pages.

76. PRINT LISTVIEW CONTENTS (54)

One of the problems with printing examples is that printing in .NET is extremely flexible so it's hard to

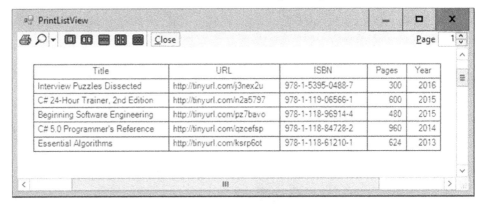

predict what you might want to do with it. For example, suppose a ListView control contains too many columns to fit on one page. Should the program split the printout across multiple pages? Should it print in landscape mode? Should it reduce the print size? Should it ignore some columns that hold less interesting data?

This example displays a print preview of the contents of a ListView control. It makes the printed rows and columns large as necessary to hold the item's and their sub-items. It assumes that the rows are not too wide to fit on the page and that all of the rows fit on a single page. If you need to print hundreds of entries, draw pictures, or display items in multiple rows, then you'll need to modify the example, but at least it should get you started.

At design time, I added a PrintPreviewDialog component named listViewPrintPreviewDialog to the program's form. I also set the dialog's Document property to a PrintDocument component named listViewPrintDocument.

When you select the File menu's Print Preview command, the following event handler starts the printing process.

```
// Print the ListView's contents.
private void printPreviewMenuItem_Click(object sender, EventArgs e)
{
    // Maximize the PrintPreviewDialog.
    Form frm = listViewPrintPreviewDialog as Form;
    frm.WindowState = FormWindowState.Maximized;

    // Start at 100% scale.
    listViewPrintPreviewDialog.PrintPreviewControl.Zoom = 1.0;

    // Display.
    listViewPrintPreviewDialog.ShowDialog();
}
```

This event handler first casts the `PrintDialog` object into a `Form`. A `PrintDialog` is a kind of `Form` so that's allowed.

The code maximizes the form, finds the `PrintPreviewControl` on the form, and sets its `Zoom` level property to 1.0 so it displays the preview at 100% scale.

The code then calls the dialog's `ShowDialog` method to display the dialog modally. The dialog invokes the `PrintDocument` to figure out what printed output it should display. The `PrintDocument` then raises its `PrintPage` event to let your program tell it what to print.

The following code shows the `PrintDocument` object's `PrintPage` event handler.

```
// Print the ListView's data.
private void listViewPrintDocument_PrintPage(object sender,
    PrintPageEventArgs e)
{
    // Print the ListView.
    booksListView.PrintData(e.MarginBounds.Location,
        e.Graphics, Brushes.Blue, Brushes.Black, Pens.Blue);
}
```

This code simply invokes the `ListView` control's `PrintData` extension method shown in the following code. This is where all of the interesting work occurs.

```
// Print the ListView's data at the indicated location
// assuming everything will fit within the column widths.
public static void PrintData(this ListView lvw, Point location, Graphics gr,
    Brush headerBrush, Brush dataBrush, Pen gridPen)
{
    const int xmargin = 5;
    const int ymargin = 3;
    float x = location.X;
    float y = location.Y;

    // See how tall rows should be.
    SizeF rowSize = gr.MeasureString(lvw.Columns[0].Text, lvw.Font);
    int rowHeight = (int)rowSize.Height + 2 * ymargin;

    // Get the column widths in printer units.
    float[] colWids = lvw.ColumnWidths(gr, 4 * xmargin);

    // Print.
    int numColumns = lvw.Columns.Count;
    using (StringFormat sf = new StringFormat())
    {
        // Draw the column headers.
        sf.Alignment = StringAlignment.Center;
        sf.LineAlignment = StringAlignment.Center;
        for (int i = 0; i < numColumns; i++)
        {
            RectangleF rect = new RectangleF(x, y, colWids[i], rowHeight);
            gr.DrawString(lvw.Columns[i].Text, lvw.Font, headerBrush, rect, sf);
            gr.DrawRectangle(gridPen, rect);
            x += colWids[i];
        }
        y += rowHeight;
        // Draw the data.
```

```
foreach (ListViewItem item in lvw.Items)
{
    x = location.X;
    for (int i = 0; i < numColumns; i++)
    {
        RectangleF rect = new RectangleF(
            x + xmargin, y, colWids[i] - 2 * xmargin, rowHeight);

        switch (lvw.Columns[i].TextAlign)
        {
            case HorizontalAlignment.Left:
                sf.Alignment = StringAlignment.Near;
                break;
            case HorizontalAlignment.Center:
                sf.Alignment = StringAlignment.Center;
                break;
            case HorizontalAlignment.Right:
                sf.Alignment = StringAlignment.Far;
                break;
        }

        gr.DrawString(item.SubItems[i].Text, lvw.Font,
            headerBrush, rect, sf);
        rect = new RectangleF(x, y, colWids[i], rowHeight);
        gr.DrawRectangle(gridPen, rect);
        x += colWids[i];
    }
    y += rowHeight;
}
```

The method takes as parameters the location where the control should be drawn and the Graphics object on which to draw. Normally, that's the Graphics object used by the PrintPage event handler to represent the printed page, although you could use this method to draw the control on a Bitmap or other drawing surface.

The method also takes parameters giving the brushes it should use to draw the data's headers and the data itself, and a pen to use when drawing a grid around the data. You could add other parameters to specify such things as background colors and fonts, but that would make this method even more complex and it's already complicated enough for an example.

The code defines constants xmargin and ymargin, which it uses to allow a bit of space between the data items and the grid lines around them. The code then initializes variables x and y to be the upper left corner of the area where the control should be printed.

Next, the code uses the Graphics object's MeasureString method to see how tall a header row should be. It adds a little space to allow some extra room.

The program then calls the ColumnWidths extension method to get the widths that the columns need to be to hold the data. I'll describe that method shortly.

At this point, the code is ready to print. It creates a `StringFormat` object and prepares it to center text vertically and horizontally.

The code then loops through the `ListView` control's columns printing each column's header. To do that, it makes a `RectangleF` object at the current x and y position to contain the header. It is as wide as the column and as tall as the previously calculated header row height.

After drawing a header, the code uses the `Graphics` object's `DrawRectangle` extension method to draw a rectangle around the text. (That method is described in, "7. Draw a Simple Histogram (37).") It then adds the column's width to the current x value.

After it has drawn all of the headers, the code adds the header row height to y so the next line of data is moved down one row.

Now the program draws the data. For each row, the code resets x to the left edge of the available area. The code then loops through the data in each row, drawing each piece of text and then drawing a rectangle around it.

The following code shows the `ColumnWidths` extension method.

```
// Return necessary column widths.
public static float[] ColumnWidths(this ListView lvw, Graphics gr, int margin)
{
    int numColumns = lvw.Columns.Count;
    float[] widths = new float[numColumns];
    for (int i = 0; i < numColumns; i++)
    {
        // Allow room for the header.
        SizeF size = gr.MeasureString(lvw.Columns[i].Text, lvw.Font);
        widths[i] = size.Width;

        // Allow room for the data.
        foreach (ListViewItem item in lvw.Items)
        {
            size = gr.MeasureString(item.SubItems[i].Text, lvw.Font);
            if (widths[i] < size.Width) widths[i] = size.Width;
        }
        widths[i] += margin;
    }
    return widths;
}
```

This method creates an array to hold the `ListView` control's column widths. It then loops through the columns. It uses the `Graphics` object's `MeasureString` method to measure the header text and sets the column's width to its size.

The code then loops through the `ListView` control's rows, measures the item in the current column, and updates the column width if necessary.

After it has checked all of the columns, the method returns the array of widths.

77. LOAD A TREEVIEW WITH XML DATA (28)

This example shows how to load a TreeView control with XML data. Because XML files hold hierarchical data, it makes sense to use them to hold data for a TreeView control, which displays hierarchical data.

When the program starts, the following Load event handler starts the loading process.

```
// Load the TreeView data.
private void Form1_Load(object sender, EventArgs e)
{
    itemsTreeView.LoadFromXmlFile("test.xml");
    itemsTreeView.ExpandAll();
}
```

This code simply calls the LoadFromXmlFile extension method described next. It then calls the TreeView control's ExpandAll method to make the control show all of its data.

The following code shows the LoadFromXmlFile extension method.

```
// Load a TreeView control from an XML file.
public static void LoadFromXmlFile(this TreeView trv, string filename)
{
    // Load the XML document.
    XmlDocument xmlDoc = new XmlDocument();
    xmlDoc.Load(filename);

    // Add the root node's children to the TreeView.
    trv.Nodes.Clear();
    AddTreeViewChildNodes(trv.Nodes, xmlDoc.DocumentElement);
}
```

This method creates a new XmlDocument object and then loads the XML file into it. It clears the TreeView control's Nodes collection and then calls the following AddTreeViewChildNodes method to do all of the real work.

```
// Add the children of this XML node to this child nodes collection.
private static void AddTreeViewChildNodes(TreeNodeCollection parentNodes,
    XmlNode xmlNode)
{
    foreach (XmlNode xmlChild in xmlNode.ChildNodes)
```

```
    {
        // Make the new TreeView node.
        TreeNode newNode = parentNodes.Add(xmlChild.Name);

        // Recursively load this node's descendants.
        AddTreeViewChildNodes(newNode.Nodes, xmlChild);
    }
}
```

This method recursively adds the children of an XML node and their descendants to a `TreeNodeCollection`.

The method loops through the XML node's children. It adds each child to the `TreeNodeCollection` and then calls itself recursively to add the child's children to the new node's `Nodes` collection.

The first time it's called, the XML parent node is the XML document's root node and the `TreeNodeCollection` is the `TreeView` control's `Nodes` collection. That means the first call loops through the XML root node's children and adds them to the `TreeView` control's `Nodes` collection. As a result, the top-level nodes in the `TreeView` are the children of the XML root node and the root node itself is ignored.

This example uses the following XML file.

```
<Items>
  <Food>
    <Vegetables>
      <Beans />
      <Peas />
      <Lettuce />
    </Vegetables>
    <Desserts>
      <Ice_Cream />
      <Cookies>
        <Peanut_Butter_Chip />
        <Chocolate_Chip />
      </Cookies>
      <Cake />
    </Desserts>
    <Fruit>
      <Bananas />
      <Peaches />
    </Fruit>
  </Food>
  <Sports>
    <Volleyball />
    <Baseball />
  </Sports>
</Items>
```

If you look at the picture at the beginning of this example, you'll see that the `TreeView` has top-level nodes Food and Sports; the `Items` node is missing.

If you want to have a single root node, just add it to the XML data inside a top-level `Items` element that the program will ignore.

Part XVII. System Interactions

This part of the book describes some examples that let a program interact with the operating system. They show how a program can get printer information, resolve relative paths, play system sounds, and get disk drive serial numbers.

78. GET DETAILED PRINTER INFORMATION (32)

Windows Management Instrumentation (WMI) provides classes that let you query the operating system. This example uses a WMI `ManagementObjectSearcher` object to query the system for information about its printers.

Before you use WMI, you need to add a reference to `System.Management`. This example makes using WMI easier by including the following two `using` directives.

```
using System.Drawing.Printing;
using System.Management;
```

When the program loads, it uses the following code to list the system's installed printers.

```
// List the installed printers.
private void Form1_Load(object sender, EventArgs e)
{
    // Find all of the installed printers.
    foreach (string printer in PrinterSettings.InstalledPrinters)
        printersComboBox.Items.Add(printer);

    // Select the first printer.
    printersComboBox.SelectedIndex = 0;
}
```

This code simply loops through the `PrinterSettings.InstalledPrinters` collection, adding the installed printers to the `printersComboBox`.

When you select a printer from the list, the program uses the following code to get information about that printer. It displays the printer's name, state, status, description, default-ness, vertical and horizontal resolution, port name, and paper sizes supported.

```
// Display information about the selected printer.
private void printersComboBox_SelectedIndexChanged(object sender, EventArgs e)
{
    // Lookup arrays.
    string[] PrinterStatuses =
    {
        "???", "Other", "Unknown", "Idle", "Printing", "Warming Up",
        "Stopped Printing", "Offline", "Paused", "Error", "Busy",
        "Not Available", "Waiting", "Processing", "Initialization",
        "Power Save", "Pending Deletion", "I/O Active", "Manual Feed",
    };
    string[] PrinterStates =
```

```
    {
        "Idle", "Paused", "Error", "Pending Deletion", "Paper Jam", "Paper Out",
        "Manual Feed", "Paper Problem", "Offline", "I/O Active", "Busy",
        "Printing", "Output Bin Full", "Not Available", "Waiting", "Processing",
        "Initialization", "Warming Up", "Toner Low", "No Toner", "Page Punt",
        "User Intervention Required", "Out of Memory", "Door Open",
        "Server_Unknown", "Power Save",
    };

    // Get a ManagementObjectSearcher for the printer.
    string query = "SELECT * FROM Win32_Printer WHERE Name='" +
        printersComboBox.SelectedItem.ToString() + "'";
    ManagementObjectSearcher searcher =
        new ManagementObjectSearcher(query);

    // Get the ManagementObjectCollection representing
    // the result of the WMI query. Loop through its
    // single item. Display some of that item's properties.
    foreach (ManagementObject service in searcher.Get())
    {
        nameTextBox.Text = service.Properties["Name"].Value.ToString();

        UInt32 state = (UInt32)service.Properties["PrinterState"].Value;
        stateTextBox.Text = PrinterStates[state];

        UInt16 status = (UInt16)service.Properties["PrinterStatus"].Value;
        statusTextBox.Text = PrinterStatuses[status];

        descriptionTextBox.Text = GetPropertyValue(service.Properties["Description"]);
        defaultTextBox.Text = GetPropertyValue(service.Properties["Default"]);
        horResTextBox.Text =
            GetPropertyValue(service.Properties["HorizontalResolution"]);
        vertResTextBox.Text =
            GetPropertyValue(service.Properties["VerticalResolution"]);
        portTextBox.Text = GetPropertyValue(service.Properties["PortName"]);

        paperSizesListBox.Items.Clear();
        string[] paperSizes = (string[])service.Properties["PrinterPaperNames"].Value;
        foreach (string size in paperSizes) paperSizesListBox.Items.Add(size);

        // List the available properties.
        foreach (PropertyData data in service.Properties)
        {
            string text = data.Name;
            if (data.Value != null)
                text += ": " + data.Value.ToString();
            Console.WriteLine(text);
        }
    }
}
}
```

This code starts by defining some arrays to convert numeric values into textual values. For example, the printer state Paper Jam has numeric code 4 so `PrinterStates[4]` is "Paper Jam."

The code then creates a new `ManagementObjectSearcher` object, passing its constructor the following query.

```
SELECT * FROM Win32_Printer WHERE Name='name'
```

Here name is replaced with the name of the printer that you selected.

That object's Get method returns a ManagementObjectCollection containing a list of ManagementObjects. This example selects information for a single printer, so the collection only holds one object.

The code examines that object and uses its Properties collection to retrieve key values. To make this a bit easier, the code uses the GetPropertyValue method described shortly.

The management object's PrinterPaperNames property contains an array of paper size names. The code loops through this array adding the paper sizes to the form's ListBox.

Finally, so you can see what values are available, the program loops through all of the object's properties writing their names into the Console window. Within WMI, the Win32_Printer class provides printer information so that class's properties are the ones that are listed. For more information about those properties, see tinyurl.com/m77cq6f.

The following GetPropertyValue method returns a string representing the value of a PropertyData object.

```
// If the data is not null and has a value, return it.
private string GetPropertyValue(PropertyData data)
{
    if ((data == null) || (data.Value == null)) return "";
    return data.Value.ToString();
}
```

If the object or its Value property is null, the method returns an empty string. If the Value isn't null, the method returns the object's Value converted into a string.

WMI is a sort of SQL-like scripting language that lets you learn about and control many parts of the system that are hard to get at through the .NET Framework or even API functions. It's pretty amazing what information is in there if you can figure out how to find it. For more information on using WMI, see tinyurl.com/ml2cbz9.

79. COMBINE AND RESOLVE RELATIVE PATHS (51)

Sometimes it's useful for a C# program to combine relative paths. For example, when you're working on a program in Visual Studio, the executable program runs in either the bin\Debug or the bin\Release subdirectory below the source code directory. If you want to manipulate a file that is in the same directory as the project's source code, you need to move two levels up the directory hierarchy from the executable program's startup location.

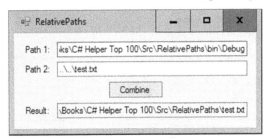

The System.IO.Path class provides several static methods for manipulating file paths. For example, the Combine method combines two paths.

Unfortunately, that method simply concatenates the paths. For example, if you combine the absolute path C:\Data\Test with the relative path ..\data.txt, you get C:\Data\Test\..\data.txt, which is probably not what you want.

The .. part of the relative path moves to the parent directory, so what you probably want in this example is C:\Data\data.txt.

Fortunately, the Path class's GetFullPath method resolves a path that contains relative elements such as this one and returns an absolute path.

The example uses the following code to combine the two paths that you enter.

```
string combined = Path.GetFullPath(
    Path.Combine(path1TextBox.Text, path2TextBox.Text));
resultTextBox.Text = combined;
```

You can use a similar technique to combine other paths in your programs. For example, a program running in Visual Studio can use the following code to find the path to its source code directory.

```
string sourceDir = Path.GetFullPath(
    Path.Combine(Application.StartupPath, "..\\.."));
```

Of course this assumes that the program is running from inside the bin\Debug or bin\Release directory.

NOTE: Another way to work with a file in the source code directory is to copy it into the startup directory. Add the file to the project. Then set its Build Action property to Content and set its Copy to Output Directory property to Copy if newer. When you run the program, Visual Studio will copy the file into the startup directory if necessary.

80. PLAY SYSTEM SOUNDS (73)

Sometimes you may want to make your program beep or make some other sound. It would be nice to just call a Beep method. Visual Basic has such a method but C# does not.

You can use `Console.Beep()`, but that produces a rather jarring sound that doesn't fit in well with the modern Windows theme. The solution is to use the `System.Media.SystemSounds` classes.

This example plays those sounds. To make things a bit more interesting, it also displays matching icons on its buttons.

At design time, I made the buttons large, set their `ImageAlign` properties to middle left, and set their `TextAlign` properties to middle right. When the program starts, the following `Load` event handler sets the button images.

```
// Add icons to the buttons.
private void Form1_Load(object sender, EventArgs e)
{
    asteriskButton.Image = SystemIcons.Asterisk.ToBitmap();
    beepButton.Image = SystemIcons.Error.ToBitmap();
    exclamationButton.Image = SystemIcons.Exclamation.ToBitmap();
    handButton.Image = SystemIcons.Hand.ToBitmap();
    questionButton.Image = SystemIcons.Question.ToBitmap();
    consoleBeepButton.Image = SystemIcons.Application.ToBitmap();
}
```

The `SystemIcons` class has no images that match the Beep or Console Beep buttons, so I used the `Error` and `Application` icons for those buttons.

When you click the Asterisk button, the following code plays the asterisk sound.

```
SystemSounds.Asterisk.Play();
```

That's all there is to it. Most of the other buttons work similarly.

The Console.Beep button is a bit different. It uses the following code to play its sound.

```
Console.Beep();
```

The exact sound that these methods produce depends on the system's sound theme. To change the system's sounds, run the Control Panel, search for "sounds," and click the "Change system sounds" entry. On the Sound Control Panel, click the Sounds tab and use it to change the sounds.

81. GET A DISK DRIVE'S SERIAL NUMBER (99)

This example shows how to get information about a disk drive including the drive's serial number. That can be useful, for example, if you want to restrict a program so it only runs if that drive is present.

The original example on C# Helper used the `GetVolumeInformation` API function to get information about a disk

DiskDriveSerialNumber				
Drive:	C:\			
Drive Type:	Fixed	Volume Name:	OS	
Name:	C:\	Serial Number:	1987243876	
Root:	C:\	Max Component Length:	255	
Is Ready:	True	File System:	NTFS	
Volume Label:	OS	Flags:	H3e700ff	
Drive Format:	NTFS			
Total Size:	985,450,672,128			
Total Free Space:	689,204,793,344			
Available Free Space:	689,204,793,344			

drive. It turns out that the `DriveInfo` class makes some of the same information available more easily, so I've modified the example to display the `DriveInfo` information, too.

When the program starts, the following `Load` event handler fills the form's `ComboBox` with the names of the systems drives.

```
// List the available drives.
private void Form1_Load(object sender, EventArgs e)
{
    driveComboBox.DataSource = DriveInfo.GetDrives();
}
```

This code simply uses the `DriveInfo` class's `GetDrives` method to get an array of information about the system's drives. It sets the `ComboBox` control's `DataSource` property equal to that array to make the `ComboBox` display the drive names.

When you select a drive from the `ComboBox`, the following code executes.

```
// Display the selected drive's information.
private void driveComboBox_SelectedIndexChanged(object sender, EventArgs e)
{
    // Get information available via DriveInfo.
    DriveInfo info = new DriveInfo(driveComboBox.Text);
    driveTypeTextBox.Text = info.DriveType.ToString();
    nameTextBox.Text = info.Name;
    rootTextBox.Text = info.RootDirectory.Name;
    isReadyTextBox.Text = info.IsReady.ToString();

    if (info.IsReady)
    {
        volumeLabelTextBox.Text = info.VolumeLabel;
        driveFormatTextBox.Text = info.DriveFormat;
        totalSizeTextBox.Text = info.TotalSize.ToString("N0");
```

```
        totalFreeSizeTextBox.Text = info.TotalFreeSpace.ToString("N0");
        availableFreeSpaceTextBox.Text = info.AvailableFreeSpace.ToString("N0");

        // Get more information.
        string volumeName, fileSystemName;
        uint serialNumber, maxComponentLength;
        UInt32 flags;
        GetVolumeInfo(driveComboBox.Text, out volumeName,
            out serialNumber, out maxComponentLength,
            out fileSystemName, out flags);

        volumeNameTextBox.Text = volumeName;
        serialNumberTextBox.Text = serialNumber.ToString();
        maxComponentLengthTextBox.Text = maxComponentLength.ToString();
        fileSystemTextBox.Text = fileSystemName;
        flagsTextBox.Text = "H" + flags.ToString("x");
    }
    else
    {
        volumeLabelTextBox.Clear();
        driveFormatTextBox.Clear();
        totalSizeTextBox.Clear();
        totalFreeSizeTextBox.Clear();
        availableFreeSpaceTextBox.Clear();

        volumeNameTextBox.Clear();
        serialNumberTextBox.Clear();
        maxComponentLengthTextBox.Clear();
        fileSystemTextBox.Clear();
        flagsTextBox.Clear();
    }
}
```

This code creates a new DriveInfo object for the selected drive. It uses that object to display various pieces of drive information such as the drive type, name, and root directory.

If the DriveInfo object's IsReady flag is true, then the code continues to display other information. It calls the GetVolumeInformation method described shortly to get even more information and displays it.

If the IsReady flag is false, then the code clears many of the form's textboxes. If the drive isn't ready, then the program cannot use the DriveInfo properties corresponding to those textboxes or it throws an exception. Similarly, if the drive isn't ready, the program cannot call the GetVolumeInfo method or it throws an exception.

The GetVolumeInfo method uses an API function. The following code shows the function's declaration.

```
[DllImport("kernel32.dll")]
private static extern long GetVolumeInformation(
    string PathName,
    StringBuilder VolumeNameBuffer,
    UInt32 VolumeNameSize,
    ref UInt32 VolumeSerialNumber,
    ref UInt32 MaximumComponentLength,
```

```
      ref UInt32 FileSystemFlags,
      StringBuilder FileSystemNameBuffer,
      UInt32 FileSystemNameSize);
```

The following code shows the GetVolumeInfo method.

```
// Get file system information.
private void GetVolumeInfo(string driveLetter, out string volumeName,
    out uint serialNumber, out uint maxComponentLength,
    out string fileSystemName, out UInt32 flags)
{
    uint serialNum = 0;
    uint maxComponentLen = 0;
    StringBuilder volumeNameSb = new StringBuilder(256);
    UInt32 fileSystemFlags = new UInt32();
    StringBuilder fileSystemNameSb = new StringBuilder(256);

    if (GetVolumeInformation(driveLetter, volumeNameSb,
        (UInt32)volumeNameSb.Capacity, ref serialNum,
        ref maxComponentLen, ref fileSystemFlags, fileSystemNameSb,
        (UInt32)fileSystemNameSb.Capacity) == 0)
    {
        throw new Exception("Error getting volume information");
    }

    volumeName = volumeNameSb.ToString();
    serialNumber = serialNum;
    maxComponentLength = maxComponentLen;
    fileSystemName = fileSystemNameSb.ToString();
    flags = fileSystemFlags;
}
```

This method prepares some variables and passes them to the GetVolumeInformation API function. If the function returns 0 to indicate an error, the method throws an exception.

If the function doesn't return 0, the method saves its results in its out parameters.

Part XVIII. Mathematics

The examples in this part of the book are mathematical. Most of them are fairly complicated. I guess people don't need help with easy things like performing multiplication or using Math class methods such as Sqrt and Sin, so posts describing those kinds of simple operations aren't in the C# Helper Top 100.

These examples demonstrate such techniques as solving systems of equations, finding least squares fits, finding prime numbers, and factoring numbers efficiently. They can be pretty challenging, but they're also quite interesting even if you don't follow every detail. (I also think they're pretty fun, but then again, I was a math major.)

82. SOLVE A SYSTEM OF EQUATIONS (64)

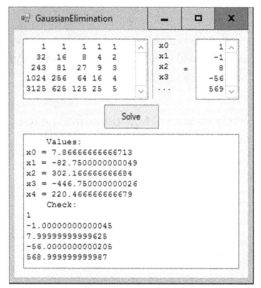

This example shows how to use Gaussian elimination to solve a linear system of equations with the following form.

```
A1*x1 + B1*x2 + ... + N1*xn = C1
A2*x1 + B2*x2 + ... + N2*xn = C2
        ...
An*x1 + Bn*x2 + ... + Nn*xn = Cn
```

The goal is to solve for the xs. For example, consider the following two equations with two unknowns x1 and x2.

```
9 * x1 + 4 * x2 = 7
4 * x1 + 3 * x2 = 8
```

The solution to these equations consists of values for x1 and x2 that make both equations true. In this example, you can verify that the values -1 and 4 work.

 NOTE: This example uses a lot of matrices, vectors, and other linear algebra stuff. If you're not comfortable with matrices and vectors, you might want to brush up a bit at Wikipedia, Kahn Academy, or an old math textbook.

You can represent a system of equations such as this one as a matrix multiplied by a vector of variables x1, x2, ..., xn, resulting in a vector of constants C1, C2, ..., Cn.

$$\begin{vmatrix} A1 & B1 & ... & N1 \\ A2 & B2 & ... & N2 \\ & & \ddots & \\ An & Bn & ... & Nn \end{vmatrix} \times \begin{vmatrix} x1 \\ x2 \\ ... \\ xn \end{vmatrix} = \begin{vmatrix} C1 \\ C2 \\ ... \\ Cn \end{vmatrix}$$

The helper method `LoadArray`, which is described shortly, loads data from textboxes into an augmented matrix that includes a column holding the constants and a final column that will eventually hold the solution. The augmented array has the following form.

$$\begin{vmatrix} A1 & B1 & ... & N1 & C1 \\ A2 & B2 & ... & N2 & C2 \\ & & \ddots & & \\ An & Bn & ... & Nn & Cn \end{vmatrix}$$

The following code shows the `LoadArray` method.

```
// Load the augmented array.
// Column numCols holds the result values.
// Column numCols + 1 will hold the variables' final values after backsolving.
private double[,] LoadArray(out int numRows, out int numCols)
{
    // Build the augmented matrix.
    string[] valueRows = valuesTextBox.Text.Split(
        new string[] { "\r\n" }, StringSplitOptions.RemoveEmptyEntries);
    string[] coefRows = coefficientsTextBox.Text.Split(
        new string[] { "\r\n" }, StringSplitOptions.RemoveEmptyEntries);
    string[] oneRow = coefRows[0].Split(
        new string[] { " " }, StringSplitOptions.RemoveEmptyEntries);
    numRows = coefRows.GetUpperBound(0) + 1;
    numCols = oneRow.GetUpperBound(0) + 1;
    double[,] arr = new double[numRows, numCols + 2];
    for (int r = 0; r < numRows; r++)
    {
        oneRow = coefRows[r].Split(
            new char[] { ' ' }, StringSplitOptions.RemoveEmptyEntries);
        for (int c = 0; c < numCols; c++)
        {
            arr[r, c] = double.Parse(oneRow[c]);
        }
        arr[r, numCols] = double.Parse(valueRows[r]);
    }

    return arr;
}
```

When you click the Solve button, the program uses row operations to zero out leading terms in every row except one.

For example, to zero out the leading term in the second row, the program multiplies each entry in the first row by $-A2/A1$ and adds the result to the second row. Multiplying $A1$ by $-A2/A1$ gives $-A2$, which cancels out the value in the first column of row two.

The program makes similar substitutions to zero out the first elements in the other rows.

After it has zeroed out the first column except in the first row, the program uses row two to zero out the second column in rows three through n. It continues in this way, using entry $[K, K]$ to zero out column K in rows K+1 through n, until it can no longer zero out any entries.

There's one problem with this method. Suppose you're trying to zero out items in column K, but the value in position $[K, K]$ is 0. Then you can't divide by that value to zero out other entries in that column. In that case, you can swap this row with one of the following rows that has a non-zero entry in column K and continue.

If there is no row to swap with, there are two possibilities. First, if every remaining entry in the array is zero, then there are an infinite number of solutions to the equations. For example, consider the following equations.

```
1 * x0 - 2 * x1 = 0
2 * x0 - 4 * x1 = 0
```

When you zero out the first entry in the second row, you get the following augmented matrix.

$$\begin{vmatrix} 1 & -2 & 0 \\ 0 & 0 & 0 \end{vmatrix}$$

In this example the equations are true for any values of x0 and x1 as long as x0 = 2*x1.

The second possibility if you cannot finish zeroing out columns is that the first n entries in the final rows are all 0 and the final column in some of those rows is not 0. In that case there is no possible solution.

For example, consider the following equations.

```
x0 + x1 = 0
x0 + x1 = 1
```

When you zero out the first entry in the second row, you get the following augmented matrix.

$$\begin{vmatrix} 1 & 1 & 0 \\ 0 & 0 & 1 \end{vmatrix}$$

In this example, the original equations do not have a solution because they require x0 + x1 to be both 0 and 1.

Assuming the program *can* zero out the leading terms, the result is an upper-triangular matrix with all zeros in the lower left as shown in the following.

$$\begin{vmatrix} v1 & * & * & * & * \\ 0 & v2 & * & * & * \\ 0 & 0 & v3 & * & * \\ 0 & 0 & 0 & v4 & * \end{vmatrix}$$

Here the vi values are non-zero and the * values can be any value zero or otherwise.

At this point the final row has the form | 0 0 ... vn Ln | for some values Kn and Ln. This represents the equation 0*x1 + 0*x2 + ... + vn*xn = Ln, so it is easy to solve for xn. In that case, xn = Ln / vn. (We've found one of the solution values! Yay!)

The program plugs that value into the second-to-last row to calculate x(n-1) and continues "backsolving" up the rows until it has a value for every variable xi.

Gaussian elimination can produce three kinds of results: a single unique solution, non-unique solutions, or no solution. The program uses the following enumeration to represent those results.

```
// Possible results.
private enum GaussianResults
```

```
{
    UniqueSolution,
    NoUniqueSolution,
    NoSolution,
}
```

The following code shows the `GaussianElimination` method.

```
// Solve the system of equations.
private GaussianResults GaussianElimination(double[,] arr)
{
    const double tiny = 0.00001;
    GaussianResults result = GaussianResults.NoSolution;

    // Get the bounds of the original (non-augmented) array.
    int numRows = arr.GetUpperBound(0) + 1;
    int numCols = arr.GetUpperBound(1) - 1;

    // Zero out leading columns.
    for (int r = 0; r < numRows - 1; r++)
    {
        // Zero out all entries in column r after this row.
        // See if this row has a non-zero entry in column r.
        if (Math.Abs(arr[r, r]) < tiny)
        {
            // Too close to zero. Try to swap with a later row.
            for (int r2 = r + 1; r2 < numRows; r2++)
            {
                if (Math.Abs(arr[r2, r]) > tiny)
                {
                    // This row will work. Swap them.
                    for (int c = 0; c <= numCols; c++)
                    {
                        double tmp = arr[r, c];
                        arr[r, c] = arr[r2, c];
                        arr[r2, c] = tmp;
                    }
                    break;
                }
            }
        }

        // If this row has a non-zero entry in column r, use it.
        if (Math.Abs(arr[r, r]) > tiny)
        {
            // Zero out this column in later rows.
            for (int r2 = r + 1; r2 < numRows; r2++)
            {
                double factor = -arr[r2, r] / arr[r, r];
                for (int c = r; c <= numCols; c++)
                {
                    arr[r2, c] = arr[r2, c] + factor * arr[r, c];
                }
            }
        }
    }

    // Display the (hopefully) upper-triangular array.
    PrintArray(arr);
```

```
// See if we have a solution.
if (arr[numRows - 1, numCols - 1] == 0)
{
    // We have no solution.
    // See if all of the entries in this row are 0.
    bool allZeros = true;
    for (int c = 0; c <= numCols + 1; c++)
    {
        if (arr[numRows - 1, c] != 0)
        {
            allZeros = false;
            break;
        }
    }
    if (allZeros) result = GaussianResults.NoUniqueSolution;
    else result = GaussianResults.NoSolution;
}
else
{
    result = GaussianResults.UniqueSolution;

    // Backsolve.
    for (int r = numRows - 1; r >= 0; r--)
    {
        double tmp = arr[r, numCols];
        for (int r2 = r + 1; r2 < numRows; r2++)
        {
            tmp -= arr[r, r2] * arr[r2, numCols + 1];
        }
        arr[r, numCols + 1] = tmp / arr[r, r];
    }
}
return result;
}
```

This method just follows the algorithm described earlier.

Here are some sample equations that you can plug in to test the program.

$$\begin{vmatrix} 1 & -3 & 1 \\ 2 & -8 & 8 \\ -6 & 3 & -15 \end{vmatrix} \times \begin{vmatrix} x1 \\ x2 \\ x3 \end{vmatrix} = \begin{vmatrix} 4 \\ -2 \\ 9 \end{vmatrix} \text{ has solution (3, -1, -2)}$$

$$\begin{vmatrix} 9 & 3 & 4 \\ 4 & 3 & 4 \\ 1 & 1 & 1 \end{vmatrix} \times \begin{vmatrix} x1 \\ x2 \\ x3 \end{vmatrix} = \begin{vmatrix} 7 \\ 8 \\ 3 \end{vmatrix} \text{ has solution (-0.2, 4, -0.8)}$$

$$\begin{vmatrix} 1 & 1 & 1 & 1 & 1 \\ 32 & 16 & 8 & 4 & 2 \\ 243 & 81 & 27 & 9 & 3 \\ 1024 & 256 & 64 & 16 & 4 \\ 3125 & 625 & 125 & 25 & 5 \end{vmatrix} \times \begin{vmatrix} x1 \\ x2 \\ x3 \\ x4 \\ x5 \end{vmatrix} = \begin{vmatrix} 1 \\ -1 \\ 8 \\ -56 \\ 569 \end{vmatrix}$$

has approximate solution (7.867, -82.750, 302.167, -446.750, 220.467).

$$\begin{vmatrix} 2 & -1 & 1 \\ 3 & 2 & -4 \\ -6 & 3 & -3 \end{vmatrix} \times \begin{vmatrix} x1 \\ x2 \\ x3 \end{vmatrix} = \begin{vmatrix} 1 \\ 4 \\ 2 \end{vmatrix}$$ has no solution

$$\begin{vmatrix} 1 & -1 & 2 \\ 4 & 4 & -2 \\ -2 & 2 & -4 \end{vmatrix} \times \begin{vmatrix} x1 \\ x2 \\ x3 \end{vmatrix} = \begin{vmatrix} -3 \\ 1 \\ 6 \end{vmatrix}$$ has no unique solution

For a more in-depth discussion of Gaussian elimination, see my article "Predicting Your Firm's Future with Least Squares, Part II" at tinyurl.com/kufuyal.

For a more general and theoretical discussion on Gaussian elimination, see the Wolfram MathWorld article "Gaussian Elimination" at tinyurl.com/723vz.

83. FIND A LINEAR LEAST SQUARES FIT (67)

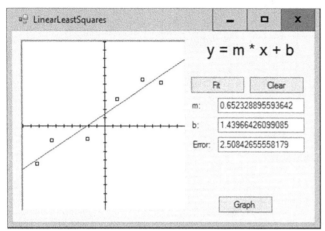

This example shows how you can make a linear least squares fit to a set of data points. Click on the `PictureBox` to select some points. Then click the Fit button to make a line to fit the points.

Suppose you have a set of data points that you believe were generated by a process that should ideally be linear. In that case, you might like to find the best parameters m and b to make the line y = m * x + b fit those points as closely as possible.

A common approach to this problem is to minimize the sum of the squares of the vertical distances between the line and the points. In the picture on the right, the vertical errors between the line and the data points are shown by dark vertical line segments.

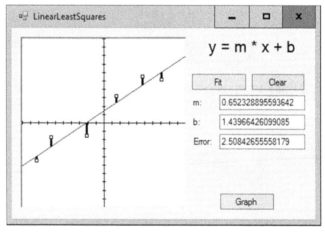

For example, suppose the point P0 = (x0, y0) is one of your data points. The vertical error for that point is the difference between y0 and the line's Y coordinate for that X position. In this case, the error is y0 - (m * x0 + b).

To calculate the total error squared, you square this error and add up the results for all of the data points.

Keep in mind that you know all of the points so, for given values of m and b, you can easily loop through all of the points and calculate the total error squared.

The following code shows a function that does just that.

```csharp
// Return the error squared.
public static double ErrorSquared(List<PointF> points, double m, double b)
{
    double total = 0;
    foreach (PointF pt in points)
    {
        double dy = pt.Y - (m * pt.X + b);
        total += dy * dy;
```

```
        }
        return total;
    }
```

This code loops through the points subtracting each point's Y coordinate from the Y coordinate of the line at the point's X position. It squares the error and adds it to the total. When it finishes its loop, the method returns the total of the squared errors.

The following equation shows the error function E as a mathematical equation.

$$E(m, b) = \sum (y_i - (m * x_i + b))^2$$

Here the sum is performed over all of the data points (x_i, y_i).

To find the least squares fit, you need to minimize this function $E(m, b)$. That sounds intimidating until you remember that the x_i and y_i values are all known–they're the values you're trying to fit with the line.

The only variables in this equation are m and b, so it's relatively easy to minimize this equation by using a little calculus. Simply take the partial derivatives of E with respect to m and b, set the two resulting equations equal to 0, and solve for m and b.

If you take the partial derivative with respect to m and rearrange a bit to gather common terms and pull constants out of the sums, you get the following.

$$\frac{\partial E}{\partial m} = \sum 2 * (y_i - (m * x_i + b)) * (-x)$$

$$= \sum -2 * (y_i * x_i - m * x_i^2 - b * x_i)$$

$$= 2 * \left(m * \sum x_i^2 + b * \sum x_i - \sum (y_i * x_i) \right)$$

Next if you take the partial derivative with respect to b and rearrange a bit, you get the following.

$$\frac{E}{\partial b} = \sum 2 * (x_i - (m * y_i + b)) * (-1)$$

$$= 2 * \left(m * \sum x_i + b * \sum 1 - \sum y_i \right)$$

To find the minimum for the error function, you set these two equations equal to 0 and solve for m and b.

To make working with the equations a bit easier, define the following values.

$$S_x = \sum x_i$$
$$S_{xx} = \sum x_i^2$$
$$S_{xy} = \sum y_i * x_i$$
$$S_y = \sum x_i$$
$$S_1 = \sum 1$$

If you make these substitutions and set the equations equal to 0, you get the following system of two equations and two unknowns.

$$0 = 2 * (m * S_{xx} + b * S_x - S_{xy})$$
$$0 = 2 * (m * S_x + b * S_1 - S_y)$$

Solving for m and b gives:

$$m = (S_{xy} * S_1 - S_x * S_y)/(S_{xx} * S_1 - S_x * S_x)$$
$$b = (S_{xy} * S_x - S_y * S_{xx})/(S_x * S_x - S_1 * S_{xx})$$

Again, these look like intimidating equations, but all of the S values are things that you can calculate given the data points that you are trying to fit.

The following code calculates the S values and uses them to find the linear least squares fit for the points in a List<PointF>.

```
// Find the least squares linear fit. Return the total error.
public static double FindLinearLeastSquaresFit(List<PointF> points,
    out double m, out double b)
{
    // Perform the calculation.
    // Find the values S1, Sx, Sy, Sxx, and Sxy.
    double S1 = points.Count;
    double Sx = 0;
    double Sy = 0;
    double Sxx = 0;
    double Sxy = 0;
    foreach (PointF pt in points)
    {
        Sx += pt.X;
        Sy += pt.Y;
        Sxx += pt.X * pt.X;
        Sxy += pt.X * pt.Y;
    }

    // Solve for m and b.
    m = (Sxy * S1 - Sx * Sy) / (Sxx * S1 - Sx * Sx);
```

```
    b = (Sxy * Sx - Sy * Sxx) / (Sx * Sx - S1 * Sxx);

    return Math.Sqrt(ErrorSquared(points, m, b));
}
```

For a slightly different explanation, see my DevX article "Predicting Your Firm's Future with Least Squares, Part I" at tinyurl.com/m3l4azh. (Free registration is required.)

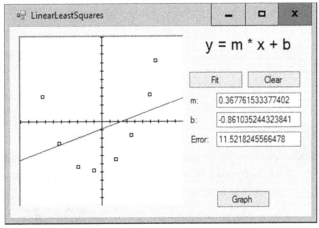

This example finds a line that fits a set of data. Naturally, that only gives you a useful result if the data points should ideally lie along a line. If the points were produced by a non-linear system then the line may not be much use. For example, in the picture on the right, the line fits the data points very poorly.

In cases such as this one, a polynomial with a higher degree may fit the points more closely. In this particular example, a quadratic equation of the form $y = Ax^2 + Bx + C$ would give a better fit.

The next example shows how to find polynomials such as that one to fit points that don't lie along a line.

84. FIND A POLYNOMIAL LEAST SQUARES FIT (33)

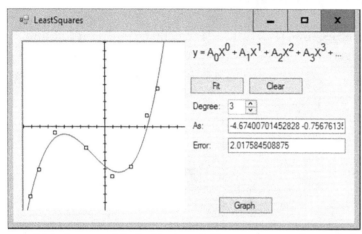

This example shows how to make a polynomial least squares fit to a set of data points. Click on the PictureBox to select some points. Then click the Fit button to make a polynomial curve to fit the points. Change the Degree and click Fit again to try different kinds of polynomials.

The calculations actually aren't too hard if you remember even the simplest calculus, but they are fairly long and intimidating. Still you can get through them if you're patient and take things one step at a time.

When you're looking for a polynomial least squares fit, the goal is to find a polynomial function that minimizes the square of the vertical distance between the curve and the data points. In the picture on the right, the dark vertical segments show the errors between the function and the data points. It's the sum of the squares of those distances that we are trying to minimize.

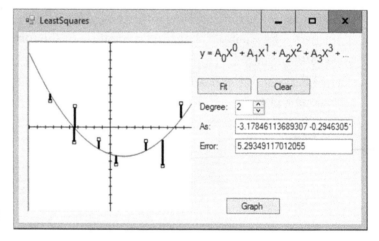

The basic approach is to make a polynomial equation where the coefficients are variables. You then subtract that function from the data values to make an error equation. Then you use some simple calculus to minimize the error equation.

That may sound scary, but we're working with a polynomial and polynomials are some of the simplest equations to minimize mathematically.

With a degree d polynomial least squares fit, we're looking for an equation with the following form.

$$F(x) = A_0 * x_i^0 + A_1 * x_i^1 + A_2 * x_i^2 + \cdots + A_N * x_i^d$$

Here the value d is given. Normally, you either suspect what value d should have based on the problem at hand, or you try different values of d until you get a fit that you like.

The coefficients A_0, A_1, …, A_d are the values that we need to find to make a good fit.

Keep in mind that you have a set of data points (x, y). If you knew the As, you could easily plug the x values into the equation to calculate the function's corresponding y values and then compare those to the data values to see how big the error is.

If you store the coefficients in a List<double>, then the following function calculates the value of the function $F(x)$ at the point x.

```
// The function.
public static double F(List<double> coeffs, double x)
{
    double total = 0;
    double xFactor = 1;
    for (int i = 0; i < coeffs.Count; i++)
    {
        total += xFactor * coeffs[i];
        xFactor *= x;
    }
    return total;
}
```

The following method uses the function F to calculate the total error squared between the data points and the polynomial curve.

```
// Return the error squared.
public static double ErrorSquared(List<PointF> points, List<double> coeffs)
{
    double total = 0;
    foreach (PointF pt in points)
    {
        double dy = pt.Y - F(coeffs, pt.X);
        total += dy * dy;
    }
    return total;
}
```

The following equation shows the error function mathematically.

$$E(A_0, A_1, ..., A_d) = \sum (y_i - (A_0 * x_i^0 + A_1 * x_i^1 + A_2 * x_i^2 + \cdots + A_N * x_i^d))^2$$

Yes, this is starting to look intimidating, but that's just because it's long. It's just a bunch of simple addition, multiplication, and exponentiation. Remember that the As are values that we're trying to find and they don't have exponents. The xs are the X coordinates of the data values, so we know those and it's easy to exponentiate them.

To simplify the error equation, let E_i be the error in the ith term. Then the equation becomes the following.

$$E(A_0, A_1, ..., A_d) = \sum E_i^2$$

The following list summarizes the steps for finding the best solution.

> ➤ Take the partial derivatives of the error function with respect to the variables that we need to find, in this case $A_0, A_1, ..., A_d$.
> ➤ Set all of the the partial derivatives equal to 0 to get d+1 equations and d+1 unknowns $A_0, A_1, ..., A_d$.
> ➤ Solve the equations for $A_0, A_1, ..., A_d$.

This may sound like a hard problem. Fortunately, the partial derivatives of the error function are simpler than you might think because that function only involves simple powers of the As. For example, the partial derivative with respect to A_k is:

$$\frac{\partial E}{\partial A_k} = \sum 2 * E_i * \frac{\partial E_i}{\partial A_k}$$

The partial derivative of E_i with respect to A_k contains lots of terms involving powers of x_i and different As, but all of those are constant with respect to A_k except for the single term $-A_k * x_{ik}$. The derivative of that term with respect to A_k is simply $-x_{ik}$. All of the other terms drop out leaving the following equation.

$$\frac{\partial E}{\partial A_k} = \sum 2 * E_i * (-x_i^k)$$

If you substitute the value of E_i, multiply the $-x_{ik}$ term through, and add the As separately, you get the following.

$$\frac{\partial E}{\partial A_k} = 2 * (\sum y_i * x_i^k - A_0 \sum x_i^k - A_1 \sum x_i^{k+1} - A_2 \sum x_i^{k+2} - \cdots - A_d \sum x_i^{k+d})$$

As usual, this looks pretty scary, but if you look closely you'll see that most of the terms are values that you can calculate using the x_i and y_i values. For example, the first term is simply the sum of the products of the y_i values and the x_i values raised to the kth power. The next term is A_0 times the sum of the x_i values raised to the kth power. Because the x_i

and y_i values are all known, this equation is the same as the following for a particular set of constants S.

$$\frac{\partial E}{\partial A_k} = 2 * (S - A_0 * S_0 - A_1 * S_1 - \cdots - A_d * S_d)$$

This is a relatively simple equation with d + 1 unknowns A_0, A_1, ..., A_d.

When you take the partial derivatives for the other values of k as k varies from 0 to d, you get d + 1 equations with d + 1 unknowns, and you can solve for the unknowns.

If d = 1, it's relatively easy to solve the equations. For the more general case, you need to use a more general method such as Gaussian elimination, which is described in the earlier example, "82. Solve a System of Equations (64)."

The following code shows how the example program finds polynomial least squares coefficients.

```
// Find the least squares linear fit.
public static List<double> FindPolynomialLeastSquaresFit(
    List<PointF> points, int degree)
{
    // Allocate space for (degree + 1) equations with
    // (degree + 2) terms each (including the constant term).
    double[,] coeffs = new double[degree + 1, degree + 2];

    // Calculate the coefficients for the equations.
    for (int j = 0; j <= degree; j++)
    {
        // Calculate the coefficients for the jth equation.

        // Calculate the constant term for this equation.
        coeffs[j, degree + 1] = 0;
        foreach (PointF pt in points)
        {
            coeffs[j, degree + 1] -= Math.Pow(pt.X, j) * pt.Y;
        }

        // Calculate the other coefficients.
        for (int aSub = 0; aSub <= degree; aSub++)
        {
            // Calculate the dth coefficient.
            coeffs[j, aSub] = 0;
            foreach (PointF pt in points)
            {
                coeffs[j, aSub] -= Math.Pow(pt.X, aSub + j);
            }
        }
    }

    // Solve the equations.
    double[] answer = GaussianElimination(coeffs);

    // Return the result converted into a List<double>.
    return answer.ToList<double>();
```

```
    }
```

The code simply builds an array holding the coefficients (the Ss in the preceding equation) and then calls the `GaussianElimination` method to find the As. It converts the result from an array into a `List<double>` for convenience and returns it.

Download the program and give it a try. It's pretty cool!

> **NOTE:** Use the smallest degree d that makes sense for your problem. If you use a very high degree, the curve will fit the points very closely, but it will probably emphasize structure that isn't really there.
>
> For example, the picture below shows the program fitting a degree four polynomial to points that really should be fit with a degree two polynomial.

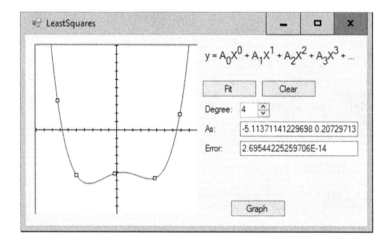

85. SIEVE OF ERATOSTHENES (63)

In the real world, a *sieve* is an object that strains solids from liquids (or big particles from smaller ones). In mathematics, a *number sieve* is a type of algorithm for finding prime numbers. The overall strategy is to make a table of values and then cross out those that are not primes. (It basically strains the primes out.) When you're done, the remaining numbers are the primes.

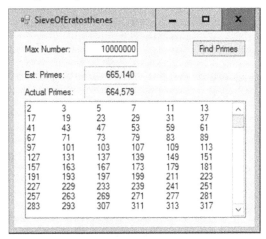

To use the sieve of Eratosthenes, you start with a table (array) containing one entry for the numbers in a range between 2 to some maximum value. This table keeps track of numbers that are primes. Initially every number is marked as prime.

Next, you look through the values in the table. If the next entry is still marked as prime, then it really *is* prime and you cross out all of the multiples of that number that appear later in the table.

> **NOTE:** The sieve used by this example is named after the Greek Eratosthenes of Cyrene (c. 276 BC–194 BC). Even though none of his works survive today, he's still a pretty interesting guy. He was a mathematician, geographer (he basically invented geography), poet, astronomer, and music theorist. He even became the head librarian of the Library at Alexandria.
>
> In addition to finding prime numbers, he calculated the circumference of the Earth, the tilt of the Earth's axis, and possibly the distance between the Earth and the Sun. For more information on Eratosthenes, see his Wikipedia article at `tinyurl.com/oc36gem`.

For example, you initially consider the number 2. That value is still marked as prime (all of them are so far), so you cross out the multiples of 2 that appear later in the table.

Next, you move to the value 3. It isn't a multiple of 2, so it's still marked as a prime. You cross out all of the multiples of 3 later in the table.

Now you move to the value 4. It was already crossed out when you examined the multiples of 2, so you don't do anything for this value.

You continue moving through the table, crossing out multiples of primes, until you reach the end of the table.

Note that you only need to consider numbers that are still marked as prime because you have already crossed out any numbers that are factors of a non-prime. For example, suppose you are considering the number 15. It was crossed out when you considered the number 3, so it will already be shown as non-prime in the table. At this point there's no need to consider multiples of 15 later in the table because they are also multiples of 3 so they were crossed out when you considered the number 3. (They were also crossed out again as multiples of 5.)

Note also that the smallest value you need to consider for the prime p is p^2. If a smaller multiple of p was a non-prime, then it would already have been crossed out by a smaller prime.

For example, suppose you're considering p = 13. Now suppose the value N = p * q is not prime and q < p. Then you would have already crossed out N when you were considering multiples of q. If q = 5, then you already crossed out N = p * q = 13 * 5 = 65 when you crossed out the multiples of 5.

Finally, the last value you need to consider is the square root of the largest value in the table. For example, suppose the table includes values up to 100, which has square root 10. You consider multiples of 7 because that is less than 10. Now think about the next prime, 11. The smallest value that you need to consider for 11 is 11^2 = 121. But that's bigger than the largest number in the table, so you don't need to cross out any more values. That means to find the primes between 2 and 100, you only need to check multiples of 2, 3, 5, and 7.

This last trick is particularly important when you're searching for lots of primes. For example, if the maximum value in the table is i = 100 million, then i^2 = 10 quadrillion, which is too big to fit in an int. That means if you even try to calculate i^2 to use it as an index in the table, the program will crash.

The following code shows how the example program uses a sieve of Eratosthenes to find prime numbers.

```
// Use a sieve of Eratosthenes to find primes.
private List<int> FindPrimes(int max)
{
    // Make an array indicating whether numbers are prime.
    // Initially 2 and odd values greater than 1 are true.
    bool[] isPrime = new bool[max + 1];
    isPrime[2] = true;
    for (int i = 3; i <= max; i += 2) isPrime[i] = true;

    // Find the square root of max.
    int maxRoot = (int)Math.Sqrt(max);

    // Cross out multiples of odd primes.
```

```
for (int i = 3; i <= max; i += 2)
{
    // If i > maxRoot, then there are no more entries to check.
    if (i > maxRoot) break;

    // See if i is prime.
    if (isPrime[i])
    {
        // Knock out multiples of i.
        for (int j = i * i; j <= max; j += i)
            isPrime[j] = false;
    }
}

// Convert the sieve into a list of primes.
List<int> result = new List<int>();
for (int i = 2; i <= max; i++) if (isPrime[i]) result.Add(i);

return result;
}
```

This method just follows the steps described earlier to build a sieve of Eratosthenes.

The main program uses the FindPrimes method to find the primes in the range that you specify. It then displays the number of primes it found, an estimate of the number of primes in the range, and a list of up to the first 1,000 primes. Most of that code isn't very interesting, so I won't include it here.

However, the equation that the program uses to estimate the number of primes *is* interesting. In 1808 the French mathematician Adrien-Marie Legendre published the following refined formula for estimating the number of primes between 1 and N.

$$\pi(N) \approx \frac{N}{log(N) - 1.08366}$$

The following code shows how the program uses that equation to displays its estimate.

```
double est = (max / (Math.Log(max) - 1.08366));
estPrimesLabel.Text = est.ToString("N0");
```

For large values of N, the estimate is remarkably close to the correct value. For example, in the picture at the beginning of this example, the program estimated that the number of primes would be 665,140. The correct value is 664,579, a difference of around 0.084%.

For more information on this kind of estimate, see the Wikipedia article "Prime Number Theorem" at tinyurl.com/1z9ev52.

86. FACTOR NUMBERS (74)

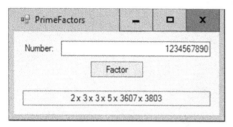

Once upon a time, I read an article where the author said something like the following.

My professor asked us whether we had prime factored our Social Security numbers yet. Being a normal person, I laughed along with everyone else. Being a nerd, I managed to resist for only three days.

Of course I immediately rushed to my computer and wrote a prime factoring program. At the time it was kind of hard because the computer I was using didn't have integers big enough to hold nine-digit numbers. This is a lot easier now.

This example uses the following `FindFactors` extension method to find a number's prime factors.

```
// Return the number's prime factors.
public static List<long> Factor(this long num)
{
    List<long> result = new List<long>();

    // Take out the 2s.
    while (num % 2 == 0)
    {
        result.Add(2);
        num /= 2;
    }

    // Take out other primes.
    long factor = 3;
    while (factor * factor <= num)
    {
        if (num % factor == 0)
        {
            // This is a factor.
            result.Add(factor);
            num /= factor;
        }
        else
        {
            // Go to the next odd number.
            factor += 2;
        }
    }

    // If num is not 1, then whatever is left is prime.
    if (num > 1) result.Add(num);

    return result;
}
```

First, while the number num is divisible by 2, the program adds 2 to the list of factors and divides num by 2.

Next, the program makes the variable factor take on odd values : 3, 5, 7, and so forth. If factor divides evenly into num, the program adds factor to the list of factors and divides num by it.

If factor does not divide num evenly, the program adds 2 to factor to check the next odd number.

The program stops when $factor^2$ is greater than num.

The following code shows how the program uses this method.

```
// Get the factors.
List<long> factors = number.Factor();
List<string> strings = factors.ConvertAll<string>(x => x.ToString());
factorsTextBox.Text = string.Join(" x ", strings.ToArray());
```

This code first uses the FindFactors extension method to get the list of number's factors.

That list contains long integers and the program needs to display strings, so the code calls the list's ConvertAll method. That's a LINQ extension method that takes as a parameter a method that converts each of the items in the list into a new data type. This example uses the lambda expression x => x.ToString() to call each value's ToString method to convert it into a string.

Finally, the code calls the string.Join method to merge the factors (now strings) into a single string. It uses the list's ToArray LINQ extension method to convert the list into an array because string.Join cannot work with a list. The code finishes by displaying the concatenated results in its textbox.

87. CONVERT BETWEEN BASES (92)

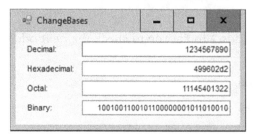

The Convert class's ToInt64 and ToString methods make it easy to convert between different numeric bases. For example, the following statement parses the hexadecimal value in the textbox named hexadecimalTextBox and saves the result in the long variable value. The second parameter's value of 16 means the method should parse the text as a base 16 (hexadecimal) value.

```
value = Convert.ToInt64(hexadecimalTextBox.Text, 16);
```

The following code does the opposite: it converts the value in variable value into a hexadecimal string and displays it in the TextBox named hexadecimalTextBox.

```
hexadecimalTextBox.Text = Convert.ToString(value, 16)
```

To parse and display values in other bases, simply replace the 16 with 8 for octal or 2 for binary.

Download the example and look over its code to see how the program responds when you type values in any of its textboxes.

Part XIX. Multimedia

The two examples in this part of the book show how a program can provide some simple multimedia support. The first example loads and displays animated GIF files in a Windows Forms application. The second shows one way a WPF program can control video playback.

88. LOAD AND DISPLAY ANIMATED GIFS (34)

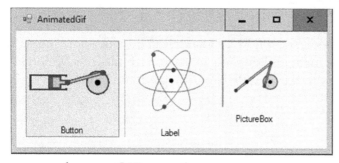

A Windows Forms application can display animated GIFs in the `Image` property of a `Button`, `Label`, `PictureBox`, or other control. The `PictureBox` control can even resize the GIF just as it can resize other images.

There are a couple of ways that you can change a GIF at runtime.

First, you can add the GIF as a resource. Open the Project menu and select Properties. On the Resources tab, open the Add Resource dropdown and select Add Existing File. Browse to the GIF file and click Open.

Now you can use the GIF resource as in the following statement.

```
gifButton.Image = Properties.Resources.piston;
```

You can also load a GIF from a file as in the following statement.

```
gifLabel.Image = new Bitmap("atom.gif");
```

The `Image.FromFile` method demonstrated by the following statement does basically the same thing.

```
gifPictureBox.Image = Image.FromFile("atom.gif");
```

This program demonstrates all three methods when you click on its `Button`, `Label`, or `PictureBox`. Download the example and look at its code to see how it cycles through the three images.

NOTE: If you display an animated GIF on a form by setting its `BackgroundImage` property, you can see the image but it's not animated. Just put it in a `PictureBox` without a border an it will look like it's on the form.

89. Control a Video with the WPF MediaElement Control (86)

WPF has some drawbacks, but one place where it really shines is its multimedia support. This example shows how you can control an MP4 video with WPF's `MediaElement` control. This control provides a surprisingly nice assortment of features that let you play, pause, position, speed, slow, and otherwise control a video.

The following XAML code shows how the example program defines its `MediaElement` control.

```
<MediaElement x:Name="flutePlayer" Margin="5"
    Grid.Row="0" Grid.Column="0"
    MediaOpened="flutePlayer_MediaOpened"
    ScrubbingEnabled="True"
    LoadedBehavior="Manual" Source="flutes.mp4"/>
```

Most of that code is self-explanatory. The control's name is `flutePlayer`. When it finishes opening some media, in this case the MP4 video named "flutes.mp4," it executes the `flutePlayer_MediaOpened` event handler.

At design time, I added the video file to the project, set its `Build Action` property to `Content`, and set its `Copy to Output Directory` property to `Copy if newer`. That way the video is available in the executable directory so the program can load it into the `MediaElement`.

Probably the least obvious part of the preceding XAML code is the `ScrubbingEnabled` property. That property is set to `true` to allow the control to update its display if the video is repositioned while the video is not running. (This isn't quite the classic definition of the term "scrubbing," but it's the term Microsoft picked. For more information on the term, see the Wikipedia article "Scrubbing (audio)" at `tinyurl.com/mtsnh44`.)

The media element's `LoadedBehavior` property is set to `Manual`, so the video doesn't start playing as soon as the control loads.

NOTE: Defining the sources for images and other media is one place where WPF does not shine. Figuring out exactly what values you need to give to the Build Action and Copy to Output Directory properties can be difficult.

Visual Studio doesn't help either. You can use the Properties window to set a control's Source property and the Window Designer will show the correct media. Unless the other properties are set correctly, however, the media are unavailable at runtime. The program won't crash; it just doesn't show you the image or video.

When it starts, the program executes the following code to prepare to run the video.

```
// A timer to display the video's location.
private DispatcherTimer VideoTimer;

// Create the timer and otherwise get ready.
private void Window_Loaded(object sender, RoutedEventArgs e)
{
    VideoTimer = new DispatcherTimer();
    VideoTimer.Interval = TimeSpan.FromSeconds(0.1);
    VideoTimer.Tick += new EventHandler(timer_Tick);
    flutePlayer.Stop();
}
```

This code creates a new `DispatcherTimer` to monitor the video's progress. It then calls the `MediaElement` control's `Stop` method. That makes the control load its media so you can see it. If you omit that statement, the control is invisible and the program's scroll bar doesn't show any position.

The following event handler executes when the media file finishes loading.

```
private void flutePlayer_MediaOpened(object sender, RoutedEventArgs e)
{
    positionScrollBar.Minimum = 0;
    positionScrollBar.Maximum =
        flutePlayer.NaturalDuration.TimeSpan.TotalSeconds;
    positionScrollBar.Visibility = Visibility.Visible;
}
```

This code sets the `ScrollBar` control's `Minimum` and `Maximum` properties so it can represent the video's full duration.

The program uses two helper methods, `ShowPosition` and `EnableButtons`. The following code shows the `ShowPosition` method.

```
// Show the play position in the ScrollBar and TextBox.
private void ShowPosition()
{
    positionScrollBar.Value = flutePlayer.Position.TotalSeconds;
    positionTextBox.Text = flutePlayer.Position.TotalSeconds.ToString("0.0");
}
```

This method displays the value of the MediaElement control's Position property in the program's ScrollBar and TextBox.

The following code shows the EnableButtons method.

```
// Enable and disable appropriate buttons.
private void EnableButtons(bool isPlaying)
{
    if (isPlaying)
    {
        playButton.IsEnabled = false;
        pauseButton.IsEnabled = true;
        playButton.Opacity = 0.5;
        pauseButton.Opacity = 1.0;
    }
    else
    {
        playButton.IsEnabled = true;
        pauseButton.IsEnabled = false;
        playButton.Opacity = 1.0;
        pauseButton.Opacity = 0.5;
    }
    VideoTimer.IsEnabled = isPlaying;
}
```

This method enables or disables the Play and Pause buttons depending on whether the video is currently playing. For example, if the video is playing, then the Play button is disabled and the Pause button is enabled.

The code sets the buttons' Opacity properties to 1.0 for enabled buttons (so they appear normally) and 0.5 for disabled buttons (so they appear grayed out).

The timer's Tick event handler, shown in the following code, simply calls the ShowPosition method to update the position display.

```
private void timer_Tick(object sender, EventArgs e)
{
    ShowPosition();
}
```

The following code shows how the buttons control the MediaElement control.

```
private void playButton_Click(object sender, RoutedEventArgs e)
{
    flutePlayer.Play();
    EnableButtons(true);
}
private void pauseButton_Click(object sender, RoutedEventArgs e)
{
    flutePlayer.Pause();
    EnableButtons(false);
}
private void stopButton_Click(object sender, RoutedEventArgs e)
{
    flutePlayer.Stop();
    EnableButtons(false);
    ShowPosition();
```

```
    }
    private void restartButton_Click(object sender, RoutedEventArgs e)
    {
        flutePlayer.Stop();
        flutePlayer.Play();
        EnableButtons(true);
    }
    private void fasterButton_Click(object sender, RoutedEventArgs e)
    {
        flutePlayer.SpeedRatio *= 1.5;
    }
    private void nextButton_Click(object sender, RoutedEventArgs e)
    {
        flutePlayer.Position += TimeSpan.FromSeconds(10);
        ShowPosition();
    }
    private void slowerButton_Click(object sender, RoutedEventArgs e)
    {
        flutePlayer.SpeedRatio /= 1.5;
    }
    private void previousButton_Click(object sender, RoutedEventArgs e)
    {
        flutePlayer.Position -= TimeSpan.FromSeconds(10);
        ShowPosition();
    }
```

The buttons' code is pretty self-explanatory.

When the video isn't playing, you can enter a time in the textbox and then click the Set Position button. When you do, the following code executes.

```
    private void setPositionButton_Click(object sender, RoutedEventArgs e)
    {
        TimeSpan timespan =
            TimeSpan.FromSeconds(double.Parse(positionTextBox.Text));
        flutePlayer.Position = timespan;
        ShowPosition();
    }
```

This code converts the time you entered into a `TimeSpan` and sets the player's `Position` property to it. It then calls `ShowPosition` to update the position display.

That's all there is to it. The `MediaPlayer` provides a lot of features for controlling the video relatively easily.

Part XX. Interoperability

The examples in this part of the book show how your C# programs can interoperate with other applications. The first example shows how you can make a DLL that provides methods for use by Excel or other Office applications. The other examples in this part of the book deal with drag and drop and the clipboard.

90. MAKE A C# DLL FOR USE WITH EXCEL (41)

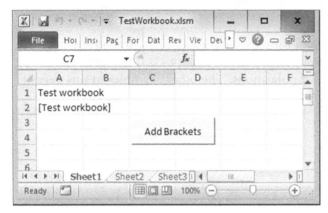

This example shows how to make a C# DLL and then use it from VBA (Visual Basic for Applications) code running in Excel. A similar procedure should work for other Microsoft Office applications.

Note that some of the steps may require modification and significant fiddling around in different versions of Windows. In particular, the number of bits used by the DLL and your Excel installation must match. My system is a 64-bit system and I have a 64-bit version of Office installed, so I needed to target the DLL for a 64-bit system.

> **NOTE:** A 32-/64-bit mismatch can be very confusing. If the DLL and Office are using different word sizes, the Excel Developer panel can see the DLL, the class inside it, and even the methods that the class exposes, but at runtime it halts with the unhelpful error message, "ActiveX Component can't create object."

Building and using the DLL isn't hard, but there are a lot of steps. The following sections explain those steps.

Building the DLL

To build the DLL, you need to run Visual Studio with elevated permissions so it can register the DLL properly. You can use `regasm` to do this yourself, but it's easier if Visual Studio does it for you.

To run with elevated privileges, open the Windows Start menu, find Visual Studio, right-click it, and select "Run as administrator."

Now use Visual Studio to create a new Class Library project. I called my library `DllForExcel`. Add a `public` class to the project (I called mine `CSharpTools`) and give that class the methods that you want the VBA code to be able to execute.

To allow the VBA code to use the class and its methods, give the class the `ComVisible` attribute. Also, give the class the `ClassInterface` attribute to create a description that VBA's IntelliSense can read so it can "see" the methods.

Optionally, you can also add the `Description` attribute to describe the class and its methods. VBA's version of IntelliSense doesn't display these descriptions, but the VBA Object Browser does.

The following code shows the class used by this example, including its attributes.

```
using System.Runtime.InteropServices;
using System.ComponentModel;

namespace DllForExcel
{
    // Put brackets around a string.
    [ComVisible(true)]
    [ClassInterface(ClassInterfaceType.AutoDual)]
    [Description("A class that contains tools for use by Office VBA code")]
    public class CSharpTools
    {
        [ComVisible(true)]
        [Description("Add brackets around the input string")]
        public string AddBrackets(string value)
        {
            return "[" + value + "]";
        }
    }
}
```

In addition to creating the class, you need to set some project properties. Open the Project menu and select Properties at the bottom. On the Application tab, click the Assembly Information button. On the Assembly Information dialog, check the "Make assembly COM-Visible" box and click OK.

Still in the project's properties, go to the Build tab. Set the platform target to match your Office installation, either x64 for 64-bit Office or x86 for 32-bit Office.

Also on the Build tab, scroll down and check the "Register for COM interop" box.

Now build the project to make Visual Studio create .dll and .tlb files. The .dll file is the library itself. The .tlb file is a type library that defines the classes and methods that are available inside the DLL so Excel can see them.

NOTE: Visual Studio cannot create the .dll and .tlb files while they are in use by another application such as Excel. At a minimum, you need to close your Excel workbook before you try to rebuild the library. Sometimes that works for me but sometimes I need to close Excel completely. If Visual Studio fails with an "access denied" error, try closing Excel.

> **NOTE:** Sometimes Visual Studio also failed to create the .tlb file for no obvious reason. When I unchecked the project's "Make assembly COM-Visible" and "Register for COM interop" boxes, saved the project, rechecked the boxes, and then rebuilt the project, everything worked fine.

At this point you should have compiled .dll and .tlb files. The next step is to use the library in Excel.

Using the DLL

To use the DLL, create an Excel workbook. Save it as a macro-enabled workbook with a .xlsm extension.

> **NOTE:** Sometimes when I later opened my workbook, Excel displayed a dialog asking if I wanted to enable macros. Other times it didn't display the dialog, disabled the macros, and then displayed a button to let me enable them if I wanted to do so. Still other times it just opened the workbook with macros enabled. Apparently, this is all due to Excel's whimsical nature.
>
> Obviously you need the macros enabled if you want to run your macro, so do whatever it takes to enable macros.

Now open Excel's VBA editor. To do that, go to the Developer tab and click the Visual Basic tool.

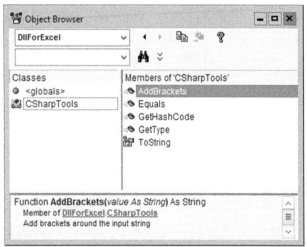

Inside the VBA editor, open the Tools menu and select References. The DLL should appear in the list. Check its box and click OK.

Now if you open the Object Browser (use the View menu or press F2), you should be able to select the DLL in the Library dropdown. Then you can click on the class and its public members to see their parameters and any description you included in the library. The picture on the left shows the Object Browser displaying information about the CSharpTools class's AddBrackets method. Notice the method's description at the bottom of the browser.

Now you can create a VBA macro to use the DLL. The DLL's namespace, class, and method should all appear to IntelliSense.

In this example, I added a button to a worksheet. To do that, go to the Developer tab, select Insert, pick the Button tool, and click and drag to position the button. When the Assign Macro dialog appears, give the macro a descriptive name and click New.

This example uses the following VBA macro.

```
Sub AddBRackets_Click()
    Dim sheet As Worksheet
    Dim tools As DllForExcel.CSharpTools
    Dim value As String
    Dim result As String

    Set sheet = ActiveSheet
    value = sheet.Cells(1, 1)

    Set tools = New DllForExcel.CSharpTools

    result = tools.AddBrackets(value)
    sheet.Cells(2, 1) = result
End Sub
```

This code gets the active worksheet and finds the value in its upper left cell. It then creates a CSharpTools object defined by the DLL, calls its AddBrackets method, and displays the result in the worksheet cell in row 2 column 1.

To run the macro, you can press F5 in the VBA editor or you can click the button on the worksheet.

91. Drag and Drop Images (46)

This example shows how to drag and drop images in C#. Drag and drop requires the interaction of two controls: a drag source and a drop target. As you can probably guess from their names, you drag from the drag source onto the drop target.

One of the first things you need to do before implementing drag and drop is set the `AllowDrop` property to `true` for the drop target. For some reason, Microsoft decided that you would never want to drop anything on a `PictureBox`, so they hid this property for `PictureBox` controls. It doesn't appear in the Properties window and IntelliSense won't admit that it exists.

However, the `Control` class implements `AllowDrop` and `PictureBox` inherits from `Control`, so the property *does* exist. You just need to set it in code at run time and you need to ignore IntelliSense's refusal to believe that it exists.

The following text shows Microsoft's official position on this issue.

> *The PictureBox control is not designed to allow drag and drop procedures. However, since PictureBox inherits from control, it also inherits the AllowDrop property. To clarify this, in the next release of the documentation, the PictureBox.AllowDrop topic will be marked with the "for internal use only" boilerplate. Also, the PictureBox.AllowDrop property will not appear in intellisense if you are using the Visual Studio text editor.*

Basically Microsoft says this is by design and most people wouldn't want to do this anyway. I have no clue what they are thinking.

Anyway, the following code shows how the example program sets this property at run time.

```
// Set the drop target PictureBox's AllowDrop property at run time.
private void Form1_Load(object sender, EventArgs e)
{
    dropTargetPictureBox.AllowDrop = true;
}
```

To start a drag, the drag source should call the `DoDragDrop` method that it inherits from the `Control` class. Most programs do that in a mouse event. The following code shows how this example calls `DoDragDrop`.

```
// Start the drag.
private void dragSourcePictureBox_MouseDown(object sender, MouseEventArgs e)
{
```

```
        // Start the drag if it's the right mouse button.
        if (e.Button == MouseButtons.Right)
        {
            dragSourcePictureBox.DoDragDrop(
                dragSourcePictureBox.Image, DragDropEffects.Copy);
        }
    }
}
```

When you press the mouse down over the dragSourcePictureBox control, this code checks which mouse button you pressed. If you pressed the right button, the code calls the control's DoDragDrop method, passing it the image to drag and the drag effect Copy.

The drag effect tells potential drop targets that this drag source only supports the copy operation and no other operations such as move.

When a drag moves over a drop target, the target receives a DragEnter event. The event handler should examine the drag data and decide what kind of operation the drop target is willing to receive.

The following code shows the DragEnter event handler used by the example program.

```
// Allow a copy of an image.
private void dropTargetPictureBox_DragEnter(object sender, DragEventArgs e)
{
    // See if this is a copy and the data includes an image.
    if (e.Data.GetDataPresent(DataFormats.Bitmap) &&
        (e.AllowedEffect & DragDropEffects.Copy) != 0)
    {
        // Allow this.
        e.Effect = DragDropEffects.Copy;
    }
    else
    {
        // Don't allow any other drop.
        e.Effect = DragDropEffects.None;
    }
}
```

This code checks the data available and the type of operation allowed by the drag source. If a bitmap is available and a copy is allowed, the code sets the e.Effect parameter to Copy. If no bitmap data is available or if the drag source won't allow the copy operation, the code sets e.Effect to None. The control automatically displays an appropriate cursor for the allowed effect.

If the user releases the mouse over a drop target, the drop target receives a DragDrop event. This only happens if the target will allow the drop; if the target set e.Effect to None, then the event doesn't occur.

The target should catch the DragDrop event and do something with the dragged data. The following code shows how the example program handles this event.

```
// Accept the drop.
private void dropTargetPictureBox_DragDrop(object sender, DragEventArgs e)
{
```

```
dropTargetPictureBox.Image =
    (Bitmap)e.Data.GetData(DataFormats.Bitmap, true);
}
```

This code uses the `e.Data` parameter's `GetData` method to get the `Bitmap` data. This code assumes that `Bitmap` data is present because if it were not, then `DragEnter` event handler would have set `e.Effect` to `None` so the `DragDrop` event wouldn't have occurred.

The `GetData` method returns a non-specific `object`, so the code casts it into a `Bitmap` and displays it in the drop target `PictureBox`.

> **NOTE:** Unfortunately, this only works between `PictureBox` controls in the same instance of the application. If you try to drag to another program, the drag and drop system tries to serialize its data.
>
> Sadly, the `Bitmap` class isn't serializable so this doesn't work.
>
> If you perform the same steps to drag and drop text, the program can drag and drop text to and from Microsoft Word, WordPad, and other programs.

92. Copy, Cut, and Paste Parts of Images to the Clipboard (53)

The first step in copying, cutting, or pasting an image to the clipboard is selecting the area to copy. This example lets you use a rubber band box to select the area.

The program's `PictureBox` has `SizeMode` property set to `Zoom`, so it scales its image to make it as large as possible without distortion. That means the program needs to scale mouse coordinates as you click and drag to account for the scaling. To do that, the example uses the techniques described in the earlier example, "40. Select an Area in a Scaled Image (48)." See that example for information about how that works.

All that remains is learning how to copy, cut, and paste to the clipboard.

The following `CopyToClipboard` method copies the selected area to the clipboard.

```
// Copy the selected area to the clipboard.
private void CopyToClipboard(Rectangle srcRect)
{
    // Copy the selected piece of image to a bitmap.
    Bitmap bm = ImagePiece(OriginalImage, srcRect);

    // Copy the selection image to the clipboard.
    Clipboard.SetImage(bm);
}
```

This code uses the `ImagePiece` method to make a `Bitmap` containing the selected part of the picture. See the previous example for a description of that method.

The code then calls the `Clipboard` object's `SetImage` method. That method clears any current contents from the clipboard and saves the new image in it.

When you select the Edit menu's Copy command (or press Ctrl+C), the program executes the following code.

```
// Copy the selected area to the clipboard.
private void copyMenuItem_Click(object sender, EventArgs e)
{
    CopyToClipboard(SelectedRect);
    SystemSounds.Beep.Play();
}
```

This code simply calls `CopyToClipboard` and beeps so you know that it did something.

When you select the Edit menu's Cut command (or press Ctrl+X), the program executes the following code.

```
// Copy the selected area to the clipboard and blank that area.
private void cutMenuItem_Click(object sender, EventArgs e)
{
    // Copy the selection to the clipboard.
    CopyToClipboard(SelectedRect);

    // Blank the selected area in the original image.
    using (Graphics gr = Graphics.FromImage(OriginalImage))
    {
        using (SolidBrush br = new SolidBrush(originalPictureBox.BackColor))
        {
            gr.FillRectangle(br, SelectedRect);
        }
    }

    // Display the result.
    originalPictureBox.Image = OriginalImage;

    // Enable the menu items appropriately.
    EnableMenuItems();
    HaveSelection = false;

    SystemSounds.Beep.Play();
}
```

This code also calls `CopyToClipboard`. To clear the selected area, it then makes a `Graphics` object for the original image and fills the selected area with the `PictureBox` control's background color.

There are several ways you could define a paste operation. This program provides two paste menu items, one that centers the pasted image on the selected area and one that stretches the pasted image to fill the selected area.

The following code shows how the program centers the pasted image.

```
// Paste the image on the clipboard, centering it on the selected area.
private void pasteCenteredMenuItem_Click(object sender, EventArgs e)
{
    // Do nothing if the clipboard doesn't hold an image.
    if (!Clipboard.ContainsImage()) return;

    // Get the clipboard's image.
    Image clipboardImage = Clipboard.GetImage();

    // Figure out where to put it.
    int cx = SelectedRect.X + (SelectedRect.Width - clipboardImage.Width) / 2;
    int cy = SelectedRect.Y + (SelectedRect.Height - clipboardImage.Height) / 2;
    Rectangle destRect = new Rectangle(
        cx, cy,
        clipboardImage.Width,
        clipboardImage.Height);
```

```
        // Copy the new image into position.
        using (Graphics gr = Graphics.FromImage(OriginalImage))
        {
            gr.DrawImage(clipboardImage, destRect);
        }

        // Display the result.
        originalPictureBox.Image = OriginalImage;

        // Discard the selection.
        HaveSelection = false;
    }
```

The code uses the `Clipboard` object's `GetImage` method to get the image that it will paste. It then calculates the position where it must put the image to center it over the selected area. It finishes by copying the image to that spot and displaying the result.

The following code shows how the program stretches the pasted image.

```
        // Paste the image on the clipboard, stretching it to fit the selected area.
        private void pasteStretchedMenuItem_Click(object sender, EventArgs e)
        {
            // Do nothing if the clipboard doesn't hold an image.
            if (!Clipboard.ContainsImage()) return;

            // Get the clipboard's image.
            Image clipboardImage = Clipboard.GetImage();

            // Get the image's bounding Rectangle.
            Rectangle srcRect = new Rectangle(0, 0,
                clipboardImage.Width, clipboardImage.Height);

            // Copy the new image into position.
            using (Graphics gr = Graphics.FromImage(OriginalImage))
            {
                gr.DrawImage(clipboardImage, SelectedRect,
                    srcRect, GraphicsUnit.Pixel);
            }

            // Display the result.
            originalPictureBox.Image = OriginalImage;

            // Discard the selection.
            HaveSelection = false;
        }
```

The code again uses the `Clipboard` object's `GetImage` method to get the image that it will paste. It then simply copies the image onto the selected area and displays the result.

93. COPY AND PASTE DATA IN MULTIPLE FORMATS (59)

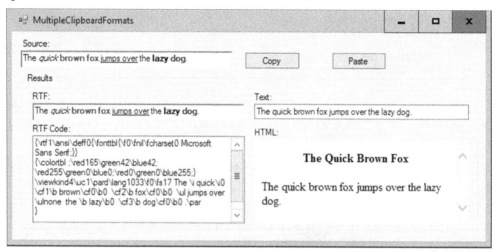

Everyone knows that the clipboard can hold pictures or text so you can copy and paste data from one program to another. Fewer people know that the clipboard can hold data in multiple formats at the same time. For example, it might hold text in Rich Text Format (RTF), ANSI, and HTML all simultaneously.

This example shows how to copy and paste data in multiple formats to the clipboard. It saves data in RTF, ANSI, and HTML formats. When you paste data into the example, the program separately displays any of those formats that are available.

The following code shows how the program copies data to the clipboard.

```
// Copy data to the clipboard in text, RTF, and HTML formats.
private void btnCopy_Click(object sender, EventArgs e)
{
    // Make a DataObject.
    DataObject data_object = new DataObject();

    // Add the data in various formats.
    data_object.SetData(DataFormats.Rtf, sourceRichTextBox.Rtf);
    data_object.SetData(DataFormats.Text, sourceRichTextBox.Text);

    string html_text;
    html_text = $@"<html>
<head><center><b>The Quick Brown Fox</b></center></head>
<p>
<body>{sourceRichTextBox.Text}
</body>
</html>";
    data_object.SetData(DataFormats.Html, html_text);

    // Place the data in the Clipboard.
```

```
        Clipboard.SetDataObject(data_object);
    }
```

First, the code makes a new **DataObject**. It calls the object's **SetData** method to save data in RTF and text formats. It then composes a small HTML document and uses the data object's **SetData** method again to save the document in the HTML format.

The program then calls the **Clipboard** object's **SetDataObject** method to save the **DataObject** and all of its data on the clipboard.

The following code shows how the program pastes data from the clipboard.

```
    // Paste data from the clipboard in text,
    // RTF, and HTML formats if they are available.
    private void btnPaste_Click(object sender, EventArgs e)
    {
        // Get the DataObject.
        IDataObject data_object = Clipboard.GetDataObject();

        if (data_object.GetDataPresent(DataFormats.Rtf))
        {
            rtfRichTextBox.Rtf = data_object.GetData(DataFormats.Rtf).ToString();
            rtfCodeTextBox.Text = data_object.GetData(DataFormats.Rtf).ToString();
        }
        else
        {
            rtfRichTextBox.Clear();
            rtfCodeTextBox.Clear();
        }

        if (data_object.GetDataPresent(DataFormats.Text))
            textTextBox.Text = data_object.GetData(DataFormats.Text).ToString();
        else textTextBox.Clear();

        if (data_object.GetDataPresent(DataFormats.Html))
        {
            HtmlDocument doc = htmlWebBrowser.Document;
            doc.Body.InnerHtml = data_object.GetData(DataFormats.Html).ToString();
        }
        else htmlWebBrowser.Navigate("about:blank");
    }
```

For each of the data RTF, text, and HTML data types, the code uses the **Clipboard** object's **GetDataPresent** method to see if the format is available. If the appropriate kind of data is present, the code uses the **Clipboard** object's **GetData** method to get the data.

Note that this method works no matter what program placed the data in the clipboard. For example, if you use Microsoft Word to copy some text, you can then paste it into the example program in RTF, text, and HTML formats. Try copying the initial text from this program into Word, and then copying it back from Word to this program. The result should be similar but slightly different from what you get when you copy from this program to itself.

Part XXI. Windows Forms Printing

The examples in this part of the book deal with printing in Windows Forms applications. Printing is an extremely complicated topic, so these examples only demonstrate the basics. They should get you started, however, so you can work on your own, more complicated printing solutions.

94. PRINT DATA IN ROWS AND COLUMNS (87)

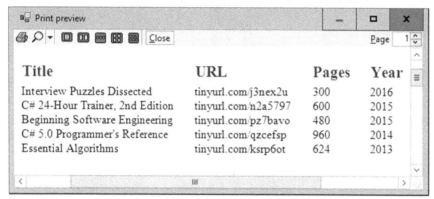

This example shows how a Windows Forms application can print data in rows and columns with column headers. To save paper, it displays a print preview dialog instead of actually printing.

This example only provides basic functionality; you can add other features such as lines between the rows and columns, multiple pages, and page numbers if you like.

The example uses the following code to initialize its data.

```
// The data to print.
private string[] Headers = { "Title", "URL", "Pages", "Year" };
private string[,] Data =
{
    {"Interview Puzzles Dissected", "tinyurl.com/j3nex2u", "300", "2016"},
    {"C# 24-Hour Trainer, 2nd Edition", "tinyurl.com/n2a5797", "600", "2015"},
    {"Beginning Software Engineering", "tinyurl.com/pz7bavo", "480", "2015"},
    {"C# 5.0 Programmer's Reference", "tinyurl.com/qzcefsp", "960", "2014"},
    {"Essential Algorithms", "tinyurl.com/ksrp6ot", "624", "2013"},
};
```

At design time, I added a `PrintPreviewDialog` component named `gridPrintPreview-Dialog` to the program's form. I also set the dialog's `Document` property to a `PrintDocument` component named `gridPrintDocument`.

When you click the program's Print Preview button, the following code invokes the `PrintPreviewDialog` component's `ShowDialog` method.

```
// Display a print preview.
private void previewButton_Click(object sender, EventArgs e)
{
    gridPrintPreviewDialog.ShowDialog();
}
```

At this point, the `PrintPreviewDialog` uses the `PrintDocument` to generate its output. The `PrintDocument` raises its `PrintPage` event when it needs to generate a new page of output. The following code shows the `PrintPage` event handler, which does most of the program's work.

```
// Print the document's page. (This version doesn't handle multiple pages.)
private void gridPrintDocument_PrintPage(object sender,
    System.Drawing.Printing.PrintPageEventArgs e)
```

```
{
    // Use this font.
    using (Font headerFont = new Font("Times New Roman", 16, FontStyle.Bold))
    {
        using (Font bodyFont = new Font("Times New Roman", 12))
        {
            // We'll skip this much space between rows.
            int lineSpacing = 20;

            // See how wide the columns must be.
            int[] columnWidths = FindColumnWidths(
                e.Graphics, headerFont, bodyFont, Headers, Data);

            // Print the headers.
            int x = e.MarginBounds.Left;
            int y = e.MarginBounds.Top;
            for (int col=0; col<Headers.Length; col++)
            {
                e.Graphics.DrawString(Headers[col],
                    headerFont, Brushes.Blue, x, y);
                x += columnWidths[col];
            }

            // Move down a bit extra before the data.
            y += (int)(lineSpacing * 1.5);

            // Print by rows.
            for (int row = 0; row <= Data.GetUpperBound(0); row++)
            {
                // Print this row's values.
                x = e.MarginBounds.Left;
                for (int col = 0; col < Headers.Length; col++)
                {
                    e.Graphics.DrawString(Data[row, col],
                        bodyFont, Brushes.Black, x, y);
                    x += columnWidths[col];
                }

                // Move down a row.
                y += lineSpacing;
            }
        }
    }
    e.HasMorePages = false;
}
```

The event handler creates fonts for the grid's column headers and the values. It then calls the FindColumnWidths method, which is described shortly, to see how wide each column must be to hold its data.

Next, the code sets variables x and y to the coordinates of the page's upper left corner inside the margins. It then draws the headers. For each header, it draws the header text and then increases x by the width of the corresponding column so the next header is drawn shifted to the right.

After it finishes drawing the headers, the code increases y to move down and then starts drawing the rows of data. For each row, the program loops through the row's data and performs the same steps it did for the column headers. It draws a data value and then increases x by the width of the corresponding column so the next value is drawn shifted to the right.

After it draws each row, the program increases y again so the next row is drawn farther down the page.

The following code shows the FindColumnWidths method.

```
// Figure out how wide each column should be.
private int[] FindColumnWidths(Graphics gr, Font headerFont, Font bodyFont,
    string[] headers, string[,] values)
{
    // Make room for the widths.
    int[] widths = new int[headers.Length];

    // Find the width for each column.
    for (int col = 0; col < widths.Length; col++)
    {
        // Check the column header.
        widths[col] = (int)gr.MeasureString(headers[col], headerFont).Width;

        // Check the items.
        for (int row = 0; row <= values.GetUpperBound(0); row++)
        {
            int valueWidth =
                (int)gr.MeasureString(values[row, col], bodyFont).Width;
            if (widths[col] < valueWidth) widths[col] = valueWidth;
        }

        // Add some extra space.
        widths[col] += 20;
    }

    return widths;
}
```

This method creates an array big enough to hold a width for each column. It then loops through the columns.

The code sets each column's width equal to the width of its header drawn in the header font. It then loops through that column's rows and updates the column width if necessary to make room for all of the row's values.

After it has finished setting the column values, the code adds some extra space to each column width so the values aren't packed too closely together.

95. PRINT MULTIPLE PAGES (96)

This example shows how a Windows Forms program can provide printing and print previews for a multipage printout.

The `PrintDocument` object plays a central role in printing and print previews. It raises its `PrintPage` event to generate graphics for each of the pages that the program needs to print.

A `PrintPreviewDialog` can display a preview for a `PrintDocument` object.

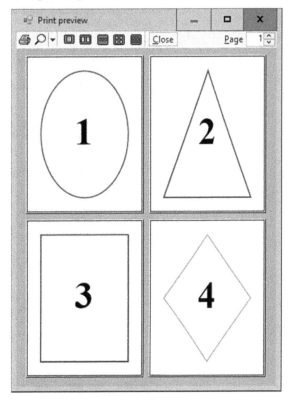

You can create these objects in code, but it's easier to create them at design time. Add a `PrintDocument` object and a `PrintPreviewDialog` object to the form. Set the `PrintPreviewDialog` object's `Document` property to the `PrintDocument` object.

When the `PrintPreviewDialog` needs to display a print preview, it uses the `PrintDocument` object to generate the graphics it should display. That object raises its `PrintPage` event when it needs to create a printed page.

Give the `PrintDocument` object a `PrintPage` event handler to generate the pages. The event handler should use the `Graphics` object provided by its `e.Graphics` parameter to draw text and other graphics.

When the event handler is finished, it should set `e.HasMorePages` to `true` or `false` to indicate whether there are more pages to print.

If it's going to print multiple pages, the program needs to keep track of the page that it is working on so the `PrintPage` event handler can draw the correct output.

The following code shows this example's `PrintPage` event handler. It displays shapes and page numbers on four pages. This is the most interesting part of the printing process.

```
// Print the document's pages.
private int NextPageNum = 0;
private void shapesPrintDocument_PrintPage(object sender,
System.Drawing.Printing.PrintPageEventArgs e)
{
```

```csharp
        e.Graphics.SmoothingMode = SmoothingMode.AntiAlias;
        e.Graphics.TextRenderingHint = TextRenderingHint.AntiAlias;

        // Draw a shape depending on the page we are printing.
        switch (NextPageNum)
        {
            case 0: // Draw an ellipse.
                using (Pen pen = new Pen(Color.Red, 10))
                {
                    e.Graphics.DrawEllipse(pen, e.MarginBounds);
                }
                break;
            case 1: // Draw a triangle.
                using (Pen pen = new Pen(Color.Green, 10))
                {
                    int xmid =
                        (int)(e.MarginBounds.X + e.MarginBounds.Width / 2);
                    Point[] pts =
                    {
                        new Point(xmid, e.MarginBounds.Top),
                        new Point(e.MarginBounds.Right, e.MarginBounds.Bottom),
                        new Point(e.MarginBounds.Left, e.MarginBounds.Bottom),
                    };
                    e.Graphics.DrawPolygon(pen, pts);
                }
                break;
            case 2: // Draw a rectangle.
                using (Pen pen = new Pen(Color.Blue, 10))
                {
                    e.Graphics.DrawRectangle(pen, e.MarginBounds);
                }
                break;
            case 3: // Draw a diamond.
                using (Pen pen = new Pen(Color.Orange, 10))
                {
                    int xmid =
                        (int)(e.MarginBounds.X + e.MarginBounds.Width / 2);
                    int ymid =
                        (int)(e.MarginBounds.Y + e.MarginBounds.Height / 2);
                    Point[] pts =
                    {
                        new Point(xmid, e.MarginBounds.Top),
                        new Point(e.MarginBounds.Right, ymid),
                        new Point(xmid, e.MarginBounds.Bottom),
                        new Point(e.MarginBounds.Left, ymid),
                    };
                    e.Graphics.DrawPolygon(pen, pts);
                }
                break;
        }

        // Draw the page number centered.
        using (StringFormat sf = new StringFormat())
        {
            sf.Alignment = StringAlignment.Center;
            sf.LineAlignment = StringAlignment.Center;

            using (Font font = new Font("Times New Roman", 200, FontStyle.Bold))
            {
```

```
            using (Brush brush = new SolidBrush(Color.Black))
            {
                e.Graphics.DrawString(String.Format("{0}", NextPageNum + 1),
                    font, brush, e.MarginBounds, sf);
            }
        }
    }

    // Next time print the next page.
    NextPageNum += 1;

    // We have more pages if we have not yet printed page 3.
    e.HasMorePages = (NextPageNum <= 3);

    // If we have no more pages, reset for the next time we print.
    if (NextPageNum > 3) NextPageNum = 0;
}
```

The class-level variable NextPageNum indicates the next page to print. Initially this is set to 0 so the program prints its first page.

The PrintPage event handler uses a switch statement to display different shapes on different pages. You can look through the code to see how the program draws each of the pages.

After it draws the appropriate shape, the code draws the page number centered on the page.

Next, the program increments NextPageNum and sets e.HasMorePages to true if NextPageNum is less than or equal to 3. (That makes it print four pages.)

Finally, if NextPageNum is greater than 3, the program has generated all of the pages. In that case, the code resets NextPageNum to 0 for the next time the program needs to generate the printout (in case you click either the Print or the Preview button again).

After you write the PrintPage event handler, the rest is easy. The following code shows how the program displays a print preview and how it generates a printout.

```
// Display a print preview.
private void previewButton_Click(object sender, EventArgs e)
{
    shapesPrintPreviewDialog.ShowDialog();
}

// Print.
private void printButton_Click(object sender, EventArgs e)
{
    shapesPrintDocument.Print();
}
```

To display a print preview, the program just calls the PrintPreviewDialog component's ShowDialog method. The dialog uses its associated PrintDocument to generate the graphics it needs, and it displays the results.

To create a printout without a preview, the program calls the `PrintDocument` object's `Print` method. The printout goes immediately to the computer's default printer.

Note that there is no easy way to tell in advance how many pages the printout will include, so you cannot print things like "Page 1 of 12." To do that, you would need to examine whatever you're printing before you start the printout and figure out how many pages there will be in advance.

Part XXII. Miscellany

The examples in this part of the book didn't fit very well anywhere else. Even though they're the "left overs," some of them are pretty interesting. They include topics such as using a `TypeConverter`, displaying Unicode symbols, and making a countdown timer.

96. USE A TYPECONVERTER WITH A PROPERTYGRID (45)

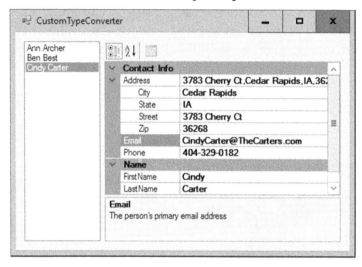

The PropertyGrid control lets you view and edit object properties at runtime much as the Properties window lets you view and edit control properties at design time. By itself, the PropertyGrid is quite powerful. Simply set the control's SelectedObject property to an object, and it displays the object's public properties.

The control even provides standard editors for properties that have common data types. For example, it can display a font selection dialog, color selection dropdown, and list of choices for enumerated types that you define.

The PropertyGrid can display simple properties easily, but if a property is an object itself, then the PropertyGrid displays whatever the object's ToString method returns and it doesn't allow the user to edit the value. This example shows how you can use a type converter to allow a PropertyGrid control to display and edit compound properties.

To let the PropertyGrid display and edit the value properly, you can provide a type converter class for that object type. A *type converter* converts an object's representation between two data types.

This example uses a Person class that has a property named Address of type StreetAddress. The StreetAddress class has Street, City, State, and Zip properties. In this example, the type converter will convert StreetAddress objects to and from strings.

To make a type converter, first decorate the class that you will convert (in this example, StreetAddress) with the TypeConverter attribute defined in the System.ComponentModel namespace. This example uses the StreetAddressConverter class to convert StreetAddress objects to and from strings, so the StreetAddress class's declaration looks like the following.

```
using System.ComponentModel;
...
[TypeConverter(typeof(StreetAddressConverter))]
class StreetAddress
{
```

```
    . . .
}
```

Next, make the type converter class. It should inherit from the `TypeConverter` base class, which is defined in the `System.ComponentModel` namespace.

```
using System.ComponentModel;
...
class StreetAddressConverter : TypeConverter
{
    ...
}
```

This class should override several methods to give the `PropertyGrid` the tools it needs to display and edit properties of the type `StreetAddress`. The following table summarizes those methods.

Method	Purpose
CanConvertFrom	Returns true if the indicated type is string to indicate that the converter can create a StreetAddress from a string.
CanConvertTo	Returns true if the indicated type is string to indicate that the converter can convert a StreetAddress into a string.
ConvertFrom	Converts a string into a StreetAddress.
ConvertTo	Converts a StreetAddress into a string.
GetProperties	Returns a collection of type descriptors to tell the PropertyGrid about the properties that the StreetAddress supports.

For example, the following code shows the converter's `CanConvertTo` method.

```
// If the type is string, return true to indicate
// that we can convert into a string.
public override bool CanConvertTo(ITypeDescriptorContext context,
    Type destinationType)
{
    if (destinationType == typeof(String)) return true;
    return base.CanConvertTo(context, destinationType);
}
```

To make converting a `StreetAddress` into a string easier, the `StreetAddress` class overrides its `ToString` method to return the object's properties separated by commas. The following code shows the `StreetAddress` class's `ToString` method.

```
// Return as a comma-delimited string.
public override string ToString()
{
    return Street + "," + City + "," + State + "," + Zip;
}
```

The two most interesting converter methods are `ConvertTo` and `ConvertFrom`. The following code shows how the `ConvertTo` method converts a `StreetAddress` object into a string.

```
// Convert the StreetAddress to a string.
public override object ConvertTo(ITypeDescriptorContext context,
    CultureInfo culture, object value, Type destinationType)
{
    if (destinationType == typeof(string)) return value.ToString();
    return base.ConvertTo(context, culture, value, destinationType);
}
```

If the destination type is `string`, this method simply calls the `StreetAddress` object's `ToString` method and returns the result. If the destination type isn't `string`, the method calls the `TypeConverter` base class's `ConvertTo` method.

The following code shows the converter's `ConvertFrom` method, which converts a string back onto a `StreetAddress`.

```
// Convert from a string.
public override object ConvertFrom(ITypeDescriptorContext context,
    CultureInfo culture, object value)
{
    if (value.GetType() == typeof(string))
    {
        // Split the string separated by commas.
        string text = (string)(value);
        string[] fields = text.Split(new char[] { ',' });

        try
        {
            StreetAddress address = new StreetAddress();
            if (fields.Length == 0) return address;
            address.Street = fields[0];
            if (fields.Length == 1) return address;
            address.City = fields[1];
            if (fields.Length == 2) return address;
            address.State = fields[2];
            if (fields.Length == 3) return address;
            address.Zip = fields[3];
            return address;
        }
        catch
        {
            string msg = "Cannot convert the string '" +
                text + "' into a StreetAddress";
            MessageBox.Show(msg);
            throw new InvalidCastException(msg);
        }
    }
    else
    {
        return base.ConvertFrom(context, culture, value);
    }
}
```

This method splits the string into fields separated by commas. It then creates a new StreetAddress object, and sets its properties to the field values that are present. It finishes by returning the new Address object.

The PropertyGrid can take advantage of special attributes intended for use with visual designers. For example, if you give a property the Description attribute, then the PropertyGrid displays the description when that property is selected. In the picture at the beginning of this example, the Email property is selected so the grid is displaying its description.

The PropertyGrid can also group properties by category if you give them the Category attribute. Any properties that don't have the Category attribute are bundled into the Misc category.

For example, the following code shows the Address class's LastName and Address properties.

```
[Description("The person's last or family name")]
[Category("Name")]
public string LastName { get; set; }

[Description("The person's street address")]
[Category("Contact Info")]
public StreetAddress Address { get; set; }
```

There are two other features of the example program that I want to mention. First, when you select a name from the list on the left, the program uses the following code to display that person's properties in the PropertyGrid.

```
// Display the selected Person in the PropertyGrid.
private void peopleListBox_SelectedIndexChanged(object sender, EventArgs e)
{
    peoplePropertyGrid.SelectedObject = peopleListBox.SelectedItem;
}
```

This code simply sets the grid's SelectedObject property to the selected Person object.

The second feature is that the program updates its list and the grid when the user changes properties. When the user modifies a property, the PropertyGrid raises its PropertyValueChanged event so the program can update itself if necessary. The example uses the following code to handle that event.

```
private void peoplePropertyGrid_PropertyValueChanged(object s,
    PropertyValueChangedEventArgs e)
{
    switch (e.ChangedItem.Label)
    {
        case "Address":
        case "Street":
        case "City":
        case "State":
        case "Zip":
            // Refresh the PropertyGrid.
```

```
            peoplePropertyGrid.Refresh();
            break;
        case "FirstName":
        case "LastName":
            // Refresh the ListBox.
            peopleListBox.DisplayMember = "FirstName";
            peopleListBox.DisplayMember = null;
            break;
    }
}
```

If the user changes the Address property or any of its sub-properties, the program refreshes the PropertyGrid to keep it synchronized. For example, if the program didn't do this and the user changed the Street property, the main Address line that displays all of the address properties in a single string wouldn't update to match.

If the user changes the person's first or last name, the program resets the ListBox control's DisplayName property to make it redraw itself so it shows the new name.

> **NOTE:** Yes, resetting the DisplayName property is a terrible kludge, but I have been unable to find a better way to force the ListBox to refresh its contents. The ListBox class has a RefreshItems method, but it's marked protected so only ListBox and any derived classes can invoke it. If you find a better way to do this, please post a comment on the book's web page.

The rest of the example is reasonably straightforward. Download it and look at its code for more details.

The PropertyGrid is a remarkably powerful control that adds a lot of features to a program with relatively little effort. For more information, see the MSDN article "Getting the Most Out of the .NET Framework PropertyGrid Control" at tinyurl.com/mrggbjg.

97. Display Unicode Symbols (56)

This example shows several ways you can display Unicode symbols in a C# program. Unicode lets you use more than one byte per symbol to represent fonts that contain a large number of characters. For example, Chinese, Japanese, Cyrillic, and Arabic fonts use Unicode to display more than the 255 characters that can fit in the simple, one-byte ASCII codes.

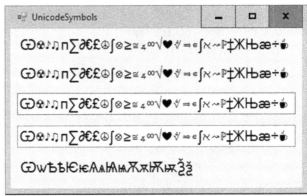

Even those of us who don't typically deal with these fonts can sometimes find Unicode characters handy. For example, Unicode can represent lots of special symbols such as $\times$, ∞, $\approx$, and $\sum$.

There are several ways that you can use Unicode in your programs. First, if you know a character's numeric code, you can add it to a character or string literal by using an escape sequence with the following form.

```
\uXXXX
```

The following code shows an example.

```
label1.Text = "\u0460";
```

You can also cast a numeric value into a Unicode character as in the following statement.

```
char ch = (char)0x460;
```

These methods are useful, but require you to know a character's numeric code.

You can also copy and paste Unicode characters directly into Visual Studio. Use Microsoft Word, WordPad, or some other program to create the character that you want. You can even select characters from a web page in your browser. Then copy and paste the characters into a character or string literal inside Visual Studio. You can even paste values into the Properties window to set a control's Text property at design time.

This example displays a Label and a TextBox that show special symbols assigned at design time. It also uses the following code to generate more symbols at run time.

```
private void Form1_Load(object sender, EventArgs e)
{
    label2.Text = "\u0460♪♫π∑∂€£∫⊗≥≅⩞∞√∜⇒∈∫∾ℙ‡ЖℋЬæ÷";
    textBox2.Text = "\u0460♪♫π∑∂€£∫⊗≥≅⩞∞√∜⇒∈∫∾ℙ‡ЖℋЬæ÷";

    string text = "";
    for (int i = 0x460; i < 0x470; i++)
    {
```

```
            text += (char)i;
        }
        label3.Text = text;
    }
```

The code first sets the text displayed in `label2` and `textBox2` equal to string literals. It then uses a loop to build a string containing Unicode characters 0x460 through 0x470 and displays them in the control `label3`.

Unicode defines more than 100 thousand characters, so examining them all is impossible. You can find some interesting symbols by searching the internet for "useful Unicode characters."

98. MAKE A COUNTDOWN TIMER (69)

This program displays a countdown in days, hours, minutes, and seconds until some event. When the event occurs, the example plays a "tada" sound and displays a full-screen window announcing the event.

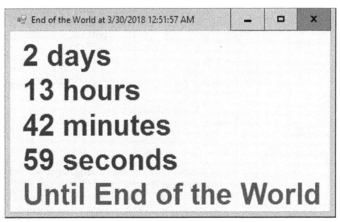

When the program starts, it uses the following code to get ready to display the countdown.

```
// Initialize information about the event.
private const string EventName = "End of the World";
private DateTime EventDate = DateTime.Now + new TimeSpan(1, 13, 42, 59);

// Get ready and start the timer.
private void Form1_Load(object sender, EventArgs e)
{
    eventLabel.Text = EventName;
    this.Text = EventName + " at " + EventDate.ToString();
    this.ClientSize = new Size(
        eventLabel.Bounds.Right, eventLabel.Bounds.Bottom);
    updateTimer.Enabled = true;
}
```

Form-level variables hold the event's name and the time at which it will occur. This example sets the event time to be the current time plus 2 days, 13 hours, 42 minutes, and 59 seconds. A real application would need to set the time in some other way such as looking up a birthday in a database, finding the end of the work day, or recording the next calendar holiday.

The form's Load event handler displays the event name in the eventLabel control. It displays the event name and time in the form's title bar and sizes the form to fit the eventLabel. It then enables the updateTimer component so the timer starts running.

The following code shows the Timer component's Tick event handler.

```
// Update the countdown.
private void updateTimer_Tick(object sender, EventArgs e)
{
    TimeSpan remaining = EventDate - DateTime.Now;
    if (remaining.TotalSeconds < 1)
    {
        updateTimer.Enabled = false;
        this.WindowState = FormWindowState.Maximized;
        this.TopMost = true;
```

```
            foreach (Control ctl in this.Controls)
            {
                if (ctl == eventLabel)
                    ctl.Location = new Point(
                        (this.ClientSize.Width - ctl.Width) / 2,
                        (this.ClientSize.Height - ctl.Height) / 2);
                else ctl.Visible = false;
            }

            using (SoundPlayer player = new SoundPlayer(Properties.Resources.tada))
            {
                player.Play();
            }
        }
        else
        {
            daysLabel.Text = remaining.Days + " days";
            hoursLabel.Text = remaining.Hours + " hours";
            minutesLabel.Text = remaining.Minutes + " minutes";
            secondsLabel.Text = remaining.Seconds + " seconds";
        }
    }
```

When the Tick event fires, the program calculates the time remaining until the event. If the event time has arrived, the program disables the Timer, maximizes the form, and makes the form topmost. It hides all controls except the one that displays the event name, which it centers. Finally, it uses a SoundPlayer object to play the sound resource named tada.

If the event's time has not arrived, the program displays the number of days, hours, minutes, and seconds remaining.

99. USE A BACKGROUNDWORKER (76)

You can use threads to perform an action in the background while a program continues running. Unfortunately using threads directly can be really confusing. The BackgroundWorker component provides a much easier way to perform simple background tasks. This example demonstrates the BackgroundWorker component.

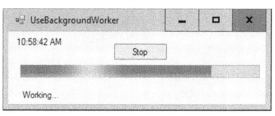

The following list summarizes the BackgroundWorker component's key features.

➤ RunWorkerAsync—The user interface (UI) thread calls this method to start the worker.

➤ DoWork—The DoWork event is where the worker does its work. It should periodically check its CancellationPending property to see if the UI thread is trying to make it stop. If the CancellationPending property is true, the event handler should set the event's e.Cancel property to true and then return.

➤ CancelAsync—The UI thread can call this method to tell worker to stop. This sets the worker's CancellationPending property to true so the DoWork event handler can see it and stop. The worker's WorkerSupportsCancel property must be true for the program to call this method.

➤ ReportProgress—The worker can call this method in its DoWork event handler to pass progress information back to the UI thread. The worker's WorkerReportsProgress property must be true for the program to call this method.

➤ ProgressChanged—This event occurs when the worker calls ReportProgress. The UI thread can update labels, progress bars, and other controls to report progress to the user. (This is a lot easier than it is when you use threads directly. In that case, you need to use InvokeRequired and Invoke to let a background thread call methods on the UI thread.)

➤ RunWorkerCompleted—This event occurs when the worker's DoEvent event handler returns. The UI thread can take action to clean up here. The e.Cancelled property tells whether the worker was stopped as opposed to finishing its task.

The code for this example is relatively straightforward. The following code starts or stops the BackgroundWorker.

```
// Use the BackgroundWorker to perform a long task.
private void goButton_Click(object sender, EventArgs e)
{
    if (goButton.Text == "Go")
    {
        // Start the process.
        statusLabel.Text = "Working...";
```

```
        goButton.Text = "Stop";
        percentCompleteProgressBar.Value = 0;
        percentCompleteProgressBar.Visible = true;

        // Start the BackgroundWorker.
        longTaskBackgroundWorker.RunWorkerAsync();
    }
    else
    {
        // Stop the process.
        longTaskBackgroundWorker.CancelAsync();
    }
}
```

If the button's caption is currently "Go," the code changes the button's text to "Stop," resets the percentCompleteProgressBar, and calls the worker's RunWorkerAsync method to start it running.

If the button's caption is "Stop," the code calls the worker's CancelAsync method to make it stop running.

The following code shows the worker's DoWork event handler.

```
// Perform the long task.
private void longTaskBackgroundWorker_DoWork(object sender, DoWorkEventArgs e)
{
    // Spend 10 seconds doing nothing.
    for (int i = 1; i <= 10; i++)
    {
        // If we should stop, do so.
        if (longTaskBackgroundWorker.CancellationPending)
        {
            // Indicate that the task was canceled.
            e.Cancel = true;
            break;
        }

        // Sleep.
        Thread.Sleep(1000);

        // Notify the UI thread of our progress.
        longTaskBackgroundWorker.ReportProgress(i * 10);
    }
}
```

This event handler enters a loop that executes 10 times. Each time through the loop, the code checks the worker's CancellationPending property to see if the UI thread is trying to stop the worker. If CancellationPending is true, the event handler sets e.Cancel to true to indicate that it didn't finish its work and then breaks out of its loop.

If CancellationPending isn't true, the code continues performing the worker's task. In this example, it simply sleeps and then calls the worker's ReportProgress method to report its progress to the UI thread.

The code passes the `ReportProgress` method a completion percentage, and that makes the following `ProgressChanged` event handler execute.

```
// Update the progress bar.
private void longTaskBackgroundWorker_ProgressChanged(object sender,
    ProgressChangedEventArgs e)
{
    percentCompleteProgressBar.Value = e.ProgressPercentage;
}
```

The `ProgressChanged` event handler simply updates the program's progress bar by setting its `Value` property to the completion percentage it receives through its parameters.

Finally, when the worker returns from its `DoWork` event handler, the following `RunWorkerComplete` event handler executes.

```
// The long task is done.
private void longTaskBackgroundWorker_RunWorkerCompleted(
    object sender, RunWorkerCompletedEventArgs e)
{
    if (e.Cancelled) statusLabel.Text = "Canceled";
    else statusLabel.Text = "Finished";

    goButton.Text = "Go";
    percentCompleteProgressBar.Visible = false;
}
```

This code makes a status label display "Canceled" or "Finished" to indicate whether the worker finished its task.

While the worker is doing all of this, the program's `Timer` executes the following code to display the current time, just to prove that the program can do something in the foreground while the worker runs in the background.

```
// Display the current time.
private void clockTimer_Tick(object sender, EventArgs e)
{
    clockLabel.Text = DateTime.Now.ToString("T");
}
```

This may seem fairly complicated, but it's easier than using a separate `Thread` object. The `BackgroundWorker` uses events to handle calls to the UI thread, so you don't have to mess with `InvokeRequired` and `Invoke`.

100. MEASURE ELAPSED TIME (98)

For most tasks, you can measure elapsed time with the Stopwatch or DateTime classes.

To use the Stopwatch class, create a Stopwatch object. Use its Start and Stop methods to start and stop it. If you use Start after stopping the object, the time picks up where it left off. That makes this class particularly useful if you want to add up several intervals.

You can use the Reset method to reset the elapsed time to 0. Use the Restart method to stop the Stopwatch, reset its time to 0, and start it running again in a single step.

Use the Stopwatch class's Elapsed property to get a TimeSpan object representing the elapsed time.

To use the DateTime class to measure elapsed time, use the static Now property to get the current time before and after you execute some code and save the results in DateTime variables. Then subtract the two times to get a TimeSpan structure representing the elapsed time.

When the example program starts, it uses the following code to get ready to run and to display information about the Stopwatch class.

```
private DateTime StartTime, StopTime;
Stopwatch Watch;
Stopwatch TotalWatch = new Stopwatch();

private void Form1_Load(object sender, EventArgs e)
{
    frequencyTextBox.Text = Stopwatch.Frequency.ToString();
    nsPerTickTextBox.Text = (1000000000 / Stopwatch.Frequency).ToString();
    isHighResTextBox.Text = Stopwatch.IsHighResolution.ToString();
}
```

The code first declares two DateTime structures and two Stopwatch objects. The form's Load event handler displays the Stopwatch class's frequency (ticks per second) and the number of nanoseconds per tick. It also indicates whether the class uses high-resolution timing. This last may return false on older computers.

When you click the Start button, the following code executes.

```
private void btnStart_Click(object sender, EventArgs e)
{
    startButton.Enabled = false;
    stopButton.Enabled = true;
    elapsed1TextBox.Clear();
    elapsed2TextBox.Clear();
    tlapsed3TextBox.Clear();
```

```
            Watch.Restart();
            TotalWatch.Start();
            StartTime = DateTime.Now;
        }
```

This code disables the Start button and enables the Stop button. It then clears the result text boxes.

Next, the code sets `StartTime` to the current time. It resets `Watch` and it restarts the `TotalWatch Stopwatch` object.

When you click the Stop button, the following code executes.

```
        private void btnStop_Click(object sender, EventArgs e)
        {
            StopTime = DateTime.Now;
            Watch.Stop();
            TotalWatch.Stop();

            TimeSpan elapsed = StopTime.Subtract(StartTime);
            elapsed1TextBox.Text = elapsed.TotalSeconds.ToString("0.000000");

            elapsed2TextBox.Text = Watch.Elapsed.TotalSeconds.ToString("0.000000");

            tlapsed3TextBox.Text = TotalWatch.Elapsed.TotalSeconds.ToString("0.000000");

            startButton.Enabled = true;
            stopButton.Enabled = false;
        }
```

This code records `DateTime.Now` in the variable `StopTime` and stops both of the `Stopwatch` objects. It then displays the elapsed time recorded by the three methods.

If you run the program several times, you'll see that the `DateTime` and `Stopwatch` classes produce very close to the same results, so it doesn't really matter which one you use. Most people use the `Stopwatch` class because it's easier.

AFTERWORD

That's the end of the 100 most popular posts on the C# Helper web site, but it's far from the end of the site itself! Currently the site contains more than 1,000 posts and it's constantly growing. Visit the site at `www.csharphelper.com` to find more examples covering topics such as the following.

- ➢ 3-D Programs
- ➢ Advanced Controls
- ➢ Algorithms
- ➢ API
- ➢ Fractals
- ➢ Many, many more!

- ➢ Multimedia
- ➢ Internationalization
- ➢ Memory Management
- ➢ Attributes
- ➢ Regular Expressions

- ➢ Databases and SQL
- ➢ Custom Dialogs
- ➢ Animation
- ➢ Formatting
- ➢ User Interface Tools

So please visit the web site and look around. You can find an index of posts at `www.csharphelper.com/howto_index.html`.

While you're there, drop in on the book's web page. See what kinds of comments and posts it's generated, and join in the discussion!

Index

Interview Puzzles Dissected

Whether you're applying for a programming job or a position on Wall Street, interview puzzles are the norm at many high-tech companies. This book explains how to solve more than 200 of the hardest and most common interview puzzles in use.

Interview Puzzles Dissected:

- Shows how to solve more than **200** challenging interview puzzles
- Reveals underlying techniques that let you solve problems that you haven't seen before
- Tells how you can show the interviewer that you can think in an organized fashion
- Explains how to get "partial credit" when all else fails and you just can't solve a puzzle
- Includes programming challenges to give you a deeper understanding of puzzles (obviously only if you're a programmer)

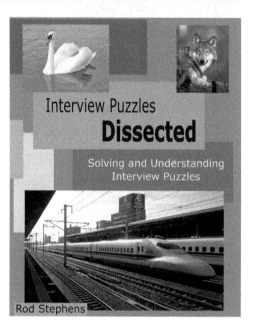

Interview Puzzles
Dissected
Solving and Understanding
Interview Puzzles

Rod Stephens

Job Candidates, Interviewers, and Puzzle Enthusiasts

Interviewers When used incorrectly an interview puzzle tells you little more than whether the job candidate has seen the puzzle before. This book explains new techniques that you can use to get a better understanding of the candidate's capabilities and answer that all-important question, "Is this someone my team can work with effectively?" **Interview Puzzles Dissected**:

- Tells how to discover the ways that a candidate analyzes and solves complex problems
- Describes variations and follow-up questions that you can use to see if the candidate truly understands a puzzle and hasn't simply seen it before
- Explains techniques for creating new, challenging puzzles
- Shows how you can solve puzzles together to further understand a candidate's thought processes and to decide whether the candidate can work in a group

Interview Puzzles Dissected not only shows you how to solve the puzzles, it explains why the solutions work. It exposes the underlying principles that you can use to solve similar puzzles and to invent new puzzles and variations of your own. This book will give you the tools you need to get the most out of interviews both as an interviewer and as a job candidate.

Also by Rod Stephens

C# 24-Hour Trainer, 2nd Edition is your quick and easy guide to programming in C#, even if you have no programming experience at all. A comprehensive beginner's guide, with each lesson supplemented by video screencasts, for over ten hours of video training. Each chapter covers a specific concept or technique and includes detailed, easy-to-follow explanations followed by hands-on exercises.

> ➤ Jump right in with the latest C# techniques
> ➤ Learn at your own pace, with hands-on practice
> ➤ Build Windows, .NET, and mobile applications

Beginning Software Engineering demystifies the software engineering methodologies and techniques that professional developers use to design and build robust, efficient, and consistently reliable software. Free of jargon and assuming no previous experience, this accessible guide explains important concepts that can be applied to any programming language. A great introduction to many development models including:

- Waterfall
- RAD
- XP
- Sashimi
- Scrum
- Crystal
- Agile
- Kanban
- Many Others!

Essential Algorithms provides a friendly and accessible introduction to the most useful computer algorithms. Computer algorithms are the recipes that programmers use to solve difficult problems. Written in simple, intuitive English, this book describes how and when to use practical classic algorithms, and even how to create new algorithms to meet future needs. The book also includes a collection of questions that can help readers prepare for a programming job interview.

- Parallel Algorithms
- Randomization
- Cryptography
- Sorting
- Network Flow
- Routing
- Searching
- Matching
- Many More!

Machine Learning Made Easy

Covering the entry-level topics needed to get you up and running with machine learning, this hands-on, friendly guide helps you make sense of the programming languages and tools you need to turn machine learning-based tasks into a reality. Whether you're maddened by the math behind machine learning, apprehensive about AI, or perplexed by preprocessing data, Machine Learning For Dummies makes it easier to understand and implement machine learning in today's useful world.

- Grasp how day-to-day activities are powered by machine learning
- Learn to 'speak' Python and R to teach machines to perform pattern-oriented tasks and data analysis
- Learn to code in R using R Studio
- Find out how to code in Python using Anaconda

Dive into this complete beginner's guide so you are armed with all you need to know about machine learning!

About the Authors

John Mueller is a freelance author and technical editor. He has writing in his blood, having produced 103 books and more than 600 articles to date. **Luca Massaron** is a data scientist specialized in organizing and interpreting big data and transforming it into smart data by means of the simplest and most effective data mining and machine learning techniques.

 Available wherever books and ebooks are sold.

www.ingramcontent.com/pod-product-compliance
Lightning Source LLC
Chambersburg PA
CBHW062046050326
40690CB00016B/3003